Piracy in the West Indies and Its Suppression

THE "JOLLY ROGER"

PENDANT STIFFENED
WITH LIGHT BATTENS,
1704.

1704.

1719.

1746.

JACK of
BARTHOLOMEW ROBERTS.

1721.

19th CENTURY.

ENSIGN AT MIZEN-PEAK,
BARTHOLOMEW ROBERTS.

U. S. SCHOONER "SHARK"

Type of a light draft vessel used in chasing Pirates.
From a print in the collection of F. B. C. Bradlee.

PIRACY IN THE WEST INDIES
AND ITS SUPPRESSION

FRANCIS B.C.BRADLEE

The Rio Grande Press, Inc.

GLORIETA, NEW MEXICO · 87535

First edition from which
this edition was copied supplied by
INTERNATIONAL BOOKFINDERS, INC.
P O. Box 1
Pacific Palisades, Calif., 90272

A RIO GRANDE CLASSIC
First Published in 1923

ISBN 0-87380-170-9

1990

The Rio Grande Press, Inc.

GLORIETA, NEW MEXICO · 87535

Piracy in the West Indies
and Its Suppression

By FRANCIS B. C. BRADLEE

AUTHOR OF "THE DREADNOUGHT OF NEWBURYPORT," "THE
KEARSARGE-ALABAMA BATTLE," "A FORGOTTEN CHAP-
TER IN OUR NAVAL HISTORY," "HISTORY OF STEAM
NAVIGATION IN NEW ENGLAND," HISTORY OF
THE EASTERN RAILROAD," "HISTORY OF
THE BOSTON & MAINE RAILROAD,"
AND OTHERS

THE ESSEX INSTITUTE

SALEM, MASSACHUSETTS

1923

NEWCOMB & GAUSS, PRINTERS

SALEM, MASS.

1923

LIST OF ILLUSTRATIONS

EXECUTION OF CAPTAIN NATHANIEL GORDON, AT NEW YORK, FEBRUARY 22, 1862

The only person ever hanged in the United States for the crime of slave smuggling

From a sketch in the New York Illustrated News, March, 1862

THE SUPPRESSION OF PIRACY IN THE WEST INDIES, 1820-1832.

By Francis B. C. Bradlee.

The struggle of the Spanish-American colonies for independence was accompanied by lawless depredations on commerce which finally developed into piracy on an unprecedented scale.

Revolutionary governments are, at best, generally attended by acts of violence, but when undertaken by the ignorant and depraved people of the South American colonies, it not only, as before stated, led to rapine and piracy, but adventurers and outlaws from all over the world flocked to these provinces as soon as the standard of rebellion was raised, ostensibly to serve against Spain, but in reality attracted by the prospects of plunder.

Shortly after the close of the Napoleonic wars, the republics of Buenos Ayres and Venezuela commissioned swift-sailing vessels, manned each by twenty-five to one hundred men, as privateers to prey on Spanish merchantmen. However, it was not long before these ships began to plunder vessels of neutral nations, and, as their first acts of violence were not nipped in the bud, piracy soon spread to an alarming extent.

A few of the most desperate characters, seeing their opportunity, captured defenceless merchantmen at the very entrance to such large ports as Havana and Vera Cruz, resulting so successfully that recruits flocked to their standards, making the pirates so formidable that squadrons from various naval powers had to be sent to capture them.

In the files of the Boston and Salem newspapers of those days are to be found many accounts of the atrocities of the pirates, which caused the greatest excitement, as the United States then had a very large commerce with the West Indies. In 1822, a bold, but, thanks to the courage of the captain and crew, unsuccessful attempt

(1)

was made by these highwaymen of the deep to seize the brig "Belvidere" of Beverly, Massachusetts. As this episode has, as far as is known, never yet been published, the full account of it, as printed in the *Essex* (Salem) *Register* for June 22d and 26th and July 17th, 1822, is well worth reproducing. Curiously enough, too, no mention is made of the "Belvidere" in the usually minute and all-embracing "Ship Registers of the District of Salem and Beverly, Massachusetts," published by the Essex Institute, but possibly she was registered at another port. The story follows:

"An account has already been published of an attack made by a piratical vessel upon the brig 'Belvidere', Capt. Lamson, of Beverly, on her passage from Port-au-Prince to New Orleans, and of the successful defence of the 'Belvidere'. Capt. Lamson has arrived at the Balize, and furnished the following particulars, which appear in the New Orleans papers. He was hailed by the piratical Capt. and ordered on board his vessel. Capt. L. replied that he was coming, and after some delay, during which the crew of the 'Belvidere' were preparing to defend themselves, the commander of the pirates came alongside in his boat and jumped on board the 'Belvidere.' Capt. L. instantly shot him down with a musket, and a severe conflict ensued between the crew of the boat and that of the 'Belvidere', the issue of which was the total defeat of the pirates, with the loss of six of their number killed. One man of the 'Belvidere' was mortally wounded.

"Capt. Lamson (who on a former voyage was robbed and shamefully abused by pirates, and determined to resist any further attacks from them, had prepared his vessel and crew accordingly) is certainly entitled to great praise for his gallant and spirited conduct. A few such checks as this will as effectually prevent a repetition of the outrages perpetrated by these lawless sea-monsters as anything which our Seventy-fours or Frigates can do."

"Extract from the log-book of the 'Belvidere', Capt. Lamson, arr. at New Orleans from Port-au-Prince."

"May 2, fell in with a sch'r and three launches, which gave chase; blowing heavy and being to windward, succeeded in getting from them the next day. At 10 A. M. made a sch. on our larboard bow, lying under mainsail and jib; at 11, she was on our lee quarter, fired a shot, and coming up very fast; at 20 minutes past 11, gave us a second shot, and hoisted a red flag, with death's head and cross under it.

"Finding I had a *hard character* to deal with, I prepared for him as well as we were able, and immediately brailed up my topsails, hauled up my courses, clewed down top-gallant sails, hauled down jib, braced to the main-topsail, and kept off two points, fired a musket and hoisted colors—at 12, she came alongside, within 10 yards distance—hailed with '*God d—— you, send your boat on board, or I will murder all hands of you.*'

"He had not discovered our gun at that time—I told him I would send her directly—he immediately gave me a whole volley of musketry and blunderbusses, before I had answered him—our gun was pointed and cloth removed, and we commenced as smart a fire as possible with our 24 pound carronade, 4 muskets and 7 pistols, and on our first fire six of them were seen to fall, the captain among them, or leader, being the one that hailed me—he only discharged his long gun three times alongside, as our third shot broke his carriage, and his gun fell into the lee scupper—he then kept up as smart a fire as he was able with muskets and blunderbusses, and dropped near the stern, expecting to find more comfortable quarters, but there he got a most terrible cutting up from a brass 3 pounder, by which he was raked within 20 yards distance with a round and two bags of 40 musket balls each, which completely fixed him—I did not receive any fire from, nor even hear a word spoken on board of him, and in fact did not see any one on deck. His vessel holding such a wind and sailing so fast, she was soon clear of grapeshot range, and wore ship, when we counted 6 or 7 of them, which appeared to be all that was left; the captain I saw distinctly laid on deck. Our loss was one man killed, shot through the head; about 40 musket balls through the rudder case, tiller, skylight, companion way, our fore topsail halliards shot away and our try-sail halliards cut in 3 pieces. The pirate was 36 to 40 tons; we counted 22 men when he came alongside; he had a brass 6 or 9 pounder amidships, and muskets and blunderbusses.

"Z. G. Lamson."

"Louisiana State Insurance Company,
"June 7, 1822.

"The report of the Committee appointed to enquire into the circumstances in relation to an action between the brig 'Belvidere', Capt. Lamson, of Beverly, and a piratical vessel, on the passage of the former vessel from Port au Prince to this place, having been read, it was unanimously adopted, and on motion it was resolved that the President and Directors of the Louisiana State Insurance Company do testify their high sense of obligation for the service rendered them by Capt. Lamson of the brig 'Belvidere' in repelling the attack made on his vessel by a piratical cruizer on the 3d day of May last, on her passage from Port au Prince to this port, by which a considerable amount of property was saved to this institution, do order that the President be directed to return Capt. Lamson the thanks of this Board for his exertions on this occasion, and that a piece of plate of the value of $300 be caused to be executed under the superintendence of a committee of this board, and presented to Capt. Lamson in the name of this Company, and likewise that the sum of $200 be appropriated and placed at the disposal of Capt. Lamson, to be distributed among his crew in such proportion as he may conceive their services merit.

"E. Deflechier, Sec'ry,
Louisiana State Insurance Office."

"New Orleans, 8th June, 1822.
"Captain Z. G. Lamson of the brig 'Belvidere.'
"Sir :—

"I am directed by a vote of this board, a copy of which is enclosed, to return you the thanks of the Company for the signal service rendered them by your suc cessful exertions in repelling the attack of a Piratical Cruizer on the brig 'Belvidere', the cargo of which was insured in this office, and it affords me much pleasure to have an opportunity individually of expressing to your crew the gratification I derive from the gallant conduct displayed on the occasion, which you will please to communicate to them in distributing the amount voted to their benefit, which you will find enclosed.

"With the best wishes for your future success and happiness, I am, very respectfully, your obedient servant.

"(Signed)   R. Relf,

"President of the L. S. I. Company."

"New Orleans, June 10.

"To the President and Directors of the Louisiana State
     Insurance Company.

"Gentlemen :—

"I have received yours of the 8th inst., inclosing the
resolutions of the board of directors, as well as their
thanks to myself and crew, for the defence made on
board the brig 'Belvidere' of Beverly, under my command, off Key Sal, against a piratical cruiser.

"Gentlemen, I have to tender my best respects, as well
as those of my crew, for the marked attention with which
you have honored us, and have to say, under similar circumstances, we shall ever be ready to defend ourselves
against those pests of the ocean.   The gratuity for the
benefit of my crew has been distributed agreeably to your
direction, with which they are highly gratified.

"Accept, gentlemen, my best wishes.

"Z. G. Lamson."

Although numerous acts of piracy were committed
about this time on Salem ships, still they suffered much
less damage, in proportion, than was done to vessels hailing from other ports of the country, the reason being that
the West India trade, at that period, had largely left
Salem in favor of Boston, New York and Portland.
Nevertheless, in 1824, the merchants of Salem were sum-
moned, by circular letter, to counsel on the matter of
petitioning Congress for means of relief.   Probably one
of the worst cases of piracy against an American vessel
was in February, 1829, when the brig "New Priscilla",
Captain Hart, was found apparently abandoned a few
miles out from Havana.   The account of this tragic
affair, which, as there were no survivors, is shrouded in
mystery, is as follows, compiled from the newspaper files
of the day.

The brig "New Priscilla", Captain Hart, of and from Salem, sailed on a voyage, the ultimate destination of which was Sumatra and the pepper coast, but she never again saw her home port. Pepper cargoes were paid for in Spanish dollars, and the specie for this voyage was driven down from the banks in Essex street in several four-horse stages, and delivered at the wharf, so that it need not be on deposit over night. Upon receiving it the brig made sail, and later was found abandoned in the Gulf Stream, all on board murdered by pirates. And yet there are those who pretend to think there was nothing exciting in Salem's past!

"It was no uncommon sight," said an old stage driver, "to see several coaches coming from Boston driven down Essex street to the Asiatic Bank, loaded with silver dollars in kegs of $3000 each and canvas bags of $1000 each."

After much research, the author has collected the following items concerning the "New Priscilla." She was built at Scituate, Mass., in 1822, registered 125 tons, length 75 feet, beam 22 feet; register issued Oct. 16, 1827; owners, Stephen W. Shepard and Charles Hart. Her last clearance from the Salem Custom House was on Sept. 24, 1828, and for the West Indies, under Captain Charles Hart.

An examination of the files of the *Essex Register* shows that she arrived at Havana, via Matanzas, about Oct. 20. She next visited Charleston, S. C., from which port she made two round voyages to the West Indies. The "New Priscilla" is reported as arriving at Charleston on Jan. 22, 1829, but no record of her sailing was published. The next news of her is that regarding her piracy, which was printed in the *Essex Register* of March 16, 1829, as follows: "The Philadelphia Gazette contains the details of a horrible tragedy, communicated in a private letter from Havana, and a notarial certificate from Matanzas. The statement is made by John Conega, master of the brig 'Mary Jane' of New York. He says:

" 'On the 14th Feb. inst., the wind at S. W., entered the Keysal Bank in sight of the Dog Keys; at 2.30 P.M. saw a herm. brig and schooner in company, lying to the

wind ; at 4 P. M., not wishing to leave the Bank, tacked
to the Southward, when they immediately filled away.
At 4.15, finding we were coming up with them, they both
tacked for about fifteen minutes, when the schooner again
filled away and left the brig in the situation above mentioned. At 5 P. M., being aboard the brig 'The New
Priscilla of Salem,' on her stern, observed that her stern
boat tackles were hanging in the water, her boat gone,
and not a soul to be seen on board ; called three or four
times, but receiving no answer, stood off.'"

The next issue of the *Register*, March 19, 1829, has an
extract from a letter written by a Captain Weston, in
which he says he has "no doubt but that Captain Hart
and his crew were all cut off by pirates."

These facts, gathered from sources which cannot be
disputed, for they are matters of record, must be accepted
as conclusive.

It is worth noting, also, that there is nowhere to be
found any mention of a boy having been spiked to the
deck by the pirates. This blood-curdling yarn has generally been told in connection with the piracy of the "New
Priscilla." Another incident in connection with this
unfortunate vessel is a story told of two sailors belonging
to her. They had been allowed a day's liberty on shore
at Charleston, and, returning at night, were about to go
on board, just as a large black dog came to the ship's side
and howled. That was enough for the men. Possessing
a sailor's superstition, they felt that something was surely
going to happen to the brig. So off they ran and secreted
themselves until the vessel had proceeded to sea, and thus
their lives were spared. One of them died many years
ago in Salem, at a green old age, and he always delighted
in telling the story of his escape from the fate of the
crew of the "New Priscilla."

In September, 1832, came the seizure of the Salem
brig "Mexican", which turned out to be the very last act
of piracy perpetrated on the Atlantic ocean. As this
noted event attracted world-wide attention and has been
often written up, a short account of it will suffice here.

The "Mexican", a craft of 227 tons register, owned by
Joseph Peabody of Salem, and commanded by Captain

John G. Butman of the same place, sailed from Salem for Rio Janeiro and a market on August 29, 1832. In view of subsequent purchases, she sailed from this port in ballast, with the exception of about one hundred bags of salt petre and one hundred chests of tea, also having concealed in the run some twenty thousand dollars in specie.

Exclusive of the captain, the crew of the "Mexican" consisted of two mates, eight hands before the mast, colored cook and steward; thirteen men all told.

On September 20, 1832, when in latitude 33 north and longitude 34 1-2 west, the "Mexican" fell in with and was captured by the piratical schooner "Panda", by whom she was robbed of her specie, the crew maltreated and robbed of their own belongings. The pirates also nearly stripped the brig of provisions, sails, and ship's furniture of all kinds.

They then drove the officers and crew of the "Mexican" below, all means of egress securely fastened, the running rigging and sails of the brig cut and mutilated, her galley filled with combustibles and set on fire, and then both the crew and the brig were abandoned to the flames. Luckily, however, before the fire had gained much headway, the crew were able to break out and slowly extinquish it. They were afraid to do this too quickly, for as long as the pirates were in sight any sudden checking of the flames would be sure to draw their attention and return, which latter fact would assuredly have settled the fate of everyone on board the "Mexican." The pirates had left the unfortunate brig in a bad plight, but Captain Butman and his crew, esteeming themselves fortunate to escape with their lives, at once set to work repairing damages as speedily as possible, and before dark had bent new sails, repaired the running gear, etc.

Thanks, also, to the foresight of Captain Butman, who, when he discovered the true character of the strange vessel, had managed to hide some of the most necessary navigating appliances, such as a compass, quadrant and chart, the "Mexican" was eventually able to reach Salem, on Oct. 12, 1832.

It had been the intention of the pirate captain to have Captain Butman and his men put to death, on the principle that "dead men tell no tales." When he found that this had not been done, he put his schooner about, and with many and deep curses at his crew for their cowardice, attempted to rejoin the unfortunate brig.

The "Mexican's" crew owed their salvation to the fact that a strong wind arose soon after the two vessels separated, which in a few hours developed into a gale, and thus prevented any chance of the pirate leader, Gibert, finding his victims.

Naturally the seizure and piracy of the "Mexican" created the greatest excitement in the United States, and the news of it soon spread to all the maritime nations of the world. In those days pirates and slavers often interchanged their roles as occasion or profit demanded, and in order to put down the slave trade, both Great Britain and the United States maintained small squadrons of men-of-war off the west coast of Africa.

Not many months after the "Mexican" piracy the British brig-of-war "Curlew", Captain Henry D. Trotter, while on this station, received information that a certain slaving schooner lay in the river Nazareth, and the description given him of this vessel corresponded exactly with that of the schooner engaged in the robbery of the "Mexican".

Arriving at the river Nazareth, Captain Trotter, with a force of forty men, proceeded up the stream in boats and attacked the schooner. Her crew fled ashore, but were soon after given up to Captain Trotter by the native king; eventually they were brought to this country in H. B. M. brig "Savage", arriving in Salem Aug. 27, 1834, and were then surrendered to the United States authorities for trial. After a long and tedious trial before the Federal Court in Boston, on the strongest evidence, both circumstantial and direct, produced by the government against the defendants, the jury returned a verdict of "Guilty" as to Gibert, de Soto, Ruiz, Boyza, Castillo, Garcia and Montenegro, and "Not Guilty" as to Costa, Ferrer, Guzman, Portana and Velaquez, it having been satisfactorily proven to the jury that they were not on board the "Panda" at the time of the commission of the offence charged. In the hush that followed the announcement of the verdict, the foreman of the jury drew from his pocket a paper and read to the Court the following recommendation to mercy:

"The sympathies of the jury have been strongly moved in behalf of Bernado de Soto on account of his generous and self-sacrificing conduct in saving the lives of more than seventy human beings, constituting the passengers and crew of the ship 'Minerva'; and they desire that his case should be presented to the merciful consideration of the Government." The testimony of Mr. Daniel F. Hale for the defence had showed that the ship "Minerva", Captain Putnam, in the course of her voyage from New York to New Orleans, loaded with lime, naval stores and other freight, and having on board, besides the crew, some sixty passengers, on the night of October 19, 1830, struck the "Little Isaacs", on the Bahama banks, and lost both boats and anchors trying to get off. By reason of the ship springing aleak, the lime coming in contact with the water, set fire to the ship. The light of the burning ship brought to their rescue the brig "Leon", commanded by de Soto, who, after a while, succeeded in getting them all safe on board his little craft, and in about a week landed the sufferers at Havana.

It was also proved that in rescuing these people, de Soto was put to considerable loss and self-sacrifice, as he was obliged, in order to accommodate them, to throw overboard a considerable quantity of freight with which his brig was loaded, and in which he was financially interested.

On December 16, 1834, Judge Story pronounced sentence of death upon all those convicted. The defence, by appeal, protest and declaration, attempted in every way to overthrow the verdict of the jury, but without success, and execution was done June 11, 1835, at Boston, upon five of those under sentence, viz: Gibert, Boyza, Castillo, Garcia and Montenegro.

A respite was granted in the case of de Soto and Ruiz by President Jackson. Before its expiration de Soto was fully pardoned by the President, mainly on account of his humane conduct in the case referred to, and duly discharged from custody. By reason of a claim on the part of the defence that Ruiz had become mentally deranged,

CAPTAIN Z. G. LAMSON
of the brig "Belvidere"

CAPTAIN CHARLES HART
of the brig "New Priscilla"

COMMODORE DAVID PORTER

Commander of the West India Squadron.
From an engraving in the collection of F. B. C. Bradlee

the President ordered a further respite of sixty days, at the end of which time, this claim having been disproved by medical examination, he, also, was hung, September 12, 1835.

The piracy of the "Mexican" may be said to mark the very end of the era of marine highwaymen. It will not be uninteresting, therefore, to mention some of the piratical acts in the West Indies which took place at other periods, and the multiplicity of which caused the United States to send a squadron into those seas to stamp out this nefarious trade.

The exploits of our navy in connection with these events has been slightly passed over by most historians, but as a whole it compares favorably as regards courage, resourcefulness and daring, with the deeds of the United States navy a quarter of a century before in its struggle with the Barbary corsairs in the Mediterranean, when it earned the gratitude of the seafaring world by curbing and finally putting an end to these pests.

The magnitude of the piratical operations in the West Indies has never been fully ascertained, and the following account of it has only been revealed to the author by means of the most diligent research among old newspaper files, log-books, insurance records, official reports of the various naval officers, etc. Many of the published reports, exaggerated beyond reason, were subsequently found to have been based upon terrified imagination ; but on the other hand, there is no doubt that much valuable information was covered up, some of the pirates, also, were lost at sea, with all their booty and all knowledge of the vessels they had plundered and destroyed.

There is every reason to believe that a large percentage of merchant vessels that at this period never reached their destination and were put down as "missing", were really the victims of piratical ferocity.* It would also seem that in those days the mariner was exposed to danger from pirates on land quite as much as he was from their brethren who frequented the ocean, as will be seen from the following story found in the *Salem Register* of January 29, 1820 :

*Records of the Marblehead Marine Insurance Company.

"Capt. Winslow of the schooner 'Sisters' from Havana [at New York] states that on Sat'y night while in soundings standing in for the land, in company with the brig 'Trader', from St. Salvador, he discovered a light at 11 o'clock, which he supposed to be Sandy Hook light, and shortly after he saw two more lights, which corresponded with the beacon lights which are made in coming into Sandy Hook. At 2, when close in, he saw the breakers, and was only enabled to tack ship and stand off. At 4 o'clock the light disappeared entirely, and at daylight men were seen on the beach. Capt. Winslow is confident that they were arranged for the purpose of decoying vessels on shore. The lights were seen 18 miles south of Sandy Hook. This is not the first instance that has come to our knowledge of this most infamous conduct in some desperate and abandoned wretches who inhabit the Jersey coast and expect by these deceptions to enrich themselves by plundering vessels decoyed on shore, even at the expense of the lives of the passengers and crew."

The number of vessels captured by West India pirates may be estimated from a list of 37 ships, brigs and schooners collected from notes in the Salem and Boston newspapers, which then devoted much space to marine news, during the period 1821-23. This covers less than half the period of time during which piracy prevailed, and is but a small percentage of those captured by the freebooters.

Congress, memorialized by the ship-owning interests of the country, lost no time in enacting statutes prescribing the penalty of death and giving extraordinary powers to the Executive for the purpose of apprehending the pirates; the right to search suspicious vessels, and bays and coasts suspected of being piratical nests, even though beyond American territorial jurisdiction in foreign land, if not under the direct control of the recognized de facto governments. The Spanish government afforded all the assistance in its power, but its navy, never large or well managed, was also crippled in its contest with the South American revolutionary colonies, so that the Spanish officials could only acquiesce in permitting our naval officers to operate within their territory where they had not sufficient force to stop piracy. This, notwithstanding our well-known sympathy with the colonies. A number of privateers were fitted out by the Spanish government to help its own naval force and also to fight the pirates, but, when opportunity offered, many of these armed vessels seized and plundered defenceless craft of any nationality, while others boldly renounced allegiance to Spain and hoisted the black flag. Some of the Spanish governors and alcades in remote districts secretly connived at this business, as it increased their always meagre salaries. They allowed the pirates to refit in port, and in some cases furnished supplies of arms and ammunition in consideration of a share in the booty.

In the autumn of 1821 the United States government sent the following squadron to cruise in West Indian waters, where it was expected they would capture and destroy the pirates : sloop of war "Hornet", brigs "Enterprise" and "Spark", schooners "Shark", "Porpoise" and "Grampus" ; the last three were each equipped with a large row barge fitted with a small gun ; these were especially designed to pursue the pirates when they took refuge in shallow waters.

The "Enterprise", commanded by Lieutenant L. Kearny, discovered four piratical craft in the act of plundering three American vessels off Cape Antonio, Cuba, Oct. 16, 1821. Although they were in shallow water, where the brig could not pursue them, five of her boats were soon armed and sent to cut the pirates out. This the American tars succeeded in doing after a sharp fight, in which the freebooters managed to burn two schooners ; however, the other vessels were captured, including forty pirates, who were sent to Charleston, S. C., for trial.

Soon after, on Nov. 6, 1821, the Boston newspapers contained the following story of outrage and robbery, at this period all too familiar :

"The brig 'Cobbessecontee', Capt. Jackson, arrived yesterday from the Havana, sailed thence on the morning of the 8th ult., and on the evening of the same day, about four miles from the Moro castle, at the very entrance of Havana harbor was brought to by a piratical sloop, containing about 30 men. A boat from her, with ten men‾

came alongside, and soon after they got on board commenced plundering. They took nearly all the clothing from the captain and mate—all the cooking utensils and spare rigging—unrove part of the running rigging—cut the small cable—broke the compasses—cut the mast's coats to pieces—took from the captain his watch and four boxes of cigars—and from the cargo three bales cochineal and six boxes cigars.

"They beat the mate unmercifully and hung him up by the neck under the maintop. They also beat the captain severely—broke a large broad sword across his back, and run a long knife through his thigh, so that he almost bled to death. Capt. Jackson saw the sloop at Regla the day before.

"Capt. Jackson informs us, and we have also been informed by other persons from the Havana, that this system of Piracy is openly countenanced by some of the inhabitants of that place—who say that it is a retaliation on the Americans for interfering against the Slave Trade (the foreign slave trade was abolished in 1808 by act of Congress) and for allowing Patriot (South American) privateers to refit in their ports.

"The pirates, therefore, receiving such countenance, grow more daring, and increase in number from the success which has attended this new mode of filling their pockets. Capt. Bagnon, who arrived yesterday from Charleston, spoke on the 2d inst. off the S. Shoal of Nantucket, the brig 'Three Partners', from Jamaica for St. John—had been robbed, off Cape Antonio, by a piratical vessel, of about 35 tons, and 17 men, of clothing, watches, etc., and the captain was hung up by the neck to the fore-yard arm, till he was almost dead.

"Capt. Bourn, who arrived yesterday from Cape Haytien, spoke on the 26th ult., lat. 33, lon. 78, brig 'Sea Lion', 36 days from Cape Haytien for Belfast, Ireland, which had been plundered by a pirate in the Gulf.

"The brig 'Harriet', Capt. Dimond, from St. Jago de Cuba for Baltimore, arrived at Havana on the 16th ult., having been robbed of all her cargo of sugar and $4000 in specie, off Cape Antonio, by a boat with 15 men, having two schooners in company. Capt. D was hung up by the

neck, and remained senseless for some time after he was
taken down.

The Dutch brig 'Mercury', 77 days from Marseilles,
arrived at Havana on the 16th ult., after having been
robbed of $10,000 worth of her cargo by a piratical
schooner and boat off Cape Antonio.

"Fortunately a U. S. man-of-war has arrived at the
scene of these daring robberies, and has already protected
two fleets. It is to be hoped that some of the villains
who have so long preyed with impunity on mercantile
property, and been guilty of the most savage acts, will
speedily be caught and brought to justice."

In the meantime, on Oct. 29, 1821, the sloop of war
"Hornet", Captain Robert Henley, captured the pirate
schooner "Moscow", which was sent to Norfolk in charge
of a prize crew. Two months later, Dec. 21, the U. S.
brig "Enterprise", Lieutenant L. Kearney commanding,
captured and burnt another freebooting schooner, whose
crew were able to escape on shore.   A few weeks after
this a "cutting out" party from the schooner "Porpoise",
commanded by Lieutenant J. Ramage, destroyed a nest
of pirates at Cape Antonio.   The official report of Lieutenant Ramage describes this brilliant fight as follows :

"United States Schooner 'Porpoise',
"Off North Coast of Cuba,
"20th January, 1822.

"Sir : Having completed the necessary equipments of
this vessel at New Orleans, on the 7th inst., and previously having given notice that I should sail from the
Balize on the 10th, with convoy, I now have the honor to
inform you that I proceeded to sea on the day appointed,
with five sail under my protection. On the 15th, having
seen the vessels bound to Havana and Matanzas safe to
their destined ports, I made all sail to the westward, and
on the following day boarded the brig 'Bolina', of Boston,
Gorham, master, from whom I received the following information : That, on the day previous, his vessel was captured by pirates and robbed of every material they could
carry away with them, at the same time treating the crew
and himself with inhuman cruelty.

"After supplying him from this vessel with what necessaries he required, I made sail for the land, and early the following morning (Saddle Hill, on the north coast of Cuba, then bearing S. by E.), I dispatched our boats with 40 men, under command of Lieutenant Curtis, in pursuit of these enemies of the human race.

"The boats, having crossed the reef, which here extends out a considerable distance from the shore, very soon discovered, chased and captured a piratical schooner, the crew of which made their escape to the woods; Lieutenant Curtis very judiciously manned the prize from our boats, and proceeded about ten miles to leeward, where, it was understood, the principal depot of these marauders was established. This he fortunately discovered and attacked. A slight skirmish here took place, but as our force advanced the opposition party precipitately retreated. We then took possession and burnt and destroyed their fleet, consisting of five vessels—one being a beautiful new schooner, of about 60 tons, ready for the sea, with the exception of her sails. We also took three prisoners; the others fled to the woods.

"In the affair just mentioned the officers of the expedition state the enemy's loss to be severe. Only one man was wounded in our boats; and it is worthy of remark that this man was one of their own gang, then a prisoner in our possession, and surrounded by our people.

"The destruction of this place will, I trust, be of some service. From information received by me, it was their principal depot, from which they dispatched squadrons to Cape Antonio. These returning loaded with plunder, it was transhipped to Havana in vessels sent from here for that purpose. Stores and materials were collected on the spot, not only for repairing, but building vessels.

"The prisoners now on board are recognized by a seaman in my possession, who was one of the crew of the English ship 'Alexander', of Greenock, lately burned by these pirates : and not content with destroying the vessel, they inhumanly butchered her unfortunate commander. The seaman in question I retain as an evidence in the case."

"Lieutenant Curtis speaks in the highest terms of the gallantry and good conduct of Midshipmen Pinkney, Kingston and Morris, as also of Dr. Terrill, and every other officer and man employed in the expedition. Nothing could exceed their ardor in pursuit but their enthusiasm in attack; and both affording abundant proof that more would have been done had more been required.

"I have manned one of the schooners taken, a very fine, fast-sailing vessel, and kept her with me. She will prove of great service in my further operations on this coast.

"I cannot close this letter, sir, without naming to you Lieutenant Curtis, whose conduct, not only in the present instance, but in every other respect during the period he has been under my command, has merited my warm and decided approbation.

"I have the honor to be, etc.,
"James Ramage,
"Lieutenant Commanding.
"Hon. Smith Thompson, Secretary of the Navy."

Among the multitude of West Indian pirates at that time the best known was John Lafitte, and a short account of this remarkable person may prove interesting.

His career is, naturally, shrouded in a good deal of obscurity and uncertainty, but after much searching and trouble on the author's part, it was discovered that Lafitte was born in France in 1780; some authorities giving St. Malo as the place of his birth, others maintaining that he first saw the light of day at Bordeaux. Those best informed say that this singular personage began his seafaring career as mate of a French East Indiaman, but quarreling with his captain, he left his ship at Mauritius and entered upon a course of daring and successful piracy in the Indian Ocean, varied by occasional ventures in the slave trade.   After several years spent in these pursuits, Lafitte returned to France, disposed of his prizes, sailed for the West Indies, and took out a commission as a privateer from the newly organized government of Carthagena, continuing his depredations, not only upon Spanish, but also upon British commerce.

Another account represents him as having begun his career as lieutenant of a French privateer, which was captured by a British man-of-war and taken into an English port, where the officers and crew of the privateer were thrown into prison.   Here the future marine highwayman was confined for several years under circumstances of peculiar hardship, after all his comrades had obtained their release.   The resentment towards Great Britain engendered by this real or supposed severity is stated to have been the motive that inspired his subsequent career.   Unable to gratify this resentment in the service of his native country, on account of the suspension of hostilities at the time of his release, he found means of doing so under cover of a privateer's commission (against Spain) obtained from the Carthaginian government.   Lafitte is said to have gone to New Orleans in 1807; and it is perfectly well known that about 1810-12 he was at the head of an organized and formidable band of desperadoes, whose headquarters were on the island of Grand Terre, in Barataria bay, some thirty or forty miles west of the mouth of the Mississippi.

Acting ostensibly under the flag of the republic of Carthagena (or New Grenada), it was, however, perfectly well known and admitted that these adventurers preyed practically on the vessels of any nation.   The bay of Barataria afforded a secure retreat for their fleet of small craft; and their goods were smuggled into New Orleans by being conveyed in boats through an intricate labyrinth of lakes, bayous and swamps, to a point near the Mississippi river a little above the city.   After various ineffectual presentments and prosecutions before the civil tribunals, an expedition was despatched against the Baratarians in 1814, under the command of Commodore Patterson. The settlement on Grande Terre was captured, with all the vessels that happened to be in port at the time; but

Lafitte and his comrades made their escape among the swamps and bayous of the interior, from which they returned to the same rendezvous and resumed operations as soon as Commodore Patterson's forces had retired.

About the same time the British, then maturing their plans for a descent upon the southern coast of the United States, made overtures to Lafitte for the purpose of securing his co-operation in that enterprise. A brig-of-war was despatched to Barataria, her commander bearing a letter from Commodore Percy, commanding the British naval forces in the gulf of Mexico, and one from Colonel Nichols, then in command of the land forces on the coast of Florida, offering Lafitte $30,000 and a commission in the British navy, on condition of obtaining his services in conducting the contemplated expedition to New Orleans and distributing a certain proclamation to the inhabitants of Louisiana. Lafitte dissembled with the British officer, Capt. Lockyer, of the "Sophia", who was the bearer of these tempting proposals, and asked for time to consider them.

Meantime he immediately wrote to Gov. Claiborne of Louisiana, enclosing the documents that had been handed him by Capt. Lockyer, informing the governor of the impending invasion, pointing out the importance of the position he occupied, and offering his services in defence of Louisiana, on the sole condition of pardon for himself and followers for the offences with which they stood charged. This amnesty would, of course, include in its provisions a brother of Jean Lafitte, who was then in prison in New Orleans under an indictment for piracy. After some hesitation on the part of the United States authorities, Lafitte's offer was accepted.

In connection with an officer of the U. S. corps of engineers, he was employed in fortifying the passes of Barataria bay, and rendered efficient service, in command of a party of his followers, in the battle of New Orleans, Jan. 8th, 1815. The subsequent career of Lafitte is involved in as much obscurity as his earlier life. A proclamation of President Madison confirmed the amnesty which had been granted by Governor Claiborne to all the Baratarians who had enlisted in the American service,

though it does not appear that their chief ever received
any further reward from the government.   After the war
Lafitte soon returned to his old pursuits, taking a privateer's commission, either, as formerly, from the government of New Grenada, or else from that of Mexico ; and
that, while thus engaged, he formed a settlement on the
site of the present city of Galveston, which was broken
up in 1821 by a naval force under the orders of Lieutenant,
afterwards Commodore, Kearney.

It is quite possible, however, that his brother Pierre,
who commanded one of his vessels, has been confounded
with him. His death is attributed by different authorities
to foundering at sea, to being burned with his vessel after
capture by a Spanish man-of-war, and to wounds received
in a desperate conflict with a British cruiser.   There are
yet other versions ; while one account states that he returned to France and died among his relatives on the
Garonne.   In person Lafitte is represented as having been
well-formed and handsome, about six feet two inches in
height, with large hazel eyes and black hair.   His appearance was totally unlike the popular idea of a pirate, his
manners were polished and easy, though retiring ; his
address was winning and affable ; his management of
piracy entirely business-like, just as his influence over his
followers was almost absolute.

There is every reason for believing that Lafitte came
of a respectable family, and that his early opportunities
for education had been good.

One Raphaelina was another freebooter whose name
was dreaded by merchant sailors navigating the South
Atlantic.   He also controlled a fleet of vessels, and in
July, 1822, got together in the vicinity of Cape Antonio
a formidable host of pirates, at which time it was said he
had collected $180,000 in money alone.

Other notorious pirates were : Diabolito, Cofrecina,
Brown, Gibbs, and Irvine ; the names of the last three
would indicate that they were renegades of Anglo-Saxon
lineage.   We, today, looking back on these events of a
century ago, do not begin to realize the magnitude of
these piratical depredations.   A fair estimate, in the light
of the very small amount of reliable information that is

available, would make the number of those engaged in this piracy at least 10,000, of whom over 3,000 were encountered by the vessels of the United States Navy, which alone captured about 1300 pirates.

The number of freebooters killed and those who escaped on shore after destroying their vessels cannot, naturally, be ascertained. Most of these marine highwaymen operated near the vicinity of their rendezvous on shore. They rarely made any extended cruises, but chose points of strategic importance on the routes of commerce. In and among the Keys of Bahama and Florida, Cape Antonio, Matanzas, and Mugeres Island, near the northeast point of Yucatan, Mexico, were some of the most prominent piratical lairs.

From a letter of one of the officers of the U. S. brig "Spark", published in the New England Palladium of Nov. 3, 1821, we learn the following:

"We arrived here, after a rather rough passage, in eighteen days from Boston, all well. We expect to sail again in two or three days. We found here the piratical ship which robbed the 'Orleans Packet'. She is now in possession of the Swedish government. She came into their possession in the following manner: The crew landed her cargo on a small island near this, from whence it was taken by a schooner to St. Thomas; they then run the ship into Five Island Harbor, where all the crew, except two men, deserted her. The government hearing of her being there, sent a guard and took possession of her, brought her into this harbor, and confined the two men found in her as pirates.

"It is said Capt. Elton has requested the Governor to allow him to take them to the United States for trial. This piratical ship was originally the U. S. brig 'Prometheus', which was condemned two years since, and was then sold."

Another letter, dated Oct. 31, 1821, from on board the U. S. sloop-of-war "Hornet", published in a later issue of the "Palladium", informs us of captures made by the latter:

"The pirate which we took yesterday mounted two long four-pounders, and her crew consisted of twenty gallows-looking scoundrels. After this capture the 'Hornet' spoke three merchant brigs, which would probably have fallen into the hands of the pirates, and were very happy at their escape. Captain Sisson, from Havana, reports that seventy of the pirates belonging to the vessels captured and destroyed by the 'Enterprise' (U. S. brig), have erected two forts on Cape Antonio for their defence".

Judging from the length of time that piracy prevailed at this period in the West Indies, it is not an exaggeration to estimate the prizes captured by the freebooters at 500 vessels. The value of the property destroyed by them amounted to about twenty millions of dollars; the records of the Marblehead Marine Insurance Company, a most accurate barometer of water-borne commerce, revealed the fact that insurance rates on ships and their cargoes rose nearly one hundred per cent in the short space of a year. Two thousand pirates are estimated to have been engaged during the period 1820-30; there were probably not many over 2000 at any one time, and but few who were pirates during the entire decade. Probably the average would be 2500 a year; and if each of the 10,000 pirates obtained the equivalent of $2000, including the cost of his living, armament and reckless extravagance, besides the small percentage realized on the actual value of the goods stolen, and the value of his proportion of property destroyed, the total loss suffered by commerce would amount to twenty millions of dollars. The comparative value of the property destroyed by pirates will be seen from the fact that the annual cost of running the United States government in 1821 was $19,785,000, including interest and redemption of part of the public debt.

Of the many vessels engaged in piracy in West Indian waters, the most formidable were the privateers originally fitted out by the various South American republics to prey on Spanish commerce, and which had later become marine highwaymen. Among these were the "Poloma", 6 guns, 130 men; the "Panchita", 16 guns, 120 men (she was subsequently captured by the U. S. schooner "Grampus", 12 guns); the "Pereira", 8 guns, 80 men; "Burguera", 4 guns, 60 men; "Flor de la Mar", 1 gun, 40 men; and "La Carmen", 4 guns, 50 men.

The brigantine "Pride", 16 guns, 116 men, under the immediate command of Lafitte himself, was the largest vessel fitted out specially for a pirate. It is said that the "Pride", in command of Lafitte's lieutenant, had a desperate fight with an English sloop-of-war, in which both commanders were killed, and only sixteen men left alive on the pirate, which was finally carried by boarding and taken to Jamaica, where the sixteen survivors were tried and convicted; ten of them were executed and six pardoned.

The great majority of piracies were accomplished by small craft with large forces of men concealed from view of their intended prey. These boats would go alongside of merchant vessels and capture them by surprise. In many cases all the crew would be taken out of the ship and compelled to join the pirates or be murdered.

Then the vessel herself would be carried to a Cuban port and sold, or otherwise disposed of for the benefit of the pirates and their agents. Other piratical craft whose names have been ascertained, besides those previously mentioned, were the "Cienega", "Bandera de Sangre" (which translated means "The Bloody Band"), "Moscow", "Catalina", "Palmyra", "Albert", "Pilot", "Tropic", "Mechanic", "La Cata", "Zaragozana", "Larch", "Aristidies", "Lucies", and "Emmanuel".

The pirates captured by the different navies were: United States navy, 79 vessels, 62 guns, and 1300 men; British navy, 13 vessels, 20 guns, and 291 men; Spanish navy, 5 vessels and 150 men.

In the "American Monthly Magazine" for February, 1824, is an interesting and most vivid account of an American gentleman's experiences with pirates in June, 1822, while making a voyage for his health from Philadelphia to New Orleans. It is quite worth quoting in full, showing as it does the many perils to which ocean travellers were exposed a century ago.

"In the early part of June I sailed from Philadelphia in the schooner 'Mary', on a voyage to New Orleans. My principal object in going round by sea was the restoration of my health, which had been for many months declining. Having some friends in New Orleans, whose commercial enterprises were conducted on an extensive scale, I was charged with the care of several sums of money in gold and silver, amounting altogether to nearly $18,000. This I communicated to the captain, and we concluded to secure it in the best manner our circumstances would admit. A plank was accordingly taken off the ribs of the schooner in my own cabin, and the money being deposited in the vacancy, the plank was nailed down in its original place, and the seams filled and tarred over. Being thus relieved from any apprehension that the money would be found upon us in case of an attack from pirates, my mind was somewhat easier. What other articles of value I could conveniently carry about with me, I did so.

"I had also brought a quantity of banknotes to the amount of $15,000. Part of these I caused to be carefully sewed in the left lappel of my coat, supposing that in case of my being lost at sea, my coat, should my body be found, would still contain the most valuable of my effects. The balance was carefully quilted into my black silk cravat. Our crew consisted of the captain and four men, with a supply of live stock for the voyage, and a Newfoundland dog, valuable for his fidelity and sagacity. He had once saved his master from a watery grave, when he had been stunned and knocked overboard by a sudden shifting of the boom. I was the only passenger on board. Our voyage at first was prosperous, and time went rapidly. I felt my strength increase the longer I was at sea, and when we arrived off the southern coast of Florida my feelings were like those of another man.

"It was towards the evening of the fourteenth day, two hours before sunset, that we espied a sail astern of us. As twilight came it neared us with astonishing rapidity. Night closed, and all around was impenetrable darkness. Now and then a gentle wave would break against our bow and sparkle for a moment, and at a distance behind us we could see the uneven glow of light, occasioned by the foaming of the strange vessel. The breeze that filled our canvas was gentle, though it was fresh.

"We coursed our way steadily through the night, though once or twice the roaring of the waves increased so suddenly as to make us believe we had passed a breaker.

ADMIRAL FRANCIS H. GREGORY
From a photograph taken during the Civil War

From the collection of F B. C. Bradlee

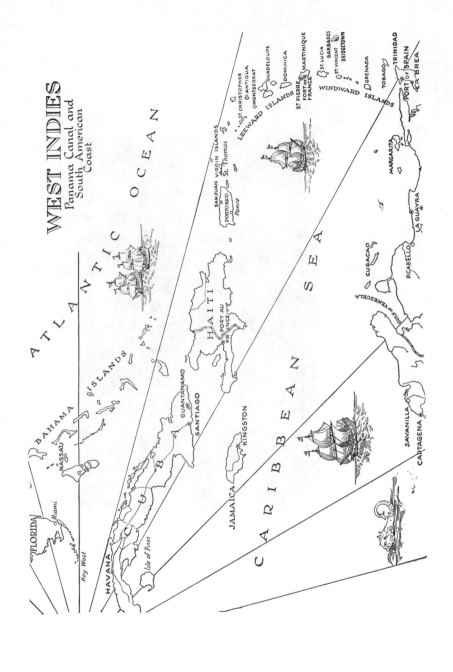

WEST INDIES
Panama Canal and
South American
Coast

ATLANTIC OCEAN

FLORIDA
Miami
Key West

BAHAMA
NASSAU
ISLANDS

HAVANA
Isle of Pines
CUBA

GUANTANAMO
SANTIAGO

JAMAICA
KINGSTON

HAITI
PORT AU PRINCE

SAN JUAN
PORTO RICO
Ponce

VIRGIN ISLANDS
St. Thomas

ST CHRISTOPHER
ANTIGUA
GUADELOUPE
MONTSERRAT
DOMINICA
LEEWARD ISLANDS

ST PIERRE
FORT DE FRANCE
MARTINIQUE
ST LUCIA
BARBADOS
ST VINCENT
BRIDGETOWN
WINDWARD ISLANDS
GRENADA
TOBAGO

CARIBBEAN SEA

MARGARITA

LA GUAYRA
PCABELLO
CURACAO

TRINIDAD
PORT OF SPAIN
BREA

MOUTHS OF VENEZUELA

SAVANILLA
CARTAGENA

"At the time it was unaccountable to me, but I now believe it to be occasioned by the schooner behind us, coming rather near in the darkness of the night. At midnight I went on deck. Nothing but an occasional sparkle was to be seen, and the ocean was undisturbed. Still it was a fearful and appalling darkness, and in spite of my endeavors I could not compose myself. At the windlass, on the forecastle, three of the sailors, like myself, unable to sleep, had collected for conversation. On joining them, I found our fears were mutual. They all kept their eyes steadily fixed upon the unknown vessel, as if anticipating some dreadful event. They informed me that they had put their arms in order and were determined to stand or die.

"At this moment a flash of light, perhaps a musket burning priming, proceeded from the vessel in pursuit, and we saw distinctly that her deck was covered with men. My heart almost failed me. I had never been in battle, and knew not what it was. Day at length dawned, and setting all her canvas, our pursuer gained alarmingly upon us. It was evident that she had followed us the whole night, being unwilling to attack us in the dark. In a few minutes she fired a gun and came alongside. She was a pirate. Her boat was lowered, and about a dozen hideous-looking objects jumped in, with a commander at their head. The boat pushed off and was fast nearing us, as we arranged ourselves for giving her a broadside. Our whole stock of arms consisted of six muskets and an old swivel—a small revolving ship's cannon in use in the eighteenth and early nineteenth centuries—used as a signal gun, belonging to the 'Mary', and a pair of pistols of my own, which I carried in my belt. The pirate boat's crew were armed with muskets, pistols, swords, cutlasses, and knives ; and when she came within her own length of us we fired five of our muskets and the swivel into her.

"Her fire was scarcely half given when she filled and went down, with all her crew. At this success we were inclined to rejoice, but looking over the pirate schooner we observed her deck still swarming with the same description of horrid-looking wretches. A second boat's crew pushed off, with their muskets pointed directly at us the whole time. When they came within the same distance as the other, we fired, but with little, if any effect. The pirate immediately returned the fire, and with horrid cries jumped aboard us. Two of our brave crew were lying dead upon the deck, and the rest of us expected nothing better. French, Spanish and English were spoken indiscriminately and all at once. The most horrid imprecations were uttered against us, and threats that fancy cannot imagine.

"A wretch whose black, shaggy whiskers covered nearly his whole face, whose eyes were only seen at intervals from beneath his bushy eyebrows, and whose whole appearance was more that of a hell-hound than of a human being, approached me with a drawn cutlass in his hand. I drew one of my pistols and snapped it in his face, but it flashed in the pan, and before I could draw the other, the pirate, with a brutality that would have disgraced a cannibal, struck me over the face with his cutlass and knocked me down. I was too much wounded to resist, and the blood ran in torrents from my forehead. In this situation the wretch seized me by the scalp, and thrusting his cutlass in my cravat cut it through completely. I felt the cold iron glide along my throat, and even now the very thought makes me shudder.

"The worst idea I had ever formed of human cruelty seemed now realized, and I could see death staring me in the face. Without stopping to examine the cravat, he put it in his pocket, and in a voice of thunder exclaimed, 'levez vous'; I accordingly rose to my feet, and he pinioned my hands behind my back, led me to the vessel's bulwark, and asked another of the gang, in French, whether he should throw me overboard. At the recollection of that scene I am still staggered. I endeavored to call the prospects of eternity before me, but could think of nothing except the cold and quiverless apathy of the tomb. His infamous companion replied, 'Il est trop bien habillé, pour l'envoyer an diable', and led me to the foremast, where he tied me with my face to the stern of the vessel. The cords were drawn so tight around my arms and legs that my agony was excruciating. In this situation he left me.

"On looking round, I found them all employed in plundering and ransacking everything we had. Over my left shoulder one of our sailors was strung up to the yard-arm, and apparently in the last agonies of death; while before me our gallant captain was on his knees and begging for his life. The wretches were endeavoring to extort from him the secret of our money; but for a while he was firm and dauntless. Provoked at his obstinacy, they extended his arms and cut them off at the elbows. At this human nature gave way, and the injured man confessed the spot where we had concealed our specie. In a few moments it was aboard their own vessel. To revenge themselves on our unhappy captain, when they had satisfied themselves that nothing else was hidden, they spread a bed of oakum on the deck, and after soaking it through with turpentine, tied the captain on it, filled his mouth with the same combustibles, and set the whole on fire. The cries of the unfortunate man were heart-rending, and his agonies must have been unutterable, but they were soon over. All this I was compelled to witness. Heart sick with the sight, I once shut my eyes, but a musket discharged close to my ear was a warning sufficient to keep them open.

"On casting my eyes towards the schooner's stern, I discovered that our boatswain had been nailed to the deck through his feet, and the body spiked through to the tiller. He was writhing in the last agonies of crucifixion. Our fifth comrade was out of sight during all this tragedy; in a few minutes, however, he was brought upon the deck blindfolded. He was then conducted to the muzzle of the swivel and commanded to kneel. The swivel was then fired off, and his head was dreadfully wounded by the discharge. In a moment after it was agonizing to behold his torments and convulsions—language is too feeble to describe them; I have seen men hung upon the gibbet, but their death is like sinking in slumber when compared with his.

"Excited with the scene of human butchery, one of those wretches fired his pistol at the captain's dog; the ball struck his shoulder and disabled him ; he finished him by shooting him again, and at last by cutting out his tongue ! At this last hell-engendered act my blood boiled with indignation at such savage brutality on a helpless, inoffensive dog ! But I was unable to give utterance or action to my feelings.

"Seeing that the crew had been every one despatched, I began to think more of myself. My old enemy, who seemed to forget me, once more approached me, but shockingly besmeared with blood and brains. He had stood by the side of the unfortunate sailor who suffered before the swivel, and supported him with the point of his bayonet. He drew a stiletto from his side, placed its point upon my heart, and gave it a heavy thrust. I felt its point touch my skin; but the quilting of my bank bills prevented its further entrance. This savage monster then ran it up my breast, as if intending to divide my lungs, and in doing so the bank notes fell upon the deck. He snatched them up greedily and exclaimed, 'Ah ! laissez mois voir ce qui reste !' My clothes in a few moments were ripped to pieces, at the peril of my life. He frequently came so near as to tear my skin and deluge me with blood ; but by the mercy of Providence, I escaped from every danger. At this moment a heavy flaw struck the schooner, and I heard one of the pirates say, 'Voila un vaisseau !' They all retreated precipitately, and gaining their own vessel, were soon out of sight.

"Helpless as I now was, I had the satisfaction of knowing that the pirates had been frightened by the appearance of a strange sail, but it was impossible for me to see it. Still tied to the foremast, I knew not what was my prospect of release. An hour or two had elapsed after they left me, and it was now noon. The sun played violently upon my head, and I felt a languor and debility that indicated approaching fever. My head gradually sank upon my breast, when I was shocked by hearing the water pouring into the cabin windows. The wretches had scuttled the schooner, and left me pinioned to go down with her. I commended my spirit to my Maker, and gave myself up for lost. I felt myself gradually dying away, and the last thing I remembered was the foaming noise of the waves. This was occasioned by a ship passing by me. I was taken in, restored to health, and am now a poor, ruined, helpless man."

On the same day, January 15, 1822, that the U. S. schooner "Porpoise" destroyed a nest of pirates on the north coast of Cuba, as previously related, the U. S. brig "Spark", master-commandant—an obsolete naval title—J. H. Elton, captured a Dutch sloop, having a crew of seven men engaged in piracy. Later, on the 1st of March, 1822, the U. S. sloop-of-war "Hornet" arrived at Norfolk, Va., escorting a convoy of 22 merchant vessels from Pensacola and Havana.

On March 7th, one of the gunboats, the "Revenge", captured a barge, but her crew escaped on shore. Next day the brig "Enterprise", Lieutenant Kearney, captured a small flotilla of the freebooters, three launches and four barges, off Cape Antonio, with their crews, numbering about 160 men.

In April, 1822, the schooner "Alligator", Lieutenant W. W. McKean, after a long chase and quite a spirited encounter, took the schooner "Cienega", five guns, thirty men, off Nuevitas, Cuba; this craft had formerly been a Colombian privateer, whose crew had mutinied at Ragged Island and turned pirates.

The United States squadron in the West Indies was increased after April, 1822, and for the rest of the year consisted of the frigates "Macedonian", 36, flagship of Commodore Biddle; frigate "Congress", 36, sloops "John Adams", 24, and "Peacock", 18; brig "Spark", 12; and schooners "Alligator", 12; "Grampus", 12; "Shark", 12; and "Porpoise", 12. The "Hornet" and "Enterprise" were at home, refitting.

It was soon found that the small vessels were better fitted for the work of running down and capturing pirates than were the heavy frigates and sloops, whose great draft of water did not permit them to pursue suspicious-looking craft in shoal water. Moreover, the flagship "Macedonian" was soon obliged to leave her station on account of the yellow fever, and arrived at Norfolk on August 5, 1822, having lost 76 of her crew, including ten officers, and fifty of the remainder were ill on her arrival. By the 24th of August the number of deaths had amounted to 103, out of her crew of 360 men.

On August 16th, 1822, Lieutenant Francis H. Gregory, commanding the schooner "Grampus", chased a brigantine which hoisted Spanish colors. .He suspected her of being a pirate, and demanded her surrender. This demand was answered by a volley from small arms and cannon. The "Grampus" fired a broadside, and in a few minutes the brigantine struck. When boarded she was nearly sinking, and had lost one man killed and six wounded. The prize proved to be the "Palmyra", 9 guns, 88 men, a privateer, but one of her officers confessed that they had robbed the American schooner "Coquette". The prize was sent to Charleston, S. C., and condemned.

In November, 1822, the U. S. schooner "Alligator", Lieutenant W. H. Allen, arriving at Matanzas, was informed that an American brig and schooner had been captured and were in possession of a large gang of pirates at a place about 45 miles east of Matanzas. The master of the brig and mate of the schooner had been sent to the latter place to procure a ransom of $7000 for the two vessels, with the threat that their vessels would be destroyed and their crews severely dealt with in case of failure to bring the money.

The master and mate were taken on board the "Alligator", which sailed immediately to the rescue. At daylight on November 9th she arrived near the bay, and hid behind intervening land, behind which they discovered a ship, two brigs and five schooners. One of the schooners, her deck black with men, was under way, and was immediately chased by the armed boats of the "Alligator". The wind was light, and the schooner using her long sweeps (oars), endeavored to escape up the bay. When the "Alligator's" boats arrived within hail, the schooner, with her bloody flag nailed to the mast, opened fire with a long brass eighteen-pound pivot gun and four smaller ones. Lieutenant Allen, Captain Freeman of the marines, and twelve men, were in the launch, far in advance of the other boats; pulling hard at the oars, they reached the pirate and took possession of her, after a desperate resistance which nothing but the most daring bravery could have overcome. The freebooters, all but one, escaped by taking to their boats and jumping overboard before the "Alligator's" boats reached them. But in the meantime the gallant Allen fell, pierced by two musket balls.

The surgeon of the "Alligator", in a letter to a friend published in many newspapers of the day, said: "Capt. Allen continued giving orders [after he was shot], and conversing with Mr. Dale and the rest of us, until a few minutes before his death, with a degree of cheerfulness that was little to be expected from a man in his condition. He said he wished his relatives and his country to know that he had fought well, and added that he died in peace and good will towards all the world, and hoped for his reward in the next."

Lieutenant Allen was wounded while standing up cheering his men in pursuit of the pirates. He was a valuable officer, and had rendered distinguished service in the U. S. brig "Argus" when she was captured by H. B. M. "Pelican" off the British coast in 1813. He commanded the "Argus" in the latter part of the action, after both his superior officers had been carried below severely wounded. He was highly commended for his skill in handling the brig, although obliged to surrender to superior force. After his death his name became the war cry in the many boat expeditions against the pirates.

After the wounding of Allen, the second pirate schooner escaped, but another heavily-armed schooner, the ship and two more "fore and afters" were captured. Besides Lieutenant Allen, the "Alligator" lost four men killed and three wounded. The pirates lost fourteen killed and several by drowning; their best armed schooner carried a long 12-pounder, two 6-pounders, two 3-pounders, and two swivel guns. In all the three piratical schooners had 125 men and 14 guns. The "Alligator's" boats' crews numbered about forty, armed with muskets, swords and pistols.

On November 19th, 1822, the "Alligator" was, unfortunately, lost on Carysford reef, a dangerous spot off the Florida coast, where many a fine ship before and since has come to grief. Her officers and crew were all saved.

The records of the old Marblehead Marine Insurance Company contain, in demands for the payment of insurance, the story, told in plain, matter-of-fact language, of the plundering by pirates, off the coast of Cuba, of the brig "Dover", from Matanzas to Charleston, S. C., and the schooner "Swan", bound from Mobile to Havana. Captain Sabins of the former reported that on January 16, 1822 : "Pan of Matanzas, bearing S., saw a boat coming to us from a small drogher, which came out of Matanzas the night before us, with five Spaniards armed with long knives, pistols, cutlasses, etc. When they got within hail, they fired a musket at us, cheered and came on board. They were the most villainous-looking rascals that any one had probably ever beheld. They immediately drew their weapons, and after beating us severely with their cutlasses, drove us below. They then robbed us of all our clothes except what we had on, our watches, and everything of value. We were afterwards called up singly. Four men with drawn knives stood over the captain and threatened him if he did not give up his money they would kill all hands and burn the vessel. After robbing the people, they commenced plundering the brig. They broke open the hatches, made us get out our boat and carry their plunder to their vessel.

"They took from us a compass, five bags of coffee, a barrel of sugar, nearly all our provisions, our colors, rigging, and cooking utensils. They then ordered us to stand to the north, or they would overhaul us, murder the crew, and burn the vessel. We made sail, and shortly after were brought to by another boat of the same charac ter,which fired into us,but left us upon being informed that we had been already robbed."

The experiences of the schooner "Swan", Captain Carter, were as follows :

"Mobile, June 1st, 1822. Schr. "Swan", Carter, arrived yesterday from Havana, and reports that on the outward passage from this port, on the 27th ult., at 8 o'clock A. M., being then within thirty miles of Havana, he was boarded by an open boat from the shore, manned with nine men, who all appeared to be Spaniards, armed with muskets, pistols, cutlasses and knives, who plundered the vessel of everything they could carry off.

"They also robbed the captain and crew of their clothing, even stripping the jackets from their backs and the shoes from their feet. The villains would not even spare the property of a Spanish priest, a passenger, but they robbed him also of his clothes, money and plate, to the value of 300 dollars ; they, however, afterwards returned his gown. A sail heaving in sight, they left the "Swan", with orders to steer E. N. E. and not go over three leagues from shore, under pain of death. From their conversation while on board, it appeared that they intended to board the schooner again in the evening, run her ashore and burn her, but she escaped by the darkness of the night."

The depredations of the pirates, nevertheless, continued to increase, and demands for ransom were frequently accompanied by threats that their hostages would be murdered if the ransom was not paid. Even at this early day the press had begun to urge that the United States should intervene in Cuba, as will be seen from the following article, which appeared in the "Baltimore Chronicle" :

"If the Spanish Government is unable to drive the pirates from their strongholds in Cuba, the Chronicle suggests the necessity of occupying the island with American forces for that purpose, as robbers and pirates have no right to protection whatever ; and in this case all civilized powers are warranted in carrying the war into the enemy's territory."

Acts of Congress were passed in 1822 giving an appropriation of $500,000 to fit out an expedition which was to wipe out the West Indian pirates. Commodore David Porter resigned his office as Navy Commissioner to take command of the expedition.

He selected and prepared the vessels personally, and organized what was known as the "Mosquito Fleet" ; owing to shallow water in many of the Cuban harbors and bays, it was necessary that some of the craft should be of small size and slight draft. This comprised what was known as the "steam galliot" "Sea Gull", 3 guns— the second steamer in the U. S. Navy, the "Fulton", in

1815, being the first—and eight small schooners, which
Commodore Porter bought for the Navy Department for
the sum of $10,190. These schooners were named:
"Fox", 51 tons; "Greyhound", 65 tons; "Jackal" 47
tons; "Beagle", 52 tons; "Terrier", 61 tons; "Weasel",
53 tons; "Wild Cat", 48 tons; and "Ferret" 51 tons.
Each of these carried three guns and a crew of 31 men.

In the fleet were, also, the transport ship "Decoy" 6
guns; five barges — "Mosquito", "Gnat", "Midge",
"Sandfly" and "Gallinipper",—together with the regular
naval vessels on the station which had been changed, and
consisted of the sloops-of-war "John Adams", 24; the
"Peacock", 18; the "Hornet", 18; the brig "Spark," 14;
and the schooners "Grampus", 12, and "Shark", 12.

As the steamer "Sea-Gull" was, without doubt, the first
steam-propelled man-of-war engaged in actual warfare, a
short description of her is not out of place. She was
built in Hartford, Conn., in 1818, for the merchant service, to run between that city and New Haven, and was
then called the "Enterprise"; she was a small craft,
measuring but slightly over 100 tons; her mode of pro-
pulsion was paddle-wheels, the engine being undoubtedly
of the "square" or "cross-head" type invented by Robert
Fulton. Like all the early steamboats, she probably had
a copper boiler carrying not over two or three pounds of
steam, and, of course, burning wood as fuel. The government paid $16,000 for the little steamer, renaming her
the "Sea-Gull", and fitting her, as before stated, with
three guns. As with all new inventions, the officers and
men of the Navy regarded a vessel propelled by steam
with anything but confidence, as is shown by the fact that
as originally built the "Sea-Gull" had little, if any, sail
power, but it is understood that the naval officers assigned
refused to go to sea in her unless she was fitted with
masts and lateen yards.

It is interesting to recall the names of her original
officers: Lieutenant Commanding, John C. Newton,—
many years later, in 1843, Lieutenant Newton, then a
captain, commanded the U. S. steam frigate "Missouri",
when she was burned while lying at anchor at Gibraltar;

acting sailing master, Arthur Bainbridge; the midshipmen were Messrs. Howard, Stockton and Taylor.

There is no record of the men who had charge of the machinery of this little craft, and we can only surmise that they were probably the same who had run her before she was a government vessel, and that their connection with the naval service was merely temporary. The grade of engineer in the United States Navy did not exist until 1836, the first person to hold it being Charles H. Haswell of New York, afterwards distinguished as a marine engine designer and naval architect.

The "Baltimore Chronicle" for January 17th, 1823, mentions the sailing of the "Sea-Gull" for the first time as a man-of-war as follows: "Yesterday Commodore Porter left this port in the steam galley 'Sea-Gull', bearing his broad pennant, to join the squadron fitting out at Norfolk for the purpose of suppressing piracy on the coast of Cuba. Every friend of humanity must wish that the efforts of the distinguished officer who has been selected to this command will be crowned with success. The means adopted are certainly the best calculated to effect the object. Frigates and sloops-of-war are totally inadequate, by means of their great draft of water; but the vessels which have been selected by Commodore Porter are precisely calculated to ferret the banditti from their lurking places.

"The aid of steam we think a most valuable addition to the squadron, and from the manner in which the 'Enterprise', now the 'Sea Gull', has been fitted out, we have every reason to believe she will completely answer the expectations formed. Commodore Porter has been indefatigable since he came here, and several of our citizens conversant in steam affairs volunteered their services to aid him in the necessary equipments for that department. We learn that she is provided with duplicates of every piece of machinery which might be carried away in action, and that her engineers are able and experienced men.

"In a very short time we hope to hear of the Commodore's arrival at his cruising ground, and we doubt not that he will soon put an end to the ravages of those law-less barbarians."

The naval career of the "Sea Gull" was but a short one ; in 1825 she was laid up at the Philadelphia Navy Yard, eventually becoming the receiving ship there until she was sold in 1840 for $4,750.

Commodore Porter sailed with his entire squadron from Norfolk on February 14th, 1823. Great publicity was given to the expedition, and this fact in itself had a good effect, because many of the pirates ceased their bloody work, while those that remained were afraid to venture far from their lairs. As soon as the fleet arrived off Porto Rico, Commodore Porter wrote to the Spanish governor on the subject of interruptions to our commerce and the illegal blockade of these coasts. On March 3d, 1823, he sent the "Greyhound", Lieutenant John Porter, into St. John's, Porto Rico, with that letter. On March 5th he sent the "Fox", Lieutenant W. H. Cocke, into the port for an answer. When the "Fox" endeavored to enter, she was fired upon by the castle, and her commander was instantly killed.

The only satisfaction offered for this insult and catas-trophe was the plea that the character of the schooner was mistaken. The Governor was profuse in his apolo-gies, and joined in paying every possible honor in the funeral services of Lieutenant Cocke, with the officers of the squadron. However, the Commodore demonstrated that the "Fox" had been fired at in a spirit of retaliation, but very wisely left Porto Rico, referring the matter to the government for action.

The squadron was then divided into small detachments and sent to thoroughly search the coasts of Porto Rico, San Domingo and Cuba. Every bay and inlet and key in all this region was visited, after which the squadron reassembled at Thompson's Island, now Key West, where Porter established a naval depot for a base of operations. On the morning of April 8th, 1823, Lieutenant C. K. Stribling—afterwards Admiral Stribling—was sent in the barge "Gallinipper" from Havana in search of a pirate, which he found three miles off, making in towards the shore. He caused muskets to be fired to bring her to, and she replied by a smart fire of round shot, grape and musketry, while working hard to escape. She was run ashore, and her crew, with the exception of one man, escaped, though it was afterwards ascertained that several of them had been wounded.

The vessel proved to be the schooner "Pilot", of Norfolk, Va., a very fast sailer, which they had captured but eight days before. She was armed with one long 12-pounder, blunderbusses, and other small arms. The notorious buccaneer Domingo commanded her; a few days before he had courteously forwarded mail for Commodore Porter and his officers that he had found on the "Pilot" when he had captured her. He sent a message with this mail that he did not wish to deprive them of the opportunity to hear from their friends; he bore them no ill-will, since they were only doing their duty.

Almost every day furnished accounts evincing the activity of Commodore Porter and the officers and men under his command; but for a long time their industry and zeal was rather shown in the suppression of piracy than the punishment of it. At length, however, an opportunity offered for inflicting the latter, as detailed in the following letter, dated Matanzas, July 10th, 1823, and afterwards printed in several New York, Boston and Salem newspapers:

"I have the pleasure of informing you of a brilliant achievement obtained against the pirates on the 5th inst. by two barges attached to Commodore Porter's squadron, the 'Gallinipper', Lieut. Watson, 18 men, and the 'Mosquito', Lieut. Inman, 10 men. The barges were returning from a cruise to windward; when they were near Jiguapa Bay, 13 leagues to windward of Matanzas, they entered it—it being a well-known rendezvous for pirates.

"They immediately discovered a large schooner under way, which they supposed to be a Patriot (South American) privateer; and as their stores were nearly exhausted, they hoped to obtain some supplies from her. They therefore made sail in pursuit. When they were within cannon shot distance, she rounded to and fired her long gun, at the same time running up the bloody flag, directing her course towards the shore, continuing to fire without effect.

"When she had got within a short distance of the shore, she came to, with springs on her cable, continuing to fire ; and when the barges were within thirty yards, they fired their muskets without touching boat or man ; our men gave three cheers, and prepared to board; the pirates discovering their intention, jumped into the water, when the bargemen, calling on the name of 'Allen', commenced a destructive slaughter, killing them in the water and as they landed. So exasperated were our men, that it was impossible for their officers to restrain them, and many were killed after orders were given to grant quarter.

"Twenty-seven dead were counted, some sunk, five taken prisoners by the bargemen, and eight taken by a party of Spaniards on shore. The officers calculated that from thirty to thirty-five were killed. The schooner mounted a long nine-pounder on a pivot and four four-pounders, with every other necessary armament, and a crew of fifty to sixty men, and ought to have blown the barges to atoms. She was commanded by the notorious Diableto, or 'Little Devil'. This statement I have from Lieut. Watson himself, and it is certainly the most decisive operation that has been effected against those murderers, either by the British or American force. This affair occurred on the same spot where the brave Allen fell about one year since. The prize was sent to Thompson's Island (now Key West)."

A few weeks before the occurrence related above, on April 16, 1823, the ship-sloop "Peacock", Captain Cassin, entered Colorados, a harbor noted for pirates. He discovered a felucca standing out, and chased her ashore, but the pirates escaped. The felucca was a new, well-coppered boat, pulling sixteen sweeps (large oars), and was evidently starting out on her first cruise. Captain Cassin broke up their establishment, and the pirates burned three of their schooners on his approach. The U. S. schooners "Greyhound" and "Beagle" left Thompson's Island (now Key West), on June 7, 1823, under the command of Lieutenants Kearney and Newton, and cruised within the

U. S. CORVETTE "JOHN ADAMS"

Flagship of the West India Squadron, 1822

From the original negative in possession of F. B. C. Bradlee

U. S. STEAMER "SEA GULL"

Second Steamer in the U. S. Navy, 1823

From the seal of the Connecticut River Banking Company

Kindness of L. F. Middlebrook, Esq.

Keys, on the south side of Cuba, as far as Cape Cruz, touching at all the intermediate ports on the island, to intercept pirates.

On July 21 they anchored off Cape Cruz, and Lieutenant Kearney went in his boat to reconnoitre the shore, when he was fired upon by a party of pirates who were concealed among the bushes. Several cannon in position on a hill a short distance off also opened fire. The boat returned, and five or six others were manned from the schooners and pushed off for the shore, but a very heavy cannonade being kept up by the pirates on the heights, the boats were compelled to retreat. Thereupon the "Greyhound" and "Beagle" were then warped in, when they discharged several broadsides, and covered the landing of the boats. After a sharp fight, the pirates retreated to another hill that they had also taken the precaution to fortify. A small hamlet, in which the pirates resided, was set on fire and destroyed. Three cannon, one a four-pounder brass fieldpiece, and two swivels, with several pistols, cutlasses, and eight large rowboats, were captured.

A cave, about 150 feet deep, was discovered near where the houses were, and after considerable difficulty, a party of seamen got to the bottom, where was found an immense quantity of plunder, consisting of broadcloths, dry goods, female dresses, saddlery, etc. Many human bones were also in the cave, supposed to have been the remains of unfortunate persons who were taken and put to death. A great many of the articles were brought away and the rest destroyed. About forty pirates escaped to the heights, but many were supposed to have been killed, from the fire of the schooners as well as from the men who landed. The bushes were so thick that it was impossible to pursue them. Several other caves were in the neighborhood, in which it was conjectured that the freebooters occasionally took shelter.

Some idea of the exacting and dangerous nature of the work undertaken by Commodore Porter, his officers and men, may be judged by the following official reports, copied from the records of the Navy Department. Indeed, the struggles of Commodore Porter's squadron in stamping out piracy compare favorably in courage and daring with that of the United States regulars in their endless fighting with savage Indians, protecting the settlers, etc., on the far western frontier during the larger part of the nineteenth century.

The schooner "Grampus" cruised in the vicinity of Campeachy from April to July, 1823, and her commander, Lieutenant, afterwards Rear-Admiral, Francis H. Gregory, reported as follows:

"United States Schooner 'Grampus',
"Thompson's Island, 3d July, 1823.

"Sir: I have the honor to inform you that this vessel sailed from the Balize on the 24th of April, with a convoy for Tobasco, where she arrived on the 1st of May. Sailed thence again on the 6th, with a convoy, towards Vera Cruz; parted with the convoy on the 9th, and arrived at Campeachy on the 13th, where I received information of several piracies committed upon merchant vessels of the United States, and that the coast of Yucatan, from Cape Catoche to Lagona, was then infested by several gangs of pirates, who had been guilty of every atrocity imaginable. Finding there were a considerable number of merchant ships at the several ports upon that coast unprotected, and others arriving almost daily, I continued thereabouts until the 25th of June, scouring the coast up and down, and occasionally, when any information was had which offered the least chance of detecting these villains, the boats were employed, and sometimes were sent along the coast twenty or thirty leagues from the vessel.

"On the 22d of May I chased a schooner ashore to windward of Sisal, which I have no doubt was a pirate, from his appearance and conduct. As it was in the night, and upon a part of the coast where I was not sufficiently acquainted, and blowing fresh upon the shore, I had not an opportunity of completing his destruction. On June 11th I seized a suspicious vessel in the harbor of Campeachy, and resigned her to the authorities there on that account. This last vessel has just come from New Malaga, or Vigia de Chiguila, a little to windward of Cape Catoche, where the pirates have a very considerable establishment, and came down to Campeachy for the purpose of procuring stores for a vessel then preparing for a cruise.

"Two seamen, who had been held as prisoners at New Malaga, informed me that this gang was sometimes a hundred and upwards in number; that they held possession of a small fort, having two 24-pounders; and that an officer named Molla, who had been placed there by the government, had joined them. This was corroborated by the authorities of Campeachy, who requested me to land and destroy the place. The pirates issue from their post in barges, small vessels, and in canoes, hover along the shores, enter the harbors, murder and destroy almost all that fall in their power.

"On the 2d of June, 1823, the American schooner 'Shiboleth', Captain Perry, of New York, being then ready for the sea, was boarded by a canoe having fourteen of these villains on board. The watch was instantly murdered, eight others of the crew were put into the forecastle, the hatch was spiked down, a ton or more of logwood put over it, the head sails set, the wind off shore, and the vessel set on fire in the cabin. By the most extraordinary exertions, these men broke out in time to save their lives. I arrived while the vessel was on fire.

"The same canoe then proceeded to windward, and two days afterward took the schooner 'Augustus and John', off Sisal, and burnt her, having turned the crew adrift in a small boat, with every probability of their perishing. The people of the country were much exasperated, and turned out to hunt them from their shores. A party of dragoons having met them, a skirmish ensued, wherein the captain of dragoons and several of his men were killed, and the pirates taking to their boats, escaped.

"One of the seamen I mentioned as having been among them, stated that he belonged to an English schooner from New Providence, called the 'Flyer', that the crew, with the exception of himself, were instantly butchered. He was detained about two months, during which time they had captured nine vessels, some of which were brought in, but the principal part destroyed; and in some instances he was certain that the whole crews were murdered. When he left the place (about twenty days since) they had a Guineaman, with 200 slaves and a large quantity of ivory and two small schooners, Americans.

"An English cutter informed me that the pirates had direct and uninterrupted intercourse with Havana, by means of small coasting vessels that ran regularly to the ports on the coast, and always touched at New Malaga. Frequently some of them would go up to the Havana, and others of the gang come down.

"That this infernal horde of villains have established themselves at New Malaga I have no doubt, and from the information given me by men of the first respectability at Campeachy, Sisal, and other places on the coast, I believe the pirates have been guilty of all the acts as herein stated.

"I have the honor to be, very respectfully, your most obedient servant,

"Francis H. Gregory,
"Lieutenant Commanding, United States Navy.
"Commodore David Porter, Commanding United States
    Naval Forces, West Indian Station."

The writer of this modest, matter-of-fact report, containing material enough to compile a thrilling sea tale, was a New Englander, born at Norwalk, Connecticut, on October 9th, 1789. Like many of our early naval officers, young Gregory began his sea career in the merchant service; he received his midshipman's warrant on January 16th, 1809. In those days the midshipmen received their professional education on shipboard, and, as it might without exaggeration be said, between battles. Midshipman Gregory's first services were near Balize, where he helped capture a slaver, a brig flying English colors and having 120 negroes on board, also a schooner fitting out for piratical purposes; shortly afterwards he took part in a night action with a privateer, which was disabled and driven off the coast, and, also, young as he was, was sent to the United States as prize-master in charge of a Spanish piratical brig mounting fourteen guns, which had been captured a few days before.

Whatever they may have lacked in some ways, it may be safely affirmed that the young officers in the early days of the navy were not wanting in the practical part of their profession.

When the war of 1812 broke out, we find Midshipman Gregory serving on Lake Ontario, under Commodore Chauncey ; he was captured in August, 1813, and sent to England, where he was confined for eighteen months as a prisoner of war ; in the meantime he had been promoted to be lieutenant, on June 28th, 1814. At the close of the war of 1812, Lieut. Gregory served for three years on the Mediterranean squadron under Commodore Shaw, whose daughter he married. From 1821 to 1823 he commanded the schooner "Grampus" in the West Indies, as we have already noted, and just before returning to the United States under orders for another station, he captured the pirate brig "Panchita", a vessel far superior to the "Grampus" in weight of metal and number of men.

On April 28th, 1828, Lieutenant Gregory was promoted to be a commander, and on January 18th, 1838, he reached the rank of full captain (equal to that of colonel in the army), then and for many years afterwards (1862) the highest grade in the United States Navy, the officers commanding squadrons being given the temporary and courtesy title of "Flag officer", or Commodore.

In connection with this antiquated and rather curious state of things, a laughable little "yarn" is not out of place. Very soon after the breaking out of the Civil war, it was naturally found necessary to restore higher grades in the navy than that of captain, and a bill to that effect was put before Congress. The late Captain A. T. Mahan, U. S. N., in his interesting reminiscences, "From Sail to Steam", recalled that the sailmaker of the ship he was then serving on, a sensible, thoughtful man, in discussing the possible higher rank, said, "Call them admirals ! never ! they will be wanting to be dukes next."

During the Mexican war, 1846-48, Captain Gregory commanded the frigate "Raritan" ; his last active sea service was a few years later, when he was placed in charge of the African squadron. The Civil war found him commandant of the Brooklyn Navy Yard, where he also superintended the construction of the early ironclads. Captain Gregory was promoted to the rank of Rear-

Admiral on July 16th, 1862. He died in Brooklyn on October 4th, 1866, having rounded out an active and glorious career of over half a century.

Lieutenant Thomas H. Newell, commanding the schooner "Ferret", reported as follows concerning a cruise made on the southern coast of Cuba:

"United States Schooner 'Ferret',
"Thompson's Island (Key West),
"June 25, 1823.

"Sir: Pursuant to your instructions, I left this place on the 14th inst., on a cruise to Trinidad, on the south side of Cuba, in company with the 'Beagle', Captain Newton. On the second day we parted company, and on the third day I made the Havana (on my way to Matanzas); from thence I commenced a diligent search in all the ports and bays.

"On Tuesday sent my boat into Canised, and obtained information that some pirates were still lurking about the coast. During that night I kept close into the land, and on Wednesday, at 10 A. M., discovered an armed barge with sixteen oars, and well manned, in a small bay called Bacuna Yeagua. I immediately sent Lieutenant Dorring with five men, the most my boat could carry, to examine all the boats, there being seven in number. He approached within fifty yards of the barge, when the crew showed their character by opening fire on him with musketry and blunderbusses, which, fortunately, did no other damage than nearly to sink the boat, she having received a ball at the water edge; five other ones were found in the boat, which, being nearly spent, had struck the water and innocently jumped into her. My boat, at no time suitable for the transportation of men, and now rendered useless, induced me to take possession of a small coaster that was near, and manned her with fifteen men, and at that time intended to stand in, if possible, with the 'Ferret', in order to cover the men while they took possession of the barge, which then had the American colors, union down; but, on approaching, found that the channel would not admit of my entering.

"It was then blowing very hard and a heavy sea on, therefore I deemed it proper to recall the coaster, which had like to have gotten ashore, for, had that catastrophe occurred, I question much whether the pirates would have had the gratification of butchering them, as they certainly would have been drowned. The sea was then breaking with great violence over the reef that covered the bay. I was then compelled to resort to making tacks, close in with the reef, and giving them 'long Tom' (a naval expression in use at that period to describe a heavy swivel gun), with round and grape shot, in hopes to destroy the boats—as to killing any of them, it was impossible, for, on the approach of the 'Ferret', they would completely secure themselves behind the rocks and trees, which hung all around the harbor; but this I was frustrated in by the enormous roughness of the sea, and the wind being on shore prevented me from taking any position from which I could annoy them much. Finding it impossible with the means then in my power, I stood out to sea, in hopes to fall in with some vessel from which I could get a suitable boat (but am sorry to say it was not until next morning that my wishes were obtained), and, if that could be done, to push to Matanzas, to concert a plan with the Governor by which the pirates, as well as their boats, may be taken.

"I, however, obtained a boat from an English vessel, and immediately bore up for the same place, which was then but a short distance off. I had not run but a short time when I discovered a Spanish brig-of-war lying to off the bay, which proved to be the 'Matae'. On the report being sent to the Governor of Matanzas that one of the United States schooners was engaged with the pirates, he dispatched this brig, and at the same time took with him a land force, and had cruised there a few minutes before me and had taken possession of a small schooner boat the pirates had abandoned, and which lay on the beach. I sent in my boat after he had left, and ordered a search, when two of the boats I had seen the day I attacked them were found, well sunk, up a lagoon, which, upon further examination, extended several miles into the island, and have no doubt but what the large barge is now at the head of it, but not being prepared with boats, I did not think it proper to send my boats out from the 'Ferret'. The two boats I have brought over, and shall await your orders relative thereto.

"On my arrival at Matanzas I found my mainmast very dangerously sprung, which has made it necessary for me to return here, but not until I had given convoy to eight of our merchantmen from Matanzas and Cuba.

"I have the honor to be, sir, very respectfully, your obedient servant,

"Thomas H. Newell.
"To Commodore David Porter, U. States Navy."

On March 1st, 1823, the famous pirate, La Cata, was captured off the Isle of Pines by the British man-of-war cutter "Grecian", after a smart action. The cutter mounted six long nine-pounders, and her crew numbered fifty; the pirate schooner had eight guns, and over one hundred in her crew; it was believed that about thirty of the latter were killed, but only three prisoners were made, the rest escaping on shore in small boats or by swimming. Considerable quantities of goods were found on board the prize.

The "Grecian" conveyed the prisoners to Jamaica, where, it seemed, the laws against piracy were more strictly enforced than in the United States. About the same date a British sloop of war captured a pirate schooner, manned by sixty men, off St. Domingo·* She had on board $200,000 in gold and silver, besides many other valuable articles. Two years later, May 16th, 1825, the "Grecian", assisted by a steamboat which, like the U. S. S. "Sea Gull", had formerly been a merchant vessel, but was chartered and fitted out by the British naval authorities at Jamaica to assist their squadron, captured a piratical brigantine and her crew of thirty-eight desperadoes, off Matanzas. Several of the pirates were killed, and the rest sent to Havana for trial. It was ascertained that some of them had assisted in capturing more than twenty American vessels, whose crews were murdered!

The British navy assisted the United States squadron in every way in their operations against the pirates, and the most cordial relations prevailed between the two

*Files of the N. Y. Shipping and Commercial List.

fleets. Unfortunately, however, the English men-of-war were constantly sent off on other duties, and they had no special squadron detailed to deal with the pirates. At this period the British West India squadron consisted of the line-of-battle ships "Forte" and "Gloucester", frigates "Dartmouth", "Hyperion" and "Seringapatam", sloops "Carnation", "Pandora", "Tyne", "Tomar" "Scout", cutter "Grecian", and "Thracian", the brigs "Redwing", "Bustard", and "Kangaroo", and the schooner "Speedwell", with four smaller craft. This formidable fleet captured, as already stated, only 13 vessels and 291 men. But the prisoners convicted of piracy were duly executed, and it is known that forty-two pirates were hung at Jamaica.

The British gave their prisoners the proper punishment for their deeds. In our country these pirates had the sympathy, strange as it may seem, of a great many people, to such an extent that very few were executed, many, too many, were pardoned, and some of the pardoned pirates were captured a second time with their former comrades.

Some idea of the desperate deeds of these marine highwaymen have been told in former pages, but no tales of fiction have pictured their crimes as black as they really were in truth. At first the reports greatly exaggerated their deeds, and the pirates themselves played upon the imaginations of their captives ; but in course of time they practiced all sorts of cruelty and tortured their victims with every possible circumstance of horror to make death welcome to the unfortunate sufferers. The reports of the many crimes and outrages demonstrate the frightful growth of marine highway robbery and the immense value of the gallant services of the United States Navy cannot be exaggerated.

The following rather minute, but most interesting account of the execution of a large number of pirates, taken from an old book on "Piracy" (which in turn copied the story from contemporaneous newspapers) is well worth reproducing.

"Ten of the pirates captured by H. B. M. sloop-of-war 'Tyne' were executed at Kingston, Jamaica, on Friday, the 7th of February, 1823. About a quarter of an hour before day dawn the wretched culprits were taken from the jail, under a guard of soldiers from the 50th regiment and the City Guard. On their arrival at the wherry wharf, the military retired, and the prisoners, with the Town Guard, were put on board two wherries, in which they proceeded to Port Royal Point, the usual place of execution in similar cases.

"They were there met by a strong party of military, consisting of 50 men, under the command of two commissioned officers. At the word of command the soldiers formed themselves into a square around the place of execution, with the sheriff and his officers with the prisoners in the centre. The gallows were of considerable length, and contrived with a drop so as to prevent the unpleasant circumstances which frequently occur. The unfortunate men had been in continual prayer from the time they were awakened out of a deep sleep till they arrived at that place, where they were to close their existence.

"They all expressed their gratitude for the attention they had met with from the Sheriff and the inferior officers. Many pressed the hands of the turnkey to their lips, others to their hearts, and, on their knees, prayed that God, Jesus Christ and the Virgin Mary would bless him and the other jailors for their goodness. They all then fervently joined in prayer. To the astonishment of all, no clerical character of any persuasion was present. They repeatedly called out, 'Adonde esta el padre' (where is the holy father?) Juan Hernandez called on all persons present to hear him—he was innocent; what they had said about his confessing himself guilty was untrue. He had admitted himself guilty because he hoped for pardon, but that now he was to die he called God, Jesus Christ, the Holy Ghost, the Virgin Mary, and the Saints, to witness that he spoke the truth—that he was no pirate, no murderer—he had been forced. The lieutenant of the pirates was a wretch, who did not fear God, and had compelled him to act.

"Juan Gutterez and Francisco de Sayas were loud in their protestations of innocence. Manuel Lima said, for himself he did not care; he felt for the old man (Miguel Jose). How could he be a pirate who could not help himself? If it were a Christian country, they would

have pardoned him for his gray hairs. He was innocent
—they had both been forced. Let none of his friends
and relations ever venture to sea—he hoped his death
would be a warning to them, that the innocent might suffer for the guilty. The language of this young man
marked him a superior to the generality of his companions
in misery. The seamen of the 'Whim' stated that he was
very kind to them when prisoners on board the piratical
vessel. Just before he was turned off he addressed the
old man—'Adios, viejo, para siempre adios' !—(Farewell,
old man, forever farewell).

"Several of the prisoners cried out for mercy, pardon,
pardon. Domingo Eucalla, the black man, then addressed
them. 'Do not look for mercy here, but pray to God ; we
are all brought here to die. This is not built for nothing ;
here we must end our lives. You know I am innocent,
but I must die the same as you all. There is not anyone
here who can do us any good, so let us think only of God
Almighty. We are not children, but men, you know that
all must die ; and in a few years those who kill us must
die, too. When I was born, God set the way of my
death ; I do not blame anyone ; I was taken by the
pirates, and they made me help them ; they would not let
me be idle.

" 'I could not show that this was the truth, and therefore they have judged me by the people they have found
me with. I am put to death unjustly, but I blame no-
body. It was my misfortune. Come, let us pray. If we
are innocent, so much the less have we to repent. I do
not come here to accuse anyone ; death must come one
day or another, better to the innocent than to the guilty.'

"He then joined in prayer with the others. He seemed
to be much reverenced by his fellow prisoners. He chose
those prayers he thought most adapted to the occasion.
Hundreds were witnesses to the manly firmness of this
negro. Observing a bystander listening attentively to the
complaints of one of his fellow-wretches, he translated
what had been said into English. With a steady pace and
a resolute and resigned countenance, he ascended the
fatal scaffold. Observing the executioner unable to untie
a knot on the collar of one of the prisoners, he with his

teeth undid it.   He then prayed most fervently until the drop fell.

"Miguel Jose protested his innocence—'No he robado, no he matado ningune, muero innocente' (I have robbed no one, I have killed no one, I die innocent. I am an old man, but my family will feel my disgraceful death.)

"Francisco Miguel prayed devoutly, but inaudibly. His soul seemed to have quitted his body before he was executed.   Breti Gullimillit called on all to witness his innocence ; it was of no use for him to say an untruth, for he was going before the face of God.   Augustus Hernandez repeatedly declared his innocence ; requested that no one would say he had made a confession; he had none to make.

"Juan Hernandez was rather obstinate when the executioner pulled the cap over his eyes. He said, rather passionately, 'Quita is de mis ojos'—(Remove it from my eyes).   He then rubbed it up against one of the posts of the gallows.   Miguel Jose made the same complaint, and drew the covering from his eyes by rubbing his head against a fellow sufferer.   Pedro Nonde was loud in his ejaculations for mercy and wept bitterly. He was covered with the marks of deep wounds.

"The whole of the ten included in the death warrant having been placed on the scaffold, and the ropes suspended, the drop was let down. Nondre, being an immensely heavy man, broke the rope and fell to the ground alive.   Juan Hernandez struggled long.   Lima was much convulsed ; the old man Gullimillit and Miguel were apparently dead before the drop fell, and Eucalla (the negro) gave one convulsion, and all was over.

"When Nondre recovered from the fall and saw his nine lifeless companions stretched in death, he gave an agonizing shriek ; he wrung his hands, screamed 'Favor, favor, me matan sin causa. O! buenos Christianos, me amparen, ampara me, ampara me, no hay Christiano en asta, tiara?' (Mercy, mercy, they kill me without cause— Oh, good Christians, protect me, protect me, protect me. Is there no Christian in this land?)

"He then lifted his eyes to Heaven and prayed long and loud. Upon being again suspended, he was for a long period convulsed. He was an immensely powerful man, and died hard.

The ship "Orleans", of Philadelphia, a large, heavily-armed vessel bound from New York to the West Indies, was robbed off Cape Antonio, in September, 1821, by an equally large piratical corvette mounting at least fourteen guns. The crew of the "Orleans" offered but a faint resistance, and were probably overawed by the size of the pirate and the number of freebooters on her; many of the "Orleans" men afterwards joined the pirate, with, it was said, but little urging. The latter was commanded by one Gasparilla, a noted desperado of the blackest die; his headquarters were in the island of Boca Grande, on the west coast of Florida; this place is now a noted and fashionable winter resort, and one of the small islands in the neighborhood is named for Gasparilla.

Goods to the value of $40,000 were taken from the "Orleans"; most of the marauders appear to have been Spaniards and Portuguese, with a liberal sprinkling of negroes. After robbing the ship, Gasparilla wrote, in the French language, a note to a United States naval officer, a passenger on the "Orleans", as follows:

"At Sea, and in Good Luck.

"Sir:

"Between buccaneers, no ceremony; I take your dry goods, and, in return, I send you pimento; therefore we are now even. I entertain no resentment.

"Bid good day to the officer of the United States, and tell him that I appreciate the energy with which he has spoken of me and my companions-in-arms. Nothing can intimidate us; we run the same fortune, and our maxim is that 'the goods of this world belong to the strong and valiant.

"The occupation of the Floridas is a pledge that the course I follow is conformable to the policy pursued by the United States.

(Signed)

"Richard Coeur de Lion."

Through the kindness of Robert S. Bradley, Esq., of Boston, president of the Charlotte Harbor and Northern

Railway Company of Florida, a most interesting, and, it is believed, accurate account of the famous, or rather infamous, Gasparilla, is here reproduced.   It was originally printed in pamphlet form, to be distributed among the patrons of the railway and the Boca Grande Hotel, but the story proved so thrilling that the little brochure went out of print rapidly and is now quite rare.

"This narrative was compiled by the writer from incidents told by John Gomez, better known as Panther Key John, a brother-in-law of Gasparilla and a member of his crew, who died at the age of one hundred and twenty years, at Panther Key, Florida, twelve miles below Marco, in the year 1900 ; also from records left by John Gomez, Jr., the cabin-boy on Gasparilla's ship, who was kidnapped by Gasparilla, and who witnessed the death of this pirate and all on board his vessel.   He died and was buried at Palmetto, Florida, in 1875, at the age of seventy years.

"While it is almost impossible to obtain exact information concerning this outlaw, owing to the numerous and conflicting accounts, the writer has tried to put into readable form a few of these stories concerning Gasparilla, and has only used such accounts where two or more sources agreed.   However, it is well to keep in mind that owing to the long lapse of time between the death of Gasparilla and the present year nearly all old landmarks have gone."

"The Story of Gasparilla."

"The romantic age of the Gulf is past, the days when pirate bands preyed upon the peaceful merchantman, stole his goods, and carried away his women passengers, have gone, but romance still holds sway in the minds of each of us, and in the pirate Gasparilla we find a story that is full of the spice of romantic adventure, that abounds with thrills, and causes the pulse to beat just a little faster at some daring exploit, the eyes to fill with water at some touching story, or the fists to clench in the good American way at the brutal butcheries that authentic documents show were committed.   Gasparilla has gone, his pirate gold lies hidden somewhere on the isles of Charlotte harbor, but the bleached bones of his murdered victims, with

COMMODORE SYDNEY S. LEE, C. S. N.
Brother of Gen. R. E. Lee

From a photograph taken during the Civil War
In the collection of F. B. C. Bradlee

U. S. SLOOP-OF-WAR "MACEDONIAN"

Originally a British Frigate, captured in the War of 1812

Cut down to a sloop-of-war in 1858

the stories that have drifted down from past generations, give to the world a synopsis of the life and death of Gasparilla, the terror of the Southern Seas.

"His name was Jose Gaspar (Gasparilla meaning Gaspar, the outlaw). He stood high in the graces of the Spanish Court, so high indeed that he filched the crown jewels. Jose was also an officer of high standing in the naval affairs of the Spaniards. Some records give him the honor of being what we would call an admiral. His theft discovered, he deserted his wife and children, gathered together a nice lot of cut-throats, stole the prize vessel of the Spanish fleet, and escaped. This happened in the year 1782. A price was declared upon his head, and, it is stated, when Gasparilla heard this decree, he swore eternal vengeance upon all Spaniards in general, and commenced to destroy the commerce of Spain.

"The Gulf of Mexico at that time being a rendezvous for pirate fleets, Gaspar settled in Charlotte Harbor and built upon the shores of what is now called Turtle Bay twelve houses, where, under guard, his female captives were placed, all male prisoners being killed when captured. The buildings were constructed of palmetto logs, and arranged in a semi-circle close to the water's edge.

"About one hundred yards further inland the burying ground was discovered several years ago, containing not only the bones of his men, but the skeletons of his murdered women captives. Many a touching story has been unearthed when the ghostly remains were uncovered— stories of great strong men who died in the fight, of women who died to save their honor, and of nobility we even find a trace, but these are only traditions, and the story of 'The Little Spanish Princess,' as told by old Panther Key John Gomez, we will relate later on.

"Close to Turtle Bay lies the little Isle of Cayopelean. Upon this island stood a burial mound fifty feet high and four hundred feet in circumference at the base, built centuries earlier, it is thought, by the Mound Builders of a prehistoric race. Excavations in this mound have produced ornaments of gold and silver, together with hundreds of human skeletons. On its summit Gasparilla constructed an observation tower, where always a grim sentinel was stationed and looked across the warm, smiling waters of the Gulf for a victim.

"The present Isle of Gasparilla the pirate named for himself. Taking the best of everything when a capture was made, he chose the best of the islands in Charlotte Harbor for his own secret haunts. It is said that Jose was saluted the King of the Pirates, and his home on Gasparilla Island was regal in its fittings.

"Some writers have said that Gasparilla joined Pierre LaFitte, the famous French pirate, while others have stated on good authority that LaFitte joined Gasparilla's band, contributing a boat and thirty men.

"While taking the census of 1900 two gentlemen stopped at Panther Key and spent the night with John Gomez. The race of the old buccaneer was nearly run, but all through that night he told a story of piracy that could scarce be believed, yet it was a dying man that was clearing his soul before his Maker. He told of the looting of ships, the massacre of innocents, and last of all, when his life had nearly passed, he told the story of 'The Little Spanish Princess,' whose name he did not remember. He told where the body would be found, and a sketch was prepared under his direction, and in recent years in the exact location as described the skeleton of a beheaded woman was found. This is the story.

"In the early days of the year 1801 a princess of Spain sailed in great state for Mexico. While in that country she was royally entertained by its Ruler, and to show her appreciation to the Mexican people she prevailed upon the nobles to allow her to take eleven of Mexico's fairest daughters away with her to be educated in Spanish customs. A treasure of much gold, bound in chests of copper, it is said, was in cargo. When about forty miles from what is now Boca Grande, Gasparilla engaged them in combat, killed the crew, took the gold, and carried away as captives the princess and the eleven Mexican girls. The princess he kept for himself, the maids were divided among his men. The little Spanish princess spurned the one-time favorite of the King, and Gasparilla swore that if she did not return of her own free will the affections lavished upon her, she would be beheaded, and the story goes the threat of Gaspar was fulfilled. Far away from her native land, alone on a tropical isle, the little princess still lies in the lonely bed made for her by Gasparilla. The night birds sing in the dusk and lull her spirit to rest in the evening, and the moon throws kindly shadows o'er the spot where royalty sleeps.

"From members of Gaspar's crew many a strange story has drifted down concerning him, his traits, his ways, his passions. He was polished in his manners and a great lover of fashionable clothes; fearless in fight, and at all times cruel in his nature. Concerning women he was fanatical, and his houses were always filled with captives. It is stated beauty was essential with him. He kept for himself a certain number of picked beauties, but so fickle was his nature that when an additional capture was made and a new face appealed to him, one of his old loves must forfeit her life to make room for the new favorite. That this was true there is no doubt, as the graveyard of Gasparilla tells its own terrible story.

"In 1819 the United States, having obtained, under the Louisiana Purchase in 1803,* the states bordering on the Gulf, made war upon the robber bands. On Sanibel Island a conference was held by all the pirates, and with the exception of Gasparilla, Baker, Caesar, and old King John, all sailed away, to be heard of no more.

"Nearly two years later, the war on piracy becoming too severe, Jose and his crew agreed to divide their wealth, which was then estimated at thirty million dollars, to give up piracy, and live as honest men the rest of their lives. This was decided upon and plans made accordingly.

"In the spring of 1822, while getting together his treasure for division, which at that time was hidden in six separate hiding places, he cited what appeared to be a large English merchantman just off Boca Grande Pass. It is said his greedy eyes lit with pleasure at the thoughts of just one more victim ere his piratical days were over. Closely following the shore-line of the Gulf, he slipped

*Florida belonged to Spain, therefore was not included in the Louisiana Purchase from France in 1803. It was acquired by the United States by special treaty in 1819.

into Charlotte Harbor through what is now known as Little Gasparilla Pass, crept around Gasparilla Island, and gathered together his crew. Great excitement reigned when the plans were unfolded. The band of eighty men was divided into two parts, he commanding thirty-five men, LaFitte thirty-five, while ten were left in charge of the camp. At about four in the afternoon Gasparilla and his men dashed through the Boca Grande Pass for the English prize; fast overtaking the fleeing ship, the black flag was hoisted, and his men stood ready with the grappling hooks, but suddenly the English flag floated down and the Stars and Stripes pulled in place; in a moment guns were uncovered on deck, and Gasparilla, realizing that he was in a trap, turned to flee. His boat, disabled by the shots from the war vessel and capture staring him in the face, he wrapped a piece of anchor chain around his waist and jumped into the sea. His age at his death was about sixty-five. His crew was hanged at the yard-arms, with the exception of the cabin-boy and the ten men left in charge of the captives, they having escaped to the mainland. Panther Key John was in this gang. The cabin-boy was carried to New Orleans, where he remained in prison ten years.

"LaFitte, watching the battle from afar, turned and fled, but the next morning his boat was captured and sunk off the mouth of the Manatee River. Whether he was captured at this point is not known, as so many conflicting stories arose concerning him, still it is a positive fact that he was buried at New Orleans.

"For thirty years the craft of Gasparilla was visible from Gasparilla Island, lying five miles off Boca Grande Pass, but the sand has now completely covered the wreck.

"The treasure of Gasparilla still lies unmoved. The bones of the bold buccaneer, with his pirate ship, have vanished, but legends from the fisher-folk say that sometimes in the dead of night, off Gasparilla Island, when the waves are singing a lullaby to the weary and the wind is whispering soft messages through the palmettos, the phantom fleets of the pirate crew arise from their ocean resting places and pursue, as in days of old, the ghost ships of the merchantmen."

Among the best known American privateers during the war of 1812-15 was the "America", owned by George Crowninshield* and Sons, of Salem, Mass. She was the fourth vessel bearing that name and belonging to the firm since 1783, and they were all lucky and profitable investments. The fourth "America", built for a merchantman at Salem in 1803-04, by Retire Becket, was always noted for her high speed, and while a privateer, her unusual number of captures and numerous escapes from British cruisers. She arrived in Salem from her last cruise in April, 1815, and never again went to sea, although she was not broken up until 1831. In 1818, however, a half interest in the "America" was sold for $4000† (the firm of George Crowninshield and Sons having been dissolved in 1817), and for a year or two there were persistent rumors that the United States Navy Department wished to buy the old privateer and make her into a small sloop of war. Her great speed would have made her useful in chasing pirates on the West India station. For some reason or other, however, the deal was never consummated, probably because the "America's" timbers may have already shown signs of dry rot.

The photograph of the old carronade inserted herewith, to show marine ordnance of one hundred years ago, is taken from one of the guns of the old "America", owned by Francis B. Crowninshield, Esq., of Marblehead, Mass., and reproduced through his kindness.

The brig "Aurilla", of Gloucester, Mass., bound from Baltimore to New Orleans, was boarded by two piratical schooners off Salt Key, May 16th, 1822. The pirates compelled the captain and crew to go below, while the captain was examined in regard to the cargo and money on board. Having besmeared the windlass with the blood of a chicken, the pirates ranged themselves in two lines, and each member of the "Aurilla's" crew was made to run the gauntlet singly, and in such manner as to lead

*George Crowninshield was the author's great-great-grandfather.

†The Private Armed Ship "America" of Salem, by Bowdoin Bradlee Crowninshield: The Essex Institute, 1901.

them to think that death awaited them at the windlass, where the blood was evidence of the fate of their ship-mates who had preceded them. They thus secured about $50,000 worth of goods and money, but they resorted to this individual inquisition in order to ascertain if the cap-tain had informed them truly.

One of the crew was found hidden below, and was brought on deck. He supposed that he was the only sur-vivor, and to escape the gauntlet he pretended that one of the passengers, a Mr. Nickoff, had stowed a box of money in the hold. Mr. Nickoff was called again, and as the money could not be found, he was stabbed in the arms and legs, blindfolded, and, with a rope round his body, was hoisted to the yard-arm and lowered into the sea. Still unable to inform them, as he really had no money, he was pulled up on deck and left apparently dead. He subsequently recovered. The freebooters confiscated all watches, clothing, and everything which could be of any use or value to them. There were a number of slaves, male and female, on the "Aurilla", bound for the south-ern market to be sold; they were badly treated, but not stolen, and this in itself seems strange, for most, if not all, the West Indian pirates were slavers also, running cargoes of negroes to Cuba, Brazil, and less often to southern ports of the United States. One of the "Auril-la's" crew was a good carpenter, and he was compelled to go with the pirates, who released the brig to resume her voyage to New Orleans.

The reader will have doubtless noticed a certain simi-larity in all the various stories of merchant vessels attacked by pirates, and the author takes the present opportunity to say that in order to avoid needless repetition, he has purposely omitted not a few accounts of merchantmen waylaid by marine highwaymen; neither has he attempted to arrange this little monograph in strictly chronological order. He has reserved his limited space in order to make pleasant reading and to mention, as far as possible, the struggles and exploits of our navy in stamping out piracy, and to record the experiences of local (Essex County, Massachusetts,) craft.

Nevertheless, in order to gratify the curiosity of the

many persons interested in the minutiae of history, a list of all ships, foreign as well as American, attacked by pirates in the South Atlantic from 1824 to 1832, will be found at the end of the book. This list, the result of much labor and trouble, has been compiled largely from the files of the New York Shipping and Commercial List, Essex (Salem) Register, and last, but not least, the Marblehead Register, which, although a small town paper, fairly teemed with marine news.

Salem was undoubtedly stirred to its depths by the following story of a piratical attack on one of its fleet of "argosies", as printed with heavily leaded headings (only reserved for the most important news in those days) in the *Register* of Feb. 9th, 1822 :

"PIRACY! PIRACY!

"Extract of a letter from Capt. Wm. Lander, of the brig 'Washington', of this port (Salem), to his owner, dated

"Havana, Jan. 16, 1822.

"I arrived at Matanzas in 18 days from Salem, and found the markets so bad, sailed for this place; on the morning of the 8th, at 10 A. M., was boarded by a small pirate schr. of about ten tons, with ten men, armed with muskets, cutlasses, pistols, and long knives. They drove all the men below, but one, whom they sent aloft, with a threat that if he saw any armed vessel in the offing and did not inform them, they would blow his brains out. They then demanded my money ; I went to my chest and handed them 16 dollars, which was all I had. The head robber threw that into a small box, and said he would burn the brig if I did not produce more. I told him I had no more. They then ordered the men on deck, and compelled them to get up bread and beef—they took 5 bbls. bread, 5 do. potatoes, 1 bbl. shoes, and 1 bbl. salt beef ; also the bag with the colors, the sounding line, a trumpet, a coil of spun yarn, a quantity of twine, and 3 or 4 light sails. They also took my trunk, with all my clothing, two watches, a spyglass, and two blankets, the mate's clothing, with all the principal part of the men's clothes, and all the cooking utensils, 2 axes, a saw, 2 buckets and a compass."

The same paper reported that : "The brig 'Dover', Sabin, of Providence, R. I., arrived at Charleston, S. C., from Matanzas, was boarded on the 16th ult., off the Pan of Matanzas, by a boat from a (sugar) drogher, which came out of Matanzas the night before. Five Spaniards, armed with long knives, pistols, cutlasses, etc., came on board, and after beating the captain and crew, drove them below, robbed them of clothes, watches, and everything of value. They were afterwards called up singly; four men with drawn knives stood over the captain and threatened him, if he did not give up his money, that they would murder all hands and burn the vessel. They then commenced plundering the brig, broke open the hatches, and made the crew carry the plunder to their vessel. They took one compass, five bags of coffee, one barrel sugar, nearly all the provisions, colors, rigging, cooking utensils, and ordered them to stand to the northward, or they would return, kill all hands, and burn the vessel." . . .

On January 7th, 1898, Capt. Charles Endicott, a well-known Salem retired shipmaster of the old school, celebrated his seventy-fifth birthday. To a few friends who assembled at his house to do him honor, Capt. Endicott related the unenviable experience of his father, Capt. Aaron Endicott, in 1822, when he was captured by pirates while in command of the brig "Niagara" of Salem, owned by Joseph Peabody. In passing it may be well to say, for the benefit of the uninitiated, that Mr. Peabody was one of the largest of the old-time Salem (and in fact of the whole country) merchants and shipowners. The "Niagara" left Salem in January, 1822, bound for Matanzas, and before her departure $50,000 in specie was stored in nail kegs and hidden among other kegs in the cargo. No person, other than the owner and commander, knew anything whatever of the money being aboard. When the brig was off Matanzas and making preparations to beat in, a piratical schooner gave chase, and when the "Niagara" was in stays came alongside.

One hundred men, armed to the teeth, jumped aboard and drove the crew below. The money was demanded of Capt. Endicott, who stoutly denied having any on board.

The cabin boy was also brutally beaten and even wounded with swords, but he could give no information. While the pirates were searching for themselves, threatening that, if any treasure were found, they would kill the entire crew, a large ship hove in sight, and believing her to be a man-of-war, the buccaneers hastily took their departure, but not before they had stolen Capt. Endicott's nautical instruments and all the clothing of his men.*

While they (the pirates) were on board the "Niagara", they headed her for the breakers, intending to leave her at the last minute, and her crew to their fate. As soon as they were gone, Capt. Endicott released his crew, 'bout ship, and was soon on his course again for the harbor of Matanzas, where he arrived in safety. There he learned that his capture had been seen from the shore, but there were no means at hand to assist him, and, quite likely, no will either, for many of the Spanish officials were in league with the pirates. It was clearly to be seen, said Capt. Endicott, that the freebooters *knew* that there was treasure hidden *somewhere* on the "Niagara"; this and several other suspicious events, including the unsuccessful attempt to plunder the steamer "Robert Fulton" (to be mentioned later), led the "initiated" to think that the pirates had agents in the seaport towns of the United States, who, by fair means or foul, found out when large sums of money were to be shipped in vessels bound to the West Indies, South America, or southern ports of this country, and were able to notify their friends to be on the lookout for them. It was even hinted that a certain consul of one of the South American republics might not be a stranger to these schemes.†

The "Niagara" was loaded with sugar at Matanzas, went from there to Cronstadt, Russia, and then returned to Salem, having made a most successful voyage; she was built on Mount Desert Island, Maine, in 1816; measured 246 tons register, and was finally lost on the Feegee Islands, March 22d, 1831. Capt. Aaron Endicott, after a prosperous career, retired from the sea, and died in Salem

---

*Accounts of this piracy may also be found in the Salem Register for Feb. 13th and 16th, 1822.

†Records of the Marblehead Marine Insurance Co.

in 1853, aged 74 years. The attack on the "Niagara" was quickly followed by a series of other piratical outrages, reported as follows in the columns of the Salem *Register :*

"Wednesday, March 6, 1822.

"Capt. Rice, from Havana, informs, that a few days before sailing he was present at the Regla, when 5 boats were taken possession of by the Police, said to be pirates. Capt. Miller, of the Jane, saw boxes of herrings, of his mark, taken from him by one of the boats. The boat he knew to be the one that boarded and robbed him. Another man, name not known, who had been robbed, saw his under coat, but dare not claim it. Two men were taken the same morning, one of them said to be the captain of one of the boats."

"New York, Feb. 28.

"Capt. Pratt, from Matanzas, informs, that a few days before he left a piratical schooner of 30 or 40 tons, with 2 brass pieces and 15 men, had been surprised and captured, three leagues to the leeward of that place, by troops dispatched for the purpose ; the captain and three men killed, and four taken prisoners. She was known to belong to Havana."

"March 2, 1822.

"The brig 'Leader', Capt. Jones, of Fair Haven, Mass., arrived at Havana, from Teneriffe, was boarded on the 6th of Feb. off the Moro, by a piratical boat, under the English flag, with 12 men. They plundered and stripped the officers and crew, and a French passenger, of everything, and threatened to take their lives. They even had a rope round the passenger's neck, and were going to hang him, but several vessels appearing in sight, induced them to desist. They robbed Mrs. Jones, the captain's lady, of her wearing apparel, took the rings from her fingers, and threatened to take her on shore. They also took part of the cargo, the vessel's provisions, stores, cabin furniture, spars, rigging, and light sails. The pirates were all Spaniards but one, who was a Frenchman. They were fitted out at Havana, and had probably not been out more than 12 hours."

"February 27, 1822.

"The U. S. Schooner 'Porpoise', Capt. Ramage, arrived at Charleston on the 10th, from a cruise. In addition to the information which we already have of the useful service rendered by this vessel, we learn that in the course of her cruise Capt. R. recaptured the Schooner 'Charles', Glavery, of Baltimore, which had been three days in the possession of pirates; and destroyed in all three piratical establishments on shore, and twelve vessels, besides two on the stocks. He has brought into port four pirates. Three others whom he had captured he discharged for want of evidence. On the day preceding the arrival of the 'Porpoise', arrived the piratical schooner 'El Bravo', Midshipman Blanchard, a prize to the 'Porpoise'.

On the 10th also arrived at Charleston the U. S. Schooner 'Revenge', Sailing Master R. I. Cox, from a cruise to the southward. On Saturday, the 2d instant, called off St. Augustine; landed Gen. Scott and Col. Archer, from St. Mary's."

"March 6, 1822.

"MORE PIRACY".

"Extract of a letter from Capt. Rufus Frink, of the schooner 'Shepherdess', dated Havana, Feb. 2, to his owner in Warren, R. I.:

"I arrived at Matanzas on the 29th ult., but finding the markets extremely unfavorable, I thought it would be most for the interest of the voyage to proceed to Havana, for which place I accordingly sailed on the 31st ult., at 4 o'clock P. M., with a fine breeze. At about 2 o'clock A. M. I discovered a boat in shore of me standing to the eastward, and was apprehensive that it was a pirate. Thinking to avail myself of the assistance and protection of the steamboat, then in sight, I continued my course. The steamboat more rapidly approached, and the pirates being nearly abreast of me, it being now 8 o'clock in the morning, I made signs to the steamboat for assistance. The pirates, thinking probably that they would not have time to effect their object before she came up, hauled their wind in shore; not so far, however, but that the steamboat passed them within half pistol shot, without taking the least notice of them. She also passed by us, totally regardless of our signal of distress and the maneuvering of the pirates, whose object she could not possibly have mistaken. A calm now succeeding, the steamboat was soon out of sight. Being thus abandoned, and in a defenceless situation, the only alternative that remained was to secrete my most valuable property and resign myself to their barbarity. The pirates now returned and boarded us. After having secured the mate and crew, beating them at the same time most inhumanly with swords and cutlasses, they ordered me into the cabin and demanded my money or my life, attempting at the same time to cut my throat. I then surrendered up to them about 60 dollars; but this only increased their savage ferocity to obtain more, and threatened to murder me and burn my vessel instantly, unless I gave up all I had. But as I persisted in saying that it was all I had by me, they ceased beating me for a moment, and commenced a general pillage of the cabin, and after rifling it of everything to the amount of a rial, they ordered me on deck and commenced beating me again with increased barbarity. Being nearly exhausted in consequence of their inhuman cruelty, they ordered me to rig a rope to hang me with, and threatened to put it into execution instantly unless I gave them more money. At this moment I cast my eyes towards the stern of my vessel and saw that she was on fire. They immediately charged me with having kindled it, and began to beat me again most unmercifully. They, however, extinguished the fire before it had arrived to a dangerous extent.

"Seeing there was no chance for my life unless I made a total surrender of all my property, I entreated them to spare my life and I would give them more money. After having surrendered up all I had, they insisted on more, and again commenced the savage work of beating me, and finally forced me overboard. They then cast loose the stern boat and let her go adrift. I was not so far exhausted but that I was able to recover the vessel.

"They then called up the mate and began to beat him most barbarously, when luckily a vessel hove in sight, having the appearance of a man-of-war. After having hastily stripped me of my clothes, their captain offered me his hand, and wished me a good passage to Havana, and they all repaired to the boat. They robbed me in money and articles to the amount of about $1200. Their boat was about 30 feet long, carrying 15 men, armed with cutlasses, muskets and blunderbusses, with a swivel mounted on the bow. I then proceeded for Havana, where I arrived yesterday, the 1st inst."

In a short while the reports of these piratical depredations spread all over the United States and Europe, and the stories lost nothing by repetition. The mercantile community became thoroughly alarmed, which was reflected in the tremendous increase, in some cases almost prohibitive, of insurance rates on vessels and cargoes bound for the "danger zone".* Congress was soon bombarded with petitions and memorials from the merchants and insurance companies calling for naval protection and the hunting down of these maritime highwaymen. The report of the Congressional Naval Committee was printed as follows in the Salem *Register* :

"Wednesday, March 13, 1822.

"Suppression of Piracy."
"Congressional Report."

"In the House of Representatives on Saturday, an interesting report was presented by Mr. M'Lane from the Committee on naval affairs, on the suppression of Piracy in the West Indies, of which the following is the substance :

*Records of the Marblehead Marine Insurance Co.

"The report states that the system of plunder in the West India seas is truly alarming, and imperiously calls for the prompt interposition of government; that every mail brings such accounts of massacre and plunder, by the vicious and depraved of all nations, that if not winked at by the authorities of Cuba, they are not restrained; that the danger of smuggling is thereby considerably increased on our coast; an ample force is therefore recommended to suppress it; that the force actually employed by our government is the 'Franklin', of 74 guns, in the Pacific, for the protection of our commerce in that quarter; that the 'Constellation', frigate of 36 guns, is in the same ocean, but ordered to return home upon the arrival of the 'Franklin'; that the schooner 'Dolphin', of 12 guns, accompanies the 'Franklin', as absolutely necessary upon so long a voyage.

"That the frigate 'Constitution', of 44 guns; sloop of war 'Ontario', of 18 guns; and schooner 'Nonesuch', of 10 guns, are cruising in the Mediterranean, to keep the Barbary powers in awe and protect our commerce in that sea; and it is believed that a less force would be inadequate for these objects.

"That the sloop of war 'Hornet', of 18 guns; the brigs 'Enterprise' and 'Spark', of 12 guns each; and the schooners 'Porpoise', 'Grampus', 'Shark', and 'Alligator', of 12 guns each, are cruising in the West India seas and Gulf of Mexico for the protection of trade, the suppression of piracy, etc.; and that the gunboats Nos. 158 and 168* are also cruising along the coasts of Georgia and Florida for the same purposes.

"That the frigate 'Macedonian' is now equipping at Boston and will soon sail on a cruise for the same object; and that it will be necessary to keep, at least, one vessel of war, either a corvette or schooner, on the coast of Africa, as the most efficient means for the suppression of the slave trade.

"The committee are of opinion that no part of the foregoing enumerated force would be withdrawn from the

*The gunboats that were numbered, instead of being named, were the remnants of a large fleet built during the war of 1812 to protect the coast. They were practically useless.

EXECUTION of the PIRATES

'Whoso sheddeth man's blood, by man shall his blood be sled.'

Particulars of the Murder perpetrated by the Pirates for which they are this day to suffer public Execution—Sketch of their Trial and of their behavior since the awful sentence of Death was passed upon them.

The Schooner [Spanish] bound from La Guira to Cadiz, captured by two Buenos Ayrean privateers in 1818. Prize crew murdered by members of the original crew who took the vessel into Scituate Harbor, Mass. They were there arrested and executed as pirates.

From a broadside in possession of F. B. C. Bradlee.

MARINE ORDNANCE OF A CENTURY AGO

Carronade used in the War of 1812 on the Privateer "America" of Salem
owned by George Crowninshield & Sons

Original in the possession of F. B. Crowninshield, Esq., of Marblehead, Msss.

service in which it is employed, without detriment to the public interest, and that the force in the West India seas and Gulf of Mexico are inadequate for the objects specified in the resolution referred to.

"That the rest of the force belonging to the Navy, consisting of the 'Java' of 44 guns, and now unworthy of repairs; the 'Erie' of 18 guns; the 'Peacock' of 18 guns; 'Congress' of 36 guns; 'Guerriere' of 44 guns; 'John Adams' of 24 guns; 'United States' of 44 guns; and 'Cyane' of 24 guns, are in ordinary at the different Navy Yards at Boston, New York, Washington and Norfolk.

"That the committee are of opinion, to afford effectual protection to the commerce in the West Indies and Gulf of Mexico, the corvettes 'Cyane' and 'John Adams', and sloops of war 'Peacock' and 'Erie', should be fitted out as soon as possible ; that the 'Erie' can be fitted out in 5 months, the 'Peacock' in 2 months, the 'John Adams' in 6 weeks, and the 'Cyane' in 5 weeks; and that the 'Constellation' frigate, should it be thought necessary, may be directed on her return from the Pacific to cruise in the West India seas, though it is believed it would be more expensive than to build additional sloops of war for the purpose, which are for many reasons superior to frigates, or smaller vessels, for such service. The first four named vessels are now undergoing repairs, and the amount necessary for this purpose is already embraced in the estimate for the present year; so that should they now be directed to be put in service, it will be necessary to increase the estimates for the present year not more than $120,000, and the committee are authorized to state that this appropriation will not materially vary the state of the public treasury, as disclosed by the Secretary's report, because since the date of that report there has been transferred to the surplus fund an amount of unexpended balances of appropriation for the naval service sufficient to meet the increased expenditure. But the committee cannot suppose that where the safety of the commerce and citizens of the United States calls imperiously for the exertion of the national force, so small an expenditure can be a matter of any moment.

"If the protection be *necessary*, it must be yielded, and the only consideration connected with the cost should be, that the money necessary to make it effectual should not be wastefully expended.

"In relation to the instructions for this service the committee think it would be *inconsistent* with public law and general usage to give any authority to destroy pirates and piratical vessels found at sea or in uninhabited places.

"The committee are of opinion that it would be dangerous and productive of great evil to vest in the commanders of our public vessels any authority to treat as pirate, and punish without trial, even such persons as those above described. It is not necessary for the accomplishment of the object in view that such an authority should be given, and it is essentially due to the rights of all, and the principles of public law and the general usage, that the consequences and punishment of piracy should follow only a legal adjudication of the fact.

"On the whole, the committee are of opinion that the employment of a sufficient number of vessels in the West India seas and Gulf of Mexico, authorized to make captures under the existing laws, etc., if the officers are properly industrious and enterprising, would afford all the protection required, and the committee therefore recommend the adoption of the following resolution :

"*Resolved*, That it is expedient forthwith to fit out and put in service the corvettes 'Cyane', 'John Adams', and sloops of war 'Peacock' and 'Erie', for the protection of commerce and the suppression of piracy in the West India seas and Gulf of Mexico, and also to employ the frigate 'Constellation', should the President of the United States deem the employment necessary for the purposes aforesaid.

"This report was ordered to be printed."

During the same year, 1822, came the bold attempt to plunder the steamer "Robert Fulton", which event more than anything else led to the belief that the pirate chiefs conducted their "affairs" on strictly "business principles", having an agent, or agents, in the principal American seaports, who gave notice in advance of vessels bound for the West Indies carrying large sums of money. The "Robert Fulton" was one of the earliest, *and if it be con-*

*sidered that she depended upon her machinery all the time, the
earliest ocean steamer in the world;* her wooden hull was
built by Henry Eckford, at New York, in 1819, for
David Dunham & Co. of the same city, to run as a regular packet between New York, Charleston, S. C., Havana
and New Orleans.   She measured 750 tons, a very large
ship for those days, 158 feet long, and 33 feet beam; the
machinery was of the "cross-head", or "square" type,
built by the Allaire Works at New York, having a 44-
inch cylinder, with a 5-foot stroke.   Two large copper
boilers, burning wood for fuel, were installed forward of
the engine.

On April 20th, 1820, the "Robert Fulton" left New
York on her first voyage, and plied regularly until 1825,
when, owing to indifferent financial results, she was sold
to the Brazilian Government and her machinery taken out.
While a steamer she had averaged four days from New
York to Charleston, four days from Charleston to Havana
and three days from Havana to New Orleans.

A century ago the merchants and bankers, and even the
government, made but little use of cheques and drafts in
transmitting money from one place to another; it was
customary, dangerous as it was, to send actual specie in
boxes or kegs; more rarely, bank notes.   It was not long
before the financial community availed themselves of the
"Robert Fulton" for the carriage of funds, offering as
she did far greater possibilities of safety.

On one of her trips, in 1822, it leaked out that she was
to have on board a very large sum of gold—over $100,000
—partly government funds, in transmission to New Orleans, besides a large consignment from a firm in New
York to some merchants in Havana.   In some way, probably through the before-mentioned confederate in the
United States, Gasparilla, the well-known pirate, learned
of the rich consignment and laid a clever trap to seize
the "Robert Fulton" and her treasure.*   Of course it
was of no use to attempt to chase the steamer with even
the swiftest sailing craft, but Gasparilla arranged that he
and a dozen or more of his most venturesome "friends"

*From Mss. material supplied by Capt. George L. Norton, for
many years editor of the N. Y. Marine Journal.

should lay in wait for her off the Cuban coast in a large open boat, impersonating shipwrecked seamen. In response to their distress signals, the "Fulton" would, naturally, stop to pick them up, and the pirates, carrying concealed weapons, would improve the opportunity by swarming on board the steamer and seizing her before the crew and passengers could recover from their surprise.

A schooner belonging to Gasparilla was to have been in the near neighborhood, to which the treasure was to be transferred, and the freebooters would then at once make off in her, first damaging the "Fulton's" machinery so that she could not pursue them. It was not, it would seem, their intention to hurt anyone on the steamer unless resistance was offered.

However, "the best laid plans o' mice and men gang aft a-gley," and in this case, it was said, one of Gasparilla's gang, having a grudge against him, revealed the whole plot, with the result that a United States man-of-war escorted the "Robert Fulton" and her rich lading safely to her destination.

In this story there seems a curious mixing of the old and the new; the pirates who make us think of seventeenth century conditions, attempting to seize a steamer, the representative of everything modern.

While on the subject of early steam navigation, it is interesting to quote an official report of Lieutenant W. H. Watson, commanding the United States steamer "Sea Gull" while in pursuit of pirates. Curiously enough, this officer makes no mention whatever of the advantages of steam over sail, nor does he refer in any way to the performances of the "Sea Gull's" machinery; all the more to be regretted, for, a century ago, a steamer was much more of an innovation and curiosity than was an aeroplane at the beginning of the World War.

In fact, Lieutenant Watson appears to have left the "Sea Gull" and given chase to the freebooters in the large sail barges (open boats) "Gallinipper" and "Mosquito"; this, however, was very likely due to the fact that the pirates, when pursued near land, always took refuge in shoal water, where the larger men-of-war could not follow them.

"United States Steam Galliot 'Sea Gull',
"Allenton, Thompson's Island (Key West),
"July 11th, 1823.

"Sir:

"Having had the honor to report the circumstances attending the cruise of the division under my orders, prior to our separation off St. John de los Remedios, I have now to communicate, for your information, my subsequent proceedings in the barges 'Gallinipper' and 'Mosquito'.

"After a strict examination of the coasts and islands, from Cayo Francisco to Cayo Blanco, in the vicinity of Point Hycacos, whilst cruising in Siguapa Bay, we discovered a large topsail-schooner, with a launch in company, working up to an anchorage, at which several merchant vessels were lying.

"Being to windward, I bore up in the 'Gallinipper', for the purpose of ascertaining their characters, and when within gunshot, perceiving the larger vessel to be well armed and her deck filled with men, I hoisted our colors, on seeing which they displayed the Spanish flag, and the schooner having brailed up her foresail, begun firing at the 'Gallinipper'. I immediately kept away and ran down upon her weather quarter, making signal at the same time for the 'Mosquito' to close. Having the advantage in sailing, they did not permit us to do so, but made all sail before the wind for the village of Siguapa, to which place we pursued them, and after a short action, succeeded in taking both their vessels and effecting the almost total destruction of their crews, amounting, as nearly as could be ascertained at the time, to 50 or 60 men, but as we are since informed, to 70 or 80. They engaged us without colors of any description, having hauled down the Spanish colors after firing the first gun; and on approaching to board, our men giving three cheers and discharging their muskets, the pirates fled precipitately, some to their launch, lying in shore, from which a fire was still kept up, whilst others endeavored to escape by swimming to the land. A volley of musketry directed at the launch completed their disorder and drove them into the sea; but the boats going rapidly through the water, cut off their retreat, with the exception of fifteen, eleven of whom were killed or desperately wounded and taken prisoners by our men, who landed in pursuit, and the remaining four apprehended by the local authorities and sent to Matanzas.

"The larger vessel was called the 'Catalina', commanded by the celebrated pirate Diabolito ('little Devil'), taken some weeks since from the Spaniards, between Havana and Matanzas, and carried to Siguapa Bay, where she received her armament. She captured nothing, this being the beginning of her piratical cruise.

"I cannot close this communication without performing a most pleasing task, in reporting the active gallantry and good conduct of my officers and men, none of whom sustained the slightest injury in the action, the result of which is, I trust, sufficient to satisfy you that all under my orders did their duty, particularly when it is considered that we had but 26 men, opposed to a force of piratical vessels well supplied with arms of all kinds, amongst which were one long 9 and two 6-pounders.

"I have much pleasure in naming as my associates Lieutenant Inman, Acting Sailing Master Bainbridge, Dr. Babbit, Midshipmen Harwood, Taylor, and S. S. Lee,* and Messrs. Webb and Grice, who obeyed and executed all orders and signals with a promptitude and zeal which could not be exceeded.

"I have the honor to be, very respectfully, your obedient servant,

"W. H. Watson,
"Lieutenant Commanding.

"Commodore David Porter, United States Navy, Commanding West India Squadron."

During the month of August, 1823, yellow fever broke out at Key West, and Commodore Porter and many of his officers and men were prostrated by it. One of the first victims was Captain John Minor Maury, U. S. N., Commodore Porter's flag captain, younger brother of Commodore Matthew Fontaine Maury, C. S. N., the well-

*Refers to Sidney Smith Lee, afterwards Commander U. S. N. and Commodore Confederate Navy, younger brother of Gen. R. E. Lee. S. S. Lee died in 1869; he was the father of Gen. Fitz Lee.

known scientist. He had had a most gallant record in the navy during the war of 1812, but died of the fever and was buried at sea almost within sight of Norfolk, Va., where his young wife and two little children were anxiously awaiting him.*

As may be imagined, the medical treatment of a century ago for yellow fever was very crude, and, possibly, did as much harm as good. Lieutenant Josiah Tattnall, afterwards Commodore, C. S. N., caught the disease and was so ill that the surgeon gave him up, telling him at the same time that he could have anything he wished to eat or drink, as he had done all he could for him. Tattnall thought he would enjoy a mint julep, which was given him, and from that time on he improved rapidly and eventually recovered. The stimulant was probably just what he needed.

There were 48 deaths in the squadron, including the gallant Watson and Lieutenant Hammersly, Chaplain Adams, Sailing Master Bainbridge, and Midshipmen Bainbridge and Reed.

Lieutenant David Glasgow Farragut, U. S. N., the future conqueror of New Orleans and admiral of the navy, added to his already gallant record during these years devoted to the extirpation of piracy. Entering the navy at the tender age of nine and one-half years, his midshipman's warrant was signed Dec. 17th, 1810, by Paul Hamilton of South Carolina, then Secretary of the Navy, when to-day boys no older would be in the lower grades of the public schools. Young Farragut was but thirteen when he took part in the desperate battle in Valparaiso bay, March 28, 1814, between the U. S. frigate "Essex" and the British frigate "Phoebe" and sloop-of-war "Cherub", resulting in the capture of the former, which had been commanded by Captain David Porter, now in charge of the West India squadron.

The "Essex" is always remembered with pride by the people of Salem, as she was built on Winter Island in that city, by Enos Briggs, in 1799, and last, but not least, the famous old frigate was completely paid for by voluntary subscriptions from the inhabitants of Essex County.

*Recollections of a Virginian, by Gen. D. H. Maury.

Her total cost, when ready for service, with twelve months' provisions, was $154,687.77.

It is, perhaps, not so well known that after her capture it had been the intention of the British naval authorities to refit the "Essex" for their own service, but she was found to be so badly knocked about as to make her useless as a man-of-war. Accordingly she was used as a stationary convict ship at Kingston, Jamaica, until 1833, and was finally sold at auction at Somerset House, in 1837, and broken up.

In 1823 Farragut's rank was what was then known as "passed midshipman", practically that of "acting lieutenant" or watch officer, and soon after received his commission as lieutenant. Promotion in those days in the navy was extremely slow.

His first independent command was that of the schooner "Greyhound", of between 50 and 60 tons; she was one of a fleet of eight, built on the model of the Chesapeake bay fast pilot schooners, and especially fitted to hunt down the pirates when they took refuge in shallow water. Each of these schooners was armed with two 18-pound brass pivot guns. For six months in 1823 the future hero of the Civil war was actively employed in ransacking the southern shores of Haiti and Cuba and the Mona Passage between Porto Rico and Haiti.

There were many encounters between the "Greyhound" and the pirates, sometimes afloat, sometimes ashore, when Farragut led his men through marsh and chaparral and cactus—a service often perilous, always painful and exhausting. It is a source of wonder that his health held out and that he did not succumb to the yellow fever, which made sad havoc among the officers and men of the American squadron. "I never owned a bed during my two years and a half in the West Indies," wrote Farragut, "but lay down to rest wherever I found the most comfortable berth."* The result, however, both directly and indirectly, was the suppression of piracy; seconded as our navy was by that of Great Britain, interested like our own in the security of commerce.

Driven off the water, with their lairs invaded, their

*"Life of Admiral Farragut," by Capt. A. T. Mahan, U. S. N.

plunder seized, their vessels burned, their occupation afloat gone, the marauders organized themselves into bandits, and turned their predatory practices against the towns and villages of Cuba. This aroused the Spanish governors from the indolent complacency, not to say more, with which they had watched robberies upon foreigners that brought profit rather than loss to their districts. When the evil was thus brought home, the Spanish troops were put in motion, and the pirates, beset on both sides, gradually disappeared.

An interesting incident of this period was the meeting of the future Admiral Farragut with his older brother William, then already a lieutenant in the navy, and whom he had not seen for thirteen years. How many Americans, even students of naval history, know that he had a brother? Lieutenant Joseph W. Revere, U. S. N. (a kinsman of Col. Paul J. Revere killed at Gettysburg and of Asst. Surgeon Edward H. R. Revere, killed at Antietam while caring for the wounded under fire), in his "Forty Years of Military and Naval Service," refers to his experiences in the West India squadron, while serving against the pirates, as follows:

"Leaving St. Augustine for Tampa and Pensacola, I was ordered to Key West from the latter place, to take command of a large felucca-rigged boat, pulling forty oars, and armed with a long twelve-pounder, and received instructions to cruise in the Old Bahama Channel and endeavor to capture a noted pirate named Benavides. Piracy was at that time a regularly organized business in the West Indies, the capital being supplied by persons in Cuba and the United States, and the cutthroats by the 'faithful isle.'

"It was very difficult to secure the trial and conviction of the corsairs in Havana, however evident their guilt, for the Spanish authorities were notoriously interested in the profits of their nefarious calling. It is well known that, not long before the time I am writing of, Commodore David Porter was tried by a court martial for landing at Foxardo to capture some of these gentlemanly marauders, —a rebuke which led to his leaving the profession of which he was so distinguished an ornament. For a week or two we saw nothing on our new cruising ground except a few small merchant vessels, and heard of no pirates, until one evening a felucca appeared, crossing from Cayo Romano to Cuba. We immediately gave chase, but lost sight of her at nightfall. At early daylight she was again seen under the land of Cuba, but suddenly disappeared up one of those estuaries which inlace the low ground of the coast. Making our way into the one we supposed she had entered, we pursued our unseen but hoped-for prize up its sinuous course, the view being limited by the banks of the estuary, which were covered by a mangrove thicket, growing down into the water, as is the habit of this plant. I landed, however, at the entrance for a few moments, in order to put on shore a couple of men provided with means to signal to us if necessary.

"After rowing in this way for about ten or fifteen miles, we came suddenly, at a turn of the estuary, upon a camp, and a barque-rigged vessel lying at a rude pier. Here we landed, with the usual precautions against surprise, and found the ship to be the French barque 'Amedee' of Bordeaux, evidently not long since captured by pirates. Her cargo had been nearly all removed and probably taken in lighters to Havana and Matanzas ; but the evidences of a hurried 'breaking bulk' were everywhere to be seen. The sails of the barque had been burned (for we found the incombustible parts), the rudder unshipped, and both anchors let go ; so that it would have been impossible to remove her from the place. Many knickknacks, which apparently did not suit the taste of the pirates, lay about, the *embarcadero* being strewn with various 'articles de Paris'. The cabin furnished evidence that it had been tenanted by passengers of both sexes; and it was fearful to think of what had probably been their fate, although we met with no positive proofs that murder had been done.

"In the afternoon I wished to return to sea, but found that some of my men had straggled away into the country ; so, leaving the galley in charge of a petty officer, I started with a small party to hunt them up, ascending the hills which rose above the landing place to a considerable height. Our search was vain, however ; we saw no traces of the stragglers, and after a walk of about two miles along the crest, we returned towards the pirates' camp down a ravine, in the hollow of which ran a brawling rivulet.

"The sides of the ravine were precipitous and covered with huge bowlders, while the dense and almost impenetrable verdure of the tropics clothed its surface. I tried to cover as much ground as possible with my men, in order to explore the country as thoroughly as we could; for I feared my lost ones had stupefied themselves with liquor obtained from the French barque. Suddenly one of my scouts high up the bank of the ravine shouted to us to ascend, and, thinking he had tidings of the runaways, we scrambled up to his elevated position. I found him at the entrance of a hole, or cave, which was partially concealed by a bowlder of great size, the ground around it bearing the marks of footprints, with staves and iron spikes scattered about. Bringing my little band together, I delegated a young and agile foretopman to enter the hole first, which he did, shoving his carbine before him as he went in, and disappeared from our sight into the bowels of the earth. We prepared to follow, but the first who entered met the second one returning, and, as neither could pass the other in the narrow entrance, we hauled the last man out by the legs. The foretopman reported that he had passed into a large chamber inside, but that, owing to the darkness, he could say nothing as to its size or contents.

"Determined to prosecute the search, I improvised tapers made of the torn leaves of a book I had in my pocket, and, thus equipped, we crawled in. At about twenty paces from the entrance we found ourselves in a circular chamber, evidently an excavation, some fifteen feet in diameter. Our means of illumination being scanty, we had not time to examine the contents of some kegs and barrels, which, together with some old rusty muskets and cutlasses, and other objects pertaining to seafaring men, composed the contents of the room.

"As we were about to withdraw, one old tar, determined not to go without carrying away some memento of the place, rolled out a keg before him, thinking, doubtless, that it contained a supply of liquor, but which, upon being upset, gave forth an ominous rattling sound, that indicated something more substantial. We rolled the keg down to the camp, which I desired to reach before the approaching sunset, after which, in the tropics, there is no twilight. I found, upon my arrival, that our stragglers had returned, my fears having been unfounded as to their drinking; for the pirates had evidently consumed, or effectually concealed, all liquors.

"While on the subject of the old-time man-of-war's men's ability to secure liquor, I heard a lieutenant say that he once sent a watch of sailors ashore for recreation on an uninhabited island in the middle of the Pacific ocean, and that they all came back drunk!

Sentinels having been placed around the camp, we went to sleep after supper, pleased with visions of untold wealth to be secured in the morning at the cave, which we imagined must contain the fabulous treasures of Aladdin; for the keg we had brought with us was filled with newly-minted Spanish dollars. Shortly after midnight my dreams were interrupted by a sentinel, who reported that a fire was burning brightly at the entrance to the estuary. As this was the signal agreed upon in case our presence was required, I had no alternative but to start at once; and we manned our row-galley and sped down the creek as fast as forty pairs of vigorous arms could propel us. The day was breaking as we arrived at our destination, ready and eager for action; for we thought it probable that the pirates were returning to their haunt, which was as secure a *puerto escondido* for those buccaneers—'friends to the sea and enemies to all who sail on it'—as could be found in Cuba.

"My lookout men reported having seen a light at sea, which we soon saw, and, boarding the vessel, found her to be H. B. M. schooner 'Monkey', on a cruise, and her commander handed me a despatch from the commander of the U. S. schooner 'Grampus', directing me to join him at Havana as soon after I received it as possible. Reluctant to abandon our promising investigations, we squared away the long yards of the felucca before the trade-wind, and next morning rounded the Moro Castle, ensign and pennant flying, and anchored near the 'Grampus'. The secret of our discovery was religiously kept, and the keg of dollars divided amongst the crew, each receiving about fifty dollars, and we cheered each other by the prospect of soon returning to the *cache* and enriching ourselves with the pirates' hoarded treasure.

"A few days after our arrival one of those terrible cyclones which periodically devastate the West Indies came on, and it seemed as if the city would be torn down by the mere power of the wind. Several vessels were destroyed by being dashed violently against the wharves at Regla. . . . The damage to vessels at sea was immense . . . in the interior plantations were ruined in a single night . . . the hurricane was long afterwards remembered . . . as the heaviest known for years. . . .

"The 'Grampus' and 'The Forty Thieves' safely rode out this tremendous gale, and after its fury had abated, our crews were instrumental in saving much property and some lives in the harbor. About a week after this catastrophe . . . we started again for our former cruising ground, and soon reached the *embarcadero,* near the underground treasury. On landing, we found everywhere marks of the passage of the hurricane. The French barque had been completely torn to pieces . . . the rude sheds which had sheltered the pirates were tossed about like paper, . . . and enormous rocks from above cumbered the ground.

"With doubting steps and hearts saddened by the sight of such terrible havoc, we took our way to the cave, . . . The entrance had disappeared. . . . Every evidence of the existence of the cave had been obliterated, and we returned to our boat as poor as we came."

Marooning, or leaving their victims on desert islands, was a favorite device of the West Indian buccaneers of the seventeenth century, but the only instance on record of this having been done by the later pirates was the case of Capt. Lincoln, whose experience was so interesting that it has been thought worth while to quote it in full from the old and rare volume, "Life on the Ocean Wave", in which it was originally published:

NARRATIVE OF CAPTAIN LINCOLN,

Who was taken by the Pirates, off Cape Cruz, Dec. 17,
1821, and subsequently left, with his crew, to
perish on a desolate island.

"I have reluctantly yielded to the urgent solicitations of friends, to give a short narrative of the capture, sufferings and escape of myself and crew, after having been taken by a piratical schooner, called the Mexican, December, 1821. The peculiar circumstances attending our situation gave us ample opportunity for learning the character of those cruisers which have lately infested our southern coasts, destroying the lives and plundering the property of so many peaceable traders. If this narrative should effect any good, or urge our government to still more vigorous measures for the protection of our commerce, my object will be attained.

"I sailed from Boston, bound for Trinidad, in the Island of Cuba, on the 13th of November, 1821, in the schooner Exertion, burden one hundred and seven tons, owned by Messrs. Joseph Ballister and Henry Farnam, with a crew consisting of the following persons:

Joshua Bracket,	mate,	Bristol
David Warren,	cook,	Saco
Thomas Goodall,	seaman,	Baltimore
Thomas Young,	"	Orangetown
Francis de Suze,	"	St. John's
George Reed,	"	Greenock, Scotland

"The cargo consisted of flour, beef, pork, lard, butter, fish, beans, onions, potatoes, apples, ham, furniture, sugar box shooks, &c., invoiced at about eight thousand dollars. Nothing remarkable occurred during the passage, except much bad weather, until my capture, which was as follows :

"Monday, December 17th, 1821,—commenced with fine breezes from the eastward. At daybreak saw some of the islands northward of Cape Cruz, called keys—stood along northwest ; everything now seemed favorable for a happy termination of our voyage. At three o'clock P. M. saw a sail coming round the Keys, into a channel called

Privateer "AMERICA," owned by the Crowninshields

From a recently discovered painting in possession of Francis B. Crowninshield, Esq.

Corvette "Hispanola" built at Boston for the U. S. Navy during the War of 1812-1815. The war ended before she was completed and the Spanish government purchased her for their navy in its efforts to suppress piracy in Cuban waters.

Model owned by the Marblehead Historical Society.

Boca de Cavolone by the chart, nearly in latitude 20.55 north, longitude 79.55 west; she made directly for us, with all sail set, sweeps on both sides (the wind being light), and was soon near enough for us to discover about forty men on her deck, armed with muskets, blunder-, busses, cutlasses, long knives, dirks, two carronades, one a twelve, the other a six-pounder; she was a schooner, wearing the Patriot flag (blue, white and blue) of the Republic of Mexico. I thought it not prudent to resist them, should they be pirates, with a crew of seven men, and only five muskets; accordingly ordered the arms and ammunition to be immediately stowed away in as secret a place as possible, and suffer her to speak us, hoping and believing that a republican flag indicated both honor and friendship from those who wore it, and which we might expect even from Spaniards. But how great was my astonishment when the schooner, having approached very near us, hailed in English, and ordered me to heave my boat out immediately and come on board of her with my papers. Accordingly my boat was hove out, but filled before I could get into her. I was then ordered to tack ship and lay by for the pirate's boat to board me; which was done by Bolidar, their first lieutenant, with six or eight Spaniards, armed with as many of the before men-tioned weapons as they could well sling about their bodies. They drove me into the boat, and two of them rowed me to their privateer (as they called their vessel), where I shook hands with her commander, Captain Jonnia, a Spaniard, who, before looking at my papers, ordered Bol-idar, his lieutenant, to follow the Mexican in, back of the Key they had left, which was done. At 6 o'clock P. M. the Exertion was anchored in eleven feet of water, near their vessel and an island, which they called Twelve League Key (called by the chart Key Largo), about thirty or thirty-five leagues from Trinidad. After this strange conduct they began examining my papers by a Scotchman who went by the name of Nickola, their sailing master. He spoke good English, had a countenance rather pleas-ing, although his beard and mustachios had a frightful appearance—his face, apparently full of anxiety, indicated something in my favor; he gave me my papers, saying, 'take good care of them, for I am afraid that you have fallen into bad hands.' The pirate's boat was then sent to the Exertion with more men and arms ; a part of them left on board her, the rest returning with three of my crew to their vessel, viz., Thomas Young, Thomas Goodall, and George Reed. They treated them with something to drink, and offered them equal shares with themselves and some money if they would enlist, but they could not prevail on them. I then requested permission to go on board my vessel, which was granted, and further requested Nickola should go with me, but was refused by the captain, who vociferated in a harsh manner, 'No, No, No,' accompanied with a heavy stamp upon the deck. When I got on board I was invited below by Bolidar, where I found they had emptied the case of liquors and broken a cheese to pieces and crumbled it on the table and cabin floor ; the pirates, elated with their prize (as they called it), had drank so much as to make them desperately abusive. I was permitted to lie down in my berth ; but, reader, if you have ever been awakened by a gang of armed desperadoes, who have taken possession of your habitation in the midnight hour, you can imagine my feelings. Sleep was a stranger to me, and anxiety was my guest. Bolidar, however, pretended friendship, and flattered me with the prospect of being soon set at liberty. But I found him, as I suspected, a consummate hypocrite; indeed, his very looks indicated it. He was a stout and well-built man, of a dark, swarthy complexion, with keen, ferocious eyes, huge whiskers, and beard under his chin and on his lips four or five inches long ; he was a Portuguese by birth, but had become a naturalized Frenchman —had a wife, if not children (as I was told) in France, and was well known there as commander of a first-rate privateer. His appearance was truly terrific ; he could talk some in English, and had a most lion-like voice.

"Tuesday, 18th—Early this morning the captain of the pirates came on board the Exertion, took a look at the cabin stores and cargo in the state rooms, and then ordered me back with him to his vessel, where he, with his crew, held a consultation for some time respecting the cargo. After which the interpreter, Nickola, told me that 'the

captain had or pretended to have a commission under
General Traspelascus, commander-in-chief of the republic
of Mexico, authorizing him to take all cargoes whatever
of provisions bound to any Spanish royalist port—that my
cargo, being bound to an enemy's port, must be condemned, but that the vessel should be given up and put
into a fair channel for Trinidad, where I was bound.' I
requested him to examine the papers thoroughly, and
perhaps he would be convinced to the contrary, and told
him my cargo was all American property taken in at
Boston and consigned to an American gentleman agent at
Trinidad. But the captain would not take this trouble,
but ordered both vessels under way immediately, and
commenced beating up amongst the Keys through most
of the day, the wind being very light. They now sent
their boats on board the Exertion for stores, and commenced plundering her of bread, butter, lard, onions, potatoes, fish, beans, &c., took up some sugar box shooks
that were on deck, and found the barrels of apples, selected the best of them, and threw the rest of them overboard. They inquired for spirits, wine, cider, &c., and
were told 'they had already taken all that was on board.'
But not satisfied, they proceeded to search the state rooms
and forecastle, ripped up the floor of the latter, and found
some boxes of bottled cider, which they carried to their
vessel, gave three cheers in an exulting manner to me,
and then began drinking it with such freedom that a violent quarrel arose between officers and men, which came
very near ending in bloodshed. I was accused of false-
hood, for saying they had already got all the liquors that
were on board, and I thought they had; the truth was, I
never had any bill of lading of the cider, and consequently
had no recollection of its being on board; yet it served
them as an excuse for being insolent. In the evening
peace was restored and they sung songs. I was suffered
to go below for the night, and they placed a guard over
me, stationed at the companion way.

Wednesday, 19th, commenced with moderate easterly
winds, beating towards the northeast, the pirate's boats
frequently going on board the Exertion for potatoes, fish,
beans, butter, &c., which were used with great waste and

extravagance. They gave me food and drink, but of bad quality, more particularly the victuals, which were wretchedly cooked. The place assigned me to eat was covered with dirt and vermin. It appeared that their great object was to hurt my feelings with threats and observations, and to make my situation as unpleasant as circumstances would admit. We came to anchor near a Key, called by them Brigantine, where myself and mate were permitted to go on shore, but were guarded by several armed pirates. I soon returned to the Mexican and my mate to the Exertion, with George Reed, one of my crew, the other two being kept on board the Mexican. In the course of this day I had considerable conversation with Nickola, who appeared well disposed towards me. He lamented most deeply his own situation, for he was one of those men whose early good impressions were not entirely effaced, although confederated with guilt. He told me, 'those who had taken me were no better than pirates, and their end would be the halter; but,' he added, with peculiar emotion, 'I will never be hung as a pirate,' showing me a bottle of laudanum which he had found in my medicine chest, saying, 'if we are taken that shall cheat the hangman before we are condemned.' I endeavored to get it from him, but did not succeed. I then asked him how he came to be in such company, as he appeared to be dissatisfied. He stated 'that he was at New Orleans last summer, out of employment, and became acquainted with one Captain August Orgamar, a Frenchman, who had bought a small schooner of about fifteen tons, and was going down to the bay of Mexico to get a commission under General Traspelascus, in order to go a privateering under the patriot flag. Captain Orgamar made him liberal offers respecting shares, and promised him a sailing master's berth, which he accepted and embarked on board the schooner, without sufficiently reflecting on the danger of such an undertaking. Soon after she sailed from Mexico, where they got a commission, and the vessel was called Mexican. They made up a complement of twenty men, and after rendering the General some little service in transporting his troops to a place called ——, proceeded on a cruise; took some small prizes off Campeachy; afterwards came on the south coast of Cuba, where they took other small prizes and the one which we were now on board of. By this time the crew was increased to about forty, nearly one-half Spaniards, the others Frenchmen and Portuguese. Several of them had sailed out of ports in the United States, with American protections; but, I confidently believe, none are natives, especially of the northern states.* I was careful in examining the men, being desirous of knowing if any of my countrymen were among the wretched crew, but am satisfied there were none, and my Scotch friend concurred in the opinion. And now, with a new vessel, which was the prize of these plunderers, they sailed up Manganeil Bay; previously, however, they fell in with an American schooner, from which they bought four barrels of beef, and paid in tobacco. At the Bay was an English brig belonging to Jamaica, owned by Mr. John Louden of that place. On board of this vessel the Spanish part of the crew commenced their depredations as pirates, although Captain Orgamar and Nickola protested against it and refused any participation; but they persisted, and like so many ferocious bloodhounds, boarded the brig, plundered the cabin stores, furniture, captain's trunk, &c., took a hogshead of rum, one twelve-pound carronade, some rigging and sails. One of them plundered the chest of a sailor, who made some resistance, so that the Spaniard took his cutlass and beat and wounded him without mercy. Nickola asked him 'why he did it?' the fellow answered, 'I will let you know,' and took up the cook's axe and gave him a cut on the head, which nearly deprived him of life.† Then they ordered Captain Orgamar to leave his vessel, allowing him his trunk, and turned him ashore to seek for himself. Nickola begged them to dismiss him with his captain, but no, no, was the answer, for they had no complete navigator but him. After Captain

*The Spaniards at Havana have been in the habit of saying to those who arrive there, after suffering the horrid abuse of cutting, beating, hanging, robbing, &c., "it is your countrymen that do this."

†He showed me the wound, which was quite large and not then healed.

Orgamar was gone, they put in his stead the present brave (or as I should call him cowardly) Captain Jonnia, who headed them in plundering the before mentioned brig, and made Bolidar their first lieutenant, and then proceeded down among those Keys or islands where I was captured. This is the amount of what my friend Nickola told me of their history.

Thursday, 20th, continued beating up, wind being light; the pirate's boats were sent to the Exertion for more stores, such as bread, lard, &c. I this day discovered on board the Mexican three black girls, of whom it is well to say no more. It is impossible to give an account of the filthiness of this crew, and were it possible it would not be expedient. In their appearance they were terrific, wearing black whiskers and long beards, the receptacles of dirt and vermin. They used continually the most profane language; had frequent quarrels, and so great was their love of gambling that the captain would play cards with the meanest man on board. All these things rendered them to me objects of total disgust (with a few exceptions, as will hereafter appear). I was told they had a stabbing match, but a few days before I was taken, and one man came near being killed; they put him ashore at a fisherman's hut and there left him to perish. I saw the wound of another, who had his nose split open.

Friday, 21st—After laying at anchor through the night in ten fathoms water, made sail and stood to the eastward —by this time I was out of my reckoning, having no quadrant, chart, or books. The pirate's boats were again sent for stores. The captain for the second time demanded of me where my wine, brandy, &c., were. I again told him they had already got the whole. They took the deep sea line and some cordage from the Exertion, and at night came to anchor.

Saturday, 22d—Both vessels under way standing to the eastward; they ran the Exertion aground on a bar, but after throwing overboard most of her deckload of shooks, she floated off; a pilot was sent to her and she was run into a narrow creek between two keys, where they moored her head and stern alongside the mangrove trees, sent down her yards and topmasts, and covered her mastheads and shrouds with bushes to prevent her being seen by vessels which might pass that way. I was then suffered to go on board my own vessel, and found her in a very filthy condition; sails torn, rigging cut to pieces, and everything in the cabin in waste and confusion. The swarms of moschetoes and sand-flies made it impossible to get any sleep or rest. The pirate's large boat was armed and manned under Bolidar, and sent off with letters to a merchant (as they called him) by the name of Dominico, residing in a town called Principe, on the main island of Cuba. I was told by one of them who could speak English that Principe was a very large and populous town, situated at the head of St. Maria, which was about twenty miles northeast from where we lay, and the Keys lying around us were called Cotton Keys. The captain pressed into his service Francis de Suze, one of my crew, saying he was one of his countrymen. Francis was very reluctant in going, and said to me, with tears in his eyes, 'I shall do nothing only what I am obliged to do, and will not aid in the least to hurt you or the vessel; I am very sorry to leave you.' He was immediately put on duty and Thomas Goodall sent back to the Exertion.

"Sunday, 23d.—Early this morning a large number of the pirates came on board of the Exertion, threw out the long boat, broke open the hatches and took out considerable of the cargo, in search of rum, gin, &c., still telling me 'I had some and that they would find it,' uttering the most awful profaneness. In the afternoon the boat returned with a perough,* having on board the captain, his first lieutenant, and seven men of a patriot or piratical vessel that was chased ashore at Cape Cruz by a Spanish armed brig. These seven men made their escape in said boat, and after four days, found our pirates and joined them, the remainder of the crew being killed or taken prisoners.

"Monday, 24th.—Their boat was manned and sent to the before mentioned town. I was informed by a line from Nickola that the pirates had a man on board, a native of Principe, who, in the garb of a sailor, was a partner

*A boat built of two halves of a large tree, hollowed out and so put together as to carry about thirty barrels.

with Dominico, but I could not get sight of him. This lets us a little into the plans by which this atrocious system of piracy has been carried on. Merchants having partners on board of these pirates! thus pirates at sea and robbers on land are associated to destroy the peaceable trader.

"The willingness exhibited by the seven above-mentioned men to join our gang of pirates seemed to look like a general understanding among them; and from there being merchants on shore so base as to encourage the plunder and vend the goods, I am persuaded there has been a systematic confederacy on the part of these unprincipled desperadoes, under cover of the patriot flag, and those on land are no better than those on the sea. If the governments to whom they belong know of the atrocities committed (and I have but little doubt they do), they deserve the execration of all mankind.

"Tuesday, 25th.—Still on board the Exertion—weather very calm and warm. The pirate's boat returned from St. Maria, and came for candles, cheese, potatoes, &c., they saying they must have them, and forbid my keeping any light on board at night—took a case of trunks for the captain's use, and departed. Their irritating conduct at this time can hardly be imagined.

"Wednesday, 26th.—I was told by Bolidar that three Spanish cruisers were in search of them, that they could fight two of them at once (which, by the way, I believe was not true), and were disappointed in not finding them. Same evening they took both of my boats, and their own men, towed their vessel out of the creek, and anchored at its mouth to get rid of sand-flies, while they obliged us to stay on deck under an awning, exposed to all the violence of these flies; we relieved ourselves in some measure by the burning of tobacco, which lasted but for a short time.

"Thursday, 27th.—A gang of the pirates came and stripped our masts of the green bushes, saying, 'she appeared more like a sail than trees'—took one barrel of bread and one of potatoes, using about one of each every day. I understood they were waiting for boats to take the cargo, for the principal merchant had gone to Trinidad.

"Friday, 28th.—Nothing remarkable occurred this day —were frequently called upon for tar and butter, and junk to make oakum. Capt. Jonnia brought on board with his new captain and officer before mentioned. Again they asked for wine, and were told as before they had gotten the whole.

"Saturday, 29th.—Same insulting conduct continued. Took a barrel of crackers.

"Sunday, 30th.—The beginning of trouble! this day, which peculiarly reminds Christians of the high duties of compassion and benevolence, was never observed by these pirates. This, of course, we might expect, as they did not often know when the day came, and if they knew it it was spent in gambling. The old saying among seamen, 'no Sunday off soundings,' was not thought of, and even this poor plea was not theirs, for they were on soundings and often at anchor. Early this morning the merchant, as they called him, came with a large boat for the cargo. I was immediately ordered into the boat with my crew, not allowed any breakfast, and carried about three miles to a small island out of sight of the Exertion, and left there by the side of a little pond of thick, muddy water, which proved to be very brackish, with nothing to eat but a few biscuit. One of the boat's men told us the merchant was afraid of being recognized, and when he had gone the boat would return for us, but we had great reason to apprehend they would deceive us, and therefore passed the day in the utmost anxiety. At night, however, the boats came and took us again on board the Exertion, when, to our surprise and astonishment, we found they had broken open the trunks and chests and taken all our wearing apparel, not even leaving a shirt or pair of pantaloons, not sparing a small miniature of my wife which was in my trunk. The little money I and my mate had, with some belonging to the owners, my mate had previously distributed about the cabin in three or four parcels, while I was on board the pirate, for we dare not keep it about us; one parcel in a butter pot they did not discover. Amidst the hurry with which I was obliged to leave my vessel to go to the before-mentioned island, I fortunately snatched my vessel's papers and hid them in my bosom, which the reader will find was a happy circumstance for me. My writing desk, with papers, accounts, &c., all Mr. Lord's letters (the gentleman to whom my cargo was consigned), and several others, were taken and maliciously destroyed. My medicine chest, which I so much wanted, was kept for their own use. What their motive could be to take my papers I could not imagine, except they had hopes of finding bills of lading for some Spaniards, to clear them of piracy. Mr. Bracket had some notes and papers of consequence to him, which shared the same fate. My quadrant, charts, books, and some bedding, were not yet taken, but I found it impossible to hide them, and they were soon gone from my sight.

"Monday, 31st.—We complained to them, expressing the necessity of having clothes to cover us, but as well might we have appealed to the winds, and rather better, for they would not have upbraided us in return. The captain, however, sent word he would see to it, and ordered their clothes-bags to be searched, where he found some of our things, but took good care to put them into his own cabin. I urgently requested him to give me the miniature, but 'no' was all I could get.

"Tuesday, January 1st, 1822.—A sad new year's day to me. Before breakfast orders came for me to cut down the Exertion's railing and bulwarks on one side, for their vessel to heave out by and clean her bottom. On my hesitating a little, they observed with anger, ' Very well, captain, suppose you no do it quick, we do it for you.' Directly afterwards another boat, full of armed men, came alongside ; they jumped on deck with swords drawn and ordered all of us into her immediately. I stepped below, in hopes of getting something which would be of service to us, but the captain hallooed, 'go in the boat directly or I will fire upon you.' Thus compelled to obey, we were carried, together with four Spanish prisoners, to a small, low island or key of sand in the shape of a half moon, and partly covered with mangrove trees, which was about one mile from and in sight of my vessel. There they left nine of us, with a little bread, flour, fish, lard, a little coffee and molasses, two or three kegs of water, which was brackish, an old sail for a covering, and a pot and some other small articles no way fit to cook in. Leaving us these, which were much less than they appear in the enumeration, they pushed off, saying, 'we will come to see you in a day or two.' Selecting the best place, we spread the old sail for an awning, but no place was free from flies, muschetoes, snakes, the venomous santipee. Sometimes they were found crawling inside of our pantaloons, but fortunately no injury was received. This afternoon the pirates hove their vessel out by the Exertion and cleaned one side, using her paints, oils, &c., for that purpose. To see my vessel in that situation and to think of our prospects was a source of the deepest distress. At night we retired to our tent, but having nothing but the cold damp ground for a bed, and the heavy dew of the night penetrating the old canvass—the situation of the island being fifty miles from the usual track of friendly vessels, and one hundred and thirty-five from Trinidad —seeing my owner's property so unjustly and wantonly destroyed—considering my condition, the hands at whose mercy I was, and deprived of all hopes, rendered sleep or rest a stranger to me.

"Wednesday, 2d.—The pirates hove out and cleaned the other side. She then commenced loading with the Exertion's cargo, which appeared to be flour and lard. In the afternoon their boat came and took two of the Spaniards with them to another island for water, and soon after returned with four kegs of poor, unwholesome water, and left us, saying they should not bring us provisions again for some time, as they were going away with goods from the prize, to be gone two or three days. Accordingly they brought a present supply of beef, pork, and a few potatoes, with some bedding for myself and mate. The mangrove wood afforded us a good fire, as one of the Spanish prisoners happened to have fireworks, and others had tobacco and paper with which we made cigars. About this time one of my men began to be unwell; his legs and body swelled considerably, but having no medicine I could not do much to relieve him.

"Thursday, 3d.—The pirates had dropped off from the Exertion, but kept their boats employed in bringing the cargo from her ; I supposed it to be kegs of lard to make stowage.   They then got under way with a perough in tow, both deeply laden, run out of the harbor, hauled on the wind to the eastward till out of sight behind the Keys, leaving a guard on board the Exertion.

"Friday, 4th.—Commenced with light wind and hot sun ; saw a boat coming from the Exertion, apparently loaded ; she passed between two small Keys to the north-ward, supposed to be bound for Cuba.   At sunset a boat came and inquired if we wanted anything, but instead of adding to our provisions, took away our molasses, and pushed off.   We found one of the Exertion's water casks and several pieces of plank, which we carefully laid up, in hopes of getting enough to make a raft.

"Saturday, 5th.—Pirates again in sight coming from the eastward ; they beat up alongside their prize and commenced loading.   In the afternoon Nickola came to us, bringing with him two more prisoners, which they had taken in a small sailboat coming from Trinidad to Man-ganeil, one a Frenchman, the other a Scotchman, with two Spaniards, who remained on board the pirate, and who afterwards joined them.   The back of one of these poor fellows was extremely sore, having just suffered a cruel beating from Bolidar with the broad side of a cutlass.   It appeared that when the officer asked him 'where their money was and how much,' he answered, 'he was not cer-tain, but believed they had only two ounces of gold.' Bolidar furiously swore, he said 'ten', and not finding any more, gave him the beating.   Nickola now related to me a singular fact, which was, that the Spanish part of the crew were determined to shoot him ; that they tied him to the mast, and the man was appointed for the purpose, but Lyon, a Frenchman, his particular friend, stepped up and told them if they shot him, they must shoot several more ; some of the Spaniards sided with him, and he was released.   Nickola told me the reason for such treatment was that he continually objected to their conduct towards me, and their opinion was if he should escape they would be discovered, as he declared he would take no prize money.   While with us he gave me a letter, written in great haste, which contains some particulars respecting the cargo, as follows :

"January 4th, 1822.

"Sir—We arrived here this morning, and before we came to anchor had five canoes alongside ready to take your cargo, part of which we had in; and as I heard you express a wish to know what they took out of her, to this moment, you may depend on this account of Jamieson* for quality and quantity; if I have the same opportunity you will have an account of the whole. The villian who bought your cargo is from the town of Principe, his name is Dominico, as to that it is all I can learn; they have taken your charts on board the Mexican, and I suppose mean to keep them, as the other captain has agreed to act the same infamous part in the tragedy of his life. Your clothes are here on board, but do not let me flatter you that you will get them back; it may be so, and it may not. Perhaps in your old age, when you recline with ease in a corner of your cottage, you will have the goodness to drop a tear of pleasure to the memory of him whose highest ambition should have been to subscribe himself, though devoted to the gallows, your friend,

"NICKOLA MONACRE.

"Excuse haste.

"P. S.   Your answer in writing when I come again.

"Sunday, 6th.—The pirates were under way at sunrise, with a full load of the Exertion's cargo, going to Principe again to sell a second freight, which was done readily for cash.   I afterwards heard that the flour brought only five dollars per barrel, when it was worth at Trinidad thirteen, so that the villain who bought my cargo at Principe made very large profits by it.

"Monday, 7th.—The pirates brought more water, but being very brackish, it was unfit for use.   We were now greatly alarmed at Thomas' ill health, being suddenly attacked with a pain in the head and swelling of the right eye, attended with derangement.   He, however, soon became better, but his eye remained swollen several days,

*This is the real name of Nickola.

without much pain. In the evening we had some heavy showers of rain, and having no secure cabin, no sheltered retreat, our exposure made us pass a very uncomfortable night.

"Tuesday, 8th.—Early this morning the pirates in sight again, with fore-topsail and top gallant sail set; beat up alongside of the Exertion and commenced loading, having, as I supposed, sold and discharged her last freight among the inhabitants of Cuba. They appeared to load in great haste, and the song 'O he ho,' which echoed from one vessel to the other, was distinctly heard by us. How wounding was this to me! How different was this sound from what it would have been had I been permitted to pass unmolested by these lawless plunderers, had been favored with a safe arrival at the port of my destination, where my cargo would have found an excellent sale. Then would the 'O he ho' on its discharging have been a delightful sound to me. In the afternoon she sailed with the perough in tow, both with a full load, having chairs, which was a part of the cargo, slung at her quarters.

"Wednesday, 9th.—Very calm and warm. The swarms of moschetoes and flies made us pass a very uncomfortable day. We dug in the sand for water, but were disappointed in finding none so good as they left us. In walking round among the bushes, I accidentally discovered a hole in the sand and saw something run into it; curiosity led me to dig about it. With the help of Mr. Bracket, I found at the distance of seven feet from its mouth and one from the surface, a large solitary rat, apparently several years old ; he had collected a large nest of grass and leaves, but there was not the least appearance of any other being on the island.

"Thursday, 10th.—No pirates in sight. The day was passed in anxious suspense, David Warren being quite sick.

"Friday, 11th. They came and hauled alongside of the Exertion, but I think took out none of her cargo, but had, as I supposed, a vendue on board, wherein was sold among themselves all our books, clothing, quadrants, charts, spyglasses, and everything belonging to us and our fellow-prisoners. I was afterwards told they brought a

The "ROBERT FULTON" of 1819, the second ocean steamer of the United States.

From the original painting owned by F. B. C. Bradlee.

ADMIRAL DAVID GLASGOW FARRAGUT

At the age of thirty-seven

good price, but what they could want of the Bible, Prayer Book, and many other books in English, was matter of astonishment to me.

"Saturday, 12th.—They remained alongside the Exertion; took the paints, oil, brushes, &c., and gave their vessel a new coat of paint all around, and a white boot top, took the perough to another key and caulked her; there was no appearance of their taking any cargo out; the Exertion, however, appeared considerably high out of water. About sunset the pirates went out of the harbor on a cruise. Here we had been staying day after day, and exposed night after night; apprehensions for our safety were much increased; what was to become of us seemed now to rush into every one's mind.

"Sunday, 13th.—Deprived of our good books, deprived in fact of everything save life, and our ideas respecting our fate so gloomy, all tended to render time, especially the Lord's day, burdensome to all. In the afternoon a boat came for cargo, from, as I supposed, that villain Dominico.

"Monday, 14th.—They again hove in sight, as usual, alongside their prize. While passing our solitary island they laughed at our misery, which was almost insupportable—looking upon us as though we had committed some heinous crime, and they had not sufficiently punished us: they hallooed to us, crying out, 'Captain, Captain,' accompanied with obscene motions and words, with which I shall not blacken these pages; yet I heard no check upon such conduct, nor could I expect it among such a gang, who have no idea of subordination on board, except when in chase of vessels, and even then but very little. My resentment was excited at such a malicious outrage, and I felt a disposition to revenge myself, should fortune ever favor me with an opportunity. It was beyond human nature not to feel and express some indignation at such treatment. Soon after, Bolidar, with five men, well armed, came to us, he having a blunderbuss, cutlass, a long knife and pair of pistols; but for what purpose did he come? He took me by the hand, saying, 'Captain, me speak with you, walk this way.' I obeyed, and when we were at some distance from my fellow-prisoners (his men

following), he said, 'the captain send me for your wash.'
I pretended not to understand what he meant and replied,
'I have no clothes, nor any soap to wash with—you have
taken them all'—for I had kept my watch about me, hoping they would not discover it. He demanded it again
as before, and was answered, 'I have nothing to wash.'
This raised his anger, and, lifting his blunderbuss, he
roared out, 'What the d—l you call him that make clock,
give it me.' I considered it imprudent to contend any
longer and submitted to his unlawful demand. As he was
going off he gave me a small bundle, in which was a pair
of linen drawers, sent to me by Nickola, and also the
Rev. Mr. Brooks' 'Family Prayer Book.' This gave me
great satisfaction. Soon after he returned with his captain, who had one arm slung up, yet with as many imple-
ments of war as his diminutive wicked self could conven-
iently carry; he told me (through an interpreter who
was a prisoner) 'that on his cruise he had fallen in with
two Spanish privateers and beat them off, but had three
of his men killed and himself wounded in the arm.'
Bolidar turned to me and said, 'It is a d—n lie,' which
words proved to be correct, for his arm was not wounded,
and when I saw him again, which was soon afterwards,
he forgot to sling it up. He further told me, 'after to-
morrow you shall go with your vessel and we will accompany you towards Trinidad.' This gave me some new
hopes, and why I could not tell. They then left us,
without rendering any assistance. This night we got
some rest.

"Tuesday, 15th.—The words 'go after to-morrow' were
used among our Spanish fellow-prisoners as though that
happy to-morrow would never come; in what manner it
came will soon be noticed.

"Wednesday, 16th.—One of their boats came to in-
quire if we had seen a boat pass by last night, for their
small sloop sailboat was gone and two men deserted. I
told them 'no'; at heart I could not but rejoice at the
escape and approve the deserters. I said nothing, however, to the pirates. On their return they manned three
of their boats and sent them in different directions to
search, but at night came back without finding boat or

men. They now took our old sail, which hitherto had somewhat sheltered us, to make, as I supposed, some small sail for their vessel. This rendered our night more uncomfortable than before, for in those islands the night dews are very heavy.

"Thursday, 17th, was passed with great impatience. The Exertion having been unmoored and swung to her anchor, gave some hopes of being restored to her, but was disappointed.

"Friday, 18th, commenced with brighter prospects of liberty than ever—the pirates were employed in setting up our devoted schooner's shrouds, stays, &c. My condition now reminded me of the hungry man, chained in one corner of the room, while at another part was a table loaded with delicious foods and fruits, the smell and sight of which he was continually to experience, but, alas! his chains were never to be loosed that he might go and partake. At almost the same moment they were thus employed the axe was applied with the greatest dexterity to both her masts, and I saw them fall over the side! Here fell my hopes—I looked at my condition, and then thought of home. Our Spanish fellow-prisoners were so disappointed and alarmed that they recommended hiding ourselves, if possible, among the mangrove trees, believing, as they said, we should now certainly be put to death; or, what was worse, compelled to serve on board the Mexican as pirates. Little else, it is true, seemed left for us; however, we kept a bright lookout for them during the day, and at night 'an anchor watch,' as we called it, determined, if we discovered their boats coming towards us, to adopt the plan of hiding, although starvation stared us in the face, yet preferred that to instant death. This night was passed with sufficient anxiety. I took the first watch.

"Saturday, 19th.—The pirate's large boat came for us. It being daylight, and supposing they could see us, determined to stand our ground and wait the result. They ordered us all into the boat, but left everything else; they rowed towards the Exertion. I noticed a dejection of spirits in one of the pirates, and inquired of him where they were going to carry us. He shook his head and re-

plied, 'I do not know.' I now had some hopes of visiting
my vessel again, but the pirates made sail, run down, took
us in tow and stood out of the harbor. Bolidar afterwards took me, my mate, and two of my men on board
and gave us some coffee. On examination I found they
had several additional light sails, made of the Exertion's.
Almost every man a pair of canvass trousers, and my
colors cut up and made into belts to carry their money.
My jolly boat was on deck, and I was informed all my
rigging was disposed of. Several of the pirates had on
some of my clothes, and the captain one of my best shirts,
a cleaner one than I had ever seen him have on before.
He kept at good distance from me, and forbid my friend
Nickola's speaking to me. I saw from the companion way
in the captain's cabin my quadrant, spyglass, and other
things which belonged to us, and observed by the compass
that the course steered was about west by south, distance
nearly twenty miles, which brought them up with a cluster
of islands called by some 'Cayman Keys.' Here they
anchored and caught some fish (one of which was named
guard fish), of which we had a taste. I observed that my
friend Mr. Bracket was somewhat dejected, and asked him
in a low tone of voice what his opinion was in respect to
our fate. He answered, 'I cannot tell, but it appears to
me the worst is to come.' I told him that I hoped not,
but thought they would give us our small boat and liberate the prisoners. But mercy even in this shape was not
left for us. Soon after, saw the captain and officers whispering for some time in private conference. When over,
their boat was manned, under the command of Bolidar,
and went to one of those Islands or Keys before mentioned.* On their return another conference took place,
—whether it was a jury upon our lives we could not tell
—I did not think conscience could be entirely extinguished
in the human breast, or that men could become fiends. In
the afternoon, while we knew not the doom which had
been fixed for us, the captain was engaged with several of

*This Key was full of mangrove trees, whose tops turn down and
take root, forming a kind of umbrella. The tide at high water flows
two feet deep under them; it is therefore impossible for human beings to live long among them, even with food and water.

his men in gambling, in hopes to get back some of the five
hundred dollars they said he lost but a few nights before,
which had made him unusually fractious. A little before
sunset he ordered us all into the large boat, with a supply
of provisions and water, and to be put on shore. While
we were getting into her, one of my fellow-prisoners, a
Spaniard, attempted, with tears in his eyes, to speak to
the captain, but was refused, with the answer, 'I'll have
nothing to say to any prisoner, go into the boat.' In the
meantime Nickola said to me, 'My friend, I will give you
your book' (being Mr. Colman's Sermons), 'it is the only
thing of yours that is in my possession, I dare not attempt
anything more.' But the captain forbid his giving it to
me, and I stepped into the boat. At that moment Nickola
said in a low voice, 'never mind, I may see you again before I die.' The small boat was well armed and manned,
and both set off together for the island, where they had
agreed to leave us to perish ! The scene to us was a
funeral scene. There were no arms in the prisoners'
boat, and, of course, all attempts to relieve ourselves
would have been throwing our lives away, as Bolidar was
near us, well armed. We were rowed about two miles
northeasterly from the pirates to a small, low island,
lonely and desolate. We arrived about sunset, and for
the support of us eleven prisoners they only left a ten-
gallon keg of water and perhaps a few quarts, in another
small vessel, which was very poor; part of a barrel of flour,
a small keg of lard, one ham and some salt fish, a small
kettle and an old broken pot, an old sail for a covering,
and a small blanket, which was thrown out as the boat
hastened away. One of the prisoners happened to have
a little coffee in his pocket, and these comprehended all
our means of sustaining life, and for what length of time
we knew not. We now felt the need of water, and our
supply was comparatively nothing. A man may live twice
as long without food as without water. Look at us now,
my friends, left benighted on a little spot of sand in the
midst of the ocean, far from the usual track of vessels,
and every appearance of a violent thunder tempest and a
boisterous night. Judge of my feelings, and the circumstances which our band of sufferers now witnessed. Per-

haps you can and have pitied us. I assure you we were very wretched, and to paint the scene is not within my power.   When the boats were moving from the shore, on recovering myself a little, I asked Bolidar 'If he was going to leave us so ?'   He answered, 'No, only two days—we go for water and wood, then come back, take you.' I requested him to give us bread and other stores, for they had plenty in the boat, and at least one hundred barrels of flour in the Mexican. 'No, no, suppose to-morrow morning me come, me give you bread, and hurried off to their vessel.   This was the last time I saw him. We then turned our attention upon finding a spot most convenient for our comfort, and soon discovered a little roof support-ed by stakes driven into the sand ;* it was thatched with the leaves of the cocoanut tree, a considerable part of which was torn or blown off. After spreading the old sail over this roof we placed our little stock of provisions under it.   Soon after came on a heavy shower of rain, which penetrated the canvass and made it nearly as un-comfortable inside as it would have been out.   We were not prepared to catch water, having nothing to put it in. Our next object was to get fire, and after gathering some of the driest fuel to be found, and having a small piece of cotton wick-yarn, with flint and steel, we kindled a fire, which was never afterwards suffered to be extin-guished.   The night was very dark, but we found a piece of old rope, which, when well lighted, served for a candle. On examining the ground under the roof, we found per-haps thousands of creeping insects, scorpions, lizards, crickets, &c.   After scraping them out as well as we could, the most of us having nothing but the damp earth for a bed, laid ourselves down in hopes of some rest, but it being so wet, gave many of us severe colds, and one of the Spaniards was quite sick for several days.

Sunday, 20th.—As soon as daylight came on we pro-ceeded to take a view of our little island, and found it to measure only one acre, of coarse, white sand, about two feet, and in some spots perhaps three feet, above the sur-face of the ocean.   On the higher part were growing some

*This was probably erected by the turtle men or fishers, who visit these islands in June for the purposes of their trade.

bushes and small mangroves (the dry part of which was
our fuel) and the wild castor oil beans. We were greatly
disappointed in not finding the latter suitable food; likewise some of the prickly pear bushes, which gave us only
a few pears about the size of our small button pear; the
outside has thorns, which if applied to the fingers or lips,
will remain there and cause a severe smarting similar to
the nettle; the inside a spongy substance full of juice and
seeds, which are red and a little tartish. Had they been
there in abundance, we should not have suffered so much
for water—but alas! even this substitute was not for us.
On the northerly side of the island was a hollow, where
the tide penetrated the sand, leaving stagnant water. We
presumed, in hurricanes the island was nearly overflowed.
According to the best calculations I could make, we were
about thirty-five miles from any part of Cuba, one hundred from Trinidad, and forty from the usual track of
American vessels, or others which might pass that way.
No vessel of any considerable size can safely pass among
these Keys, or 'Queen's Gardens' (as the Spaniards call
them), being a large number extending from Cape Cruz
to Trinidad, one hundred and fifty miles distance, and
many more than the charts have laid down, most of them
very low and some covered at high water, which makes it
very dangerous for navigators without a skilful pilot.
After taking this view of our condition, which was very
gloomy, we began to suspect we were left on this desolate
island by those merciless plunderers to perish. Of this I
am now fully convinced; still we looked anxiously for
the pirates' boat to come according to promise with more
water and provisions, but looked in vain. We saw them
soon after get under way, with all sail set, and run directly from us until out of sight, and we never saw them
again! One may partially imagine our feelings, but they
cannot be put into words. Before they were entirely out
of sight of us, we raised the white blanket upon a pole,
waving it in the air, in hopes that at two miles' distance
they would see it and be moved to pity. But pity in such
monsters was not to be found. It was not their interest
to save us from the lingering death which we now saw
before us. We tried to compose ourselves, trusting that

God, who had witnessed our sufferings, would yet make
use of some one as the instrument of his mercy towards
us. Our next care, now, was to try for water. We dug
several holes in the sand and found it, but quite too salt
for use. The tide penetrates probably through the island.
We now came on short allowance for water. Having no
means of securing what we had by lock and key, some
one in the night would slyly drink, and it was soon gone.
The next was to bake some bread, which we did by mixing flour with salt water and frying it in lard, allowing
ourselves eight quite small pancakes to begin with. The
ham was reserved for some more important occasion, and
the salt fish was lost for want of fresh water. The remainder of this day was passed in the most serious conversation and reflection. At night I read prayers from
the 'Prayer Book' before mentioned, which I most carefully concealed while last on board the pirates. This
plan was pursued morning and evening during our stay
there, then retired for rest and sleep, but realized little of
either.

Monday, 21st.—In the morning we walked round the
beach, in expectation of finding something useful. On
our way picked up a paddle about three feet long, very
similar to the Indian canoe paddle, except the handle,
which was like that of a shovel, the top part being split
off; we laid it aside for the present. We likewise found
some konchs and roasted them; they were a pretty good
shell fish, though rather tough. We discovered at low
water a bar or spit of sand extending northeasterly from
us, about three miles distant, to a cluster of Keys, which
were covered with mangrove trees, perhaps as high as our
quince tree. My friend Mr. Bracket and George attempted to wade across, being at that time of tide only up to
their armpits; but were pursued by a shark and returned
without success. The tide rises about four feet.

Tuesday, 22d.—We found several pieces of the palmetto or cabbage tree and some pieces of board, put them
together in the form of a raft and endeavored to cross,
but that proved ineffectual. Being disappointed, we sat
down to reflect upon other means of relief, intending to
do all in our power for our safety while our strength con-

tinued. While sitting here the sun was so powerful and oppressive, reflecting its rays upon the sea, which was then calm, and the white sand which dazzled the eye, was so painful that we retired under the awning ; there the mosquitoes and flies were so numerous that good rest could not be found. We were, however, a little cheered, when, in scraping out the top of the ground to clear out, I may say, thousands of crickets and bugs, we found a hatchet, which was to us peculiarly serviceable. At night the strong northeasterly wind, which prevails there at all seasons, was so cold as to make it equally uncomfortable with the day. Thus day after day our sufferings and apprehensions multiplying, we were very generally alarmed.

Wednesday, 23d.—Early this morning one of our Spanish fellow-prisoners crossed the bar, having taken with him a pole sharpened at one end ; this, he said, 'was to kill sharks,' but he saw none to trouble him. While he was gone we tried for water in several places, but still it was very salt; but not having any other, we drank it, and found it had a similar effect to that of glauber salts. We now concluded to reduce the allowance of bread, or rather pancakes, being too sensible that our little stock of provisions could last but a few days longer; we had not the faintest hope of any supplies before it would be too late to save life. Towards night the Spaniard returned, but almost famished for want of water and food. He reported that he found some plank on one of the islands (but they proved to be sugar-box shooks), which revived us a little, but no water. He said he had great difficulty to make his way through the mangrove trees, it being very swampy, so that we should not better ourselves by going there, although the key was rather larger than ours. This I understood through Joseph, the English prisoner, who could speak Spanish. After prayers, laid ourselves down upon our bed of sand, and being nearly exhausted, we obtained some sleep.

"Thursday, 24th.—This morning, after taking a little coffee, made of the water which we thought least salt, and two or three of the little cakes, we felt somewhat refreshed, and concluded to make another visit to those Keys in hopes of finding something more, which might make a

raft for us to escape the pirates and avoid perishing by
thirst.   Accordingly seven of us set off, wading across the
bar, and searched all the Keys thereabouts.   On one we
found a number of sugar-box shooks, two lashing planks
and some pieces of old spars, which were a part of the
Exertion's deckload that was thrown overboard when she
grounded on the bar, spoken of in the first part of the
narrative.   It seems they had drifted fifteen miles, and had
accidentally lodged on these very Keys within our reach.
Had the pirates known this they would undoubtedly have
placed us in another direction.   They no doubt thought
that they could not put us on a worse place.   The wind
at this time was blowing so strong on shore as to prevent
rafting our stuff round to our island, and we were obliged
to haul it upon the beach for the present; then dug for
water in the highest place, but found it as salt as ever, and
then returned to our habitation.   But hunger and thirst
began to prey upon us, and our comforts were as few as
our hopes.

"Friday, 25th.—Again passed over to those Keys to
windward, in order to raft our stuff to our island, it being
most convenient for building.   But the surf on the beach
was so very rough that we were again compelled to post-
pone it.   Our courage, however, did not fail where there
was the slightest hopes of life.   Returning without it, we
found on our way an old top timber of some vessel; it
had several spikes in it, which we afterwards found very
serviceable.   In the hollow of an old tree we found two
guarnas of small size, one male, the other female.   One
only was caught.   After taking off the skin, we judged
it weighed a pound and a half.   With some flour and lard
(the only things we had except salt water), it made us a
fine little mess. We thought it a rare dish, though a small
one for eleven half-starved persons.   At the same time a
small vessel hove in sight; we made a signal to her with
the blanket tied to a pole and placed it on the highest
tree—some took off their white clothes and waved them
in the air, hoping they would come to us.   Should they
be pirates they could do no more than kill us, and perhaps would give us some water, for which we began to
suffer most excessively; but, notwithstanding all our
efforts, she took no notice of us.

"Saturday, 26th.—This day commenced with moderate weather and smooth sea; at low tide found some cockles, boiled and eat them, but they were very painful to the stomach. David Warren had a fit of strangling, with swelling of the bowels, but soon recovered, and said 'something like salt rose in his throat and choked him.' Most of us then set off for the Keys, where the plank and shooks were put together in a raft, which we with pieces of boards paddled over to our island; when we consulted the best plan, either to build a raft large enough for us all to go on, or a boat, but the shooks having three or four nails in each, and having a piece of large reed or bamboo, previously found, of which we made pins, concluded to make a boat.

"Sunday, 27th.—Commenced our labor, for which I know we need offer no apology. We took the two planks, which were about fourteen feet long and two and a half wide, and fixed them together for the bottom of the boat; then, with moulds made of palmetto bark, cut timber and knees from mangrove trees, which spread so much as to make the boat four feet wide at the top, placed them exactly the distance apart of an Havana sugar-box. Her stern was square, and the bows tapered to a peak, making her form resemble a flatiron. We proceeded thus far and retired to rest for the night; but Mr. Bracket was too unwell to get much sleep,

"Monday, 28th.—Went on with the work as fast as possible. Some of the Spaniards had long knives about them, which proved very useful in fitting timbers, and a gimlet of mine, accidentally found on board the pirates, enabled us to use the wooden pins. And now our spirits began to revive, though water, water, was continually on our minds. We now feared the pirates might possibly come, find out our plan, and put us to death (although before we had wished to see them, being so much in want of water). Our labor was extremely burdensome, and the Spaniards considerably peevish, but they would often say to me, 'Never mind, captain, by and by Americana or Spanyola catch them, me go to see 'um hung.' We quitted work for the day, cooked some cakes, but found it necessary to reduce the quantity again, however

small before.   We found some herbs on a windward Key,
which the Spaniards called Spanish tea.   This, when well
boiled, we found somewhat palatable, although the water
was very salt.   This herb resembles pennyroyal in look
and taste, though not so pungent.   In the evening, when
we were sitting round the fire to keep off the mosquitoes,
I observed David Warren's eyes shone like glass.   The
mate said to him, 'David, I think you will die before
morning, I think you are struck with death now.'   I
thought so, too, and told him, I thought it most likely
we should all die here soon, but 'as some one of us may
survive to carry the tidings to our friends, if you have
anything to say respecting your family, now is the time.'
He then said, 'I have a mother in Saco where I belong;
she is a second time a widow; to-morrow, if you can spare
a scrap of paper and pencil, I will write something.'   But
no to-morrow came to him.   In the course of the night he
had another spell of strangling, and soon after expired,
without much pain and without a groan.   He was about
twenty-six years old.   How solemn was this scene to us!
Here we beheld the ravages of death commenced upon
us.   More than one of us considered death a happy release.   For myself I thought of my wife and children,
and wished to live if God should so order it, though extreme thirst, hunger and exhaustion had well nigh prostrated my fondest hopes.

"Tuesday, 29th.   Part of us recommenced labor on the
boat, while myself and Mr. Bracket went and selected the
highest clear spot of sand on the northern side of the
island, where we dug Warren's grave and boxed it up with
shooks, thinking it would be the most suitable spot for the
rest of us; whose turn would come next we knew not.   At
about ten o'clock A. M. conveyed the corpse to the grave,
followed by us survivors—a scene whose awful solemnity
can never be painted.   We stood around the grave, and
there I read the funeral prayer from the Rev. Mr. Brooks'
Family Prayer Book, and committed the body to the earth,
covered it with some pieces of board and sand, and returned to our labor.   One of the Spaniards, an old man
named Manuel, who was partial to me and I to him, made
a cross and placed it at the head of the grave, saying,

'Jesus Christ hath him now.' Although I did not believe in any mysterious influence of this cross, yet I was perfectly willing it should stand there. The middle part of the day being very warm, our mouths parched with thirst and our spirits so depressed, that we made but little progress during the remainder of this day, but in the evening were employed in picking oakum out of the bolt rope taken from the old sail.

"Wednesday, 30th. Returned to labor on the boat with as much vigor as our weak and debilitated state would admit, but it was a day of trial to us all, for the Spaniards and we Americans could not well understand each other's plans, and they being naturally petulent, would not work, nor listen with patience for Joseph, our English fellow-prisoner, to explain our views; they would sometimes undo what they had done, and in a few minutes replace it again; however, before night we began to calk her seams, by means of pieces of hard mangrove, made in form of a calking-iron, and had the satisfaction of seeing her in a form something like a boat.

"Thursday, 31st.—Went on with the work, some at calking, others with battening the seams with strips of canvass and pieces of pine nailed over, to keep the oakum in. Having found a suitable pole for a mast, the rest went about making a sail from the one we had used for a covering, also fitting oars of short pieces of boards, in form of a paddle, tied on a pole, we having a piece of fishing line brought by one of the prisoners. Thus, at 3 P. M., the boat was completed and put afloat. We had all this time confidently hoped that she would be sufficiently large and strong to carry us all; we made a trial and were disappointed! This was indeed a severe trial, and the emotions it called up were not easy to be suppressed. She proved leaky, for we had no carpenter's yard or smith's shop to go to. And now the question was, 'who should go and how many?' I found it necessary for six, four to row and one to steer and one to bale. Three of the Spaniards and the Frenchmen claimed the right, as being best acquainted with the nearest inhabitants; likewise, they had, when taken, two boats left at St. Maria (about forty miles distant), which they were confident of finding.

They promised to return within two or three days for the rest of us. I thought it best to consent. Mr. Bracket, it was agreed, should go in my stead, because my papers must accompany me as a necessary protection, and my men apprehended danger if they were lost. Joseph Baxter (I think was his name) they wished should go, because he could speak both languages, leaving Manuel, George, Thomas and myself to await their return. Having thus made all arrangements, and putting up a keg of the least salt water, with a few pancakes and salt fish, they set off a little before sunset, with our best wishes and prayers for their safety and return to our relief. To launch off into the wide ocean, with strength almost exhausted, and in such a frail boat as this, you will say was very hazardous, and in truth it was, but what else was left to us? Their intention was to touch at the Key where the Exertion was, and if no boat was to be found there, to proceed on to St. Maria, and if none there, to go to Trinidad and send us relief. But alas! it was the last time I ever saw them! Our suffering this day was most acute.

"Tuesday, February 1st. This day we rose early and traversed the beach in search of cockles, &c., but found very few. I struck my foot against something in the sand, which proved to be a curious shell, and soon found two others of a different kind, but they were to me like Crusoe's lump of gold, of no value. I could not drink them, so laid them by. I returned to our tent, and we made some skillygolee, or flour and salt water boiled together, which we found better than clear salt water. We passed the day very uncomfortably, and my people were dissatisfied at not having an equal chance, as they called it, with the others in the boat; but it is not always that we know what is for our good.

"Saturday, 2d. Thomas and George made another visit to the windward Keys, where they found some more shooks and two pieces of spars; towed them round as before. We now had some hopes of finding enough to make us a raft, which would carry us to some place of relief, in case the boat should not return.

"Sunday, 3d. A calm, warm day, but a very gloomy one to us, it being more difficult to support life—our pro-

A GROUP OF OFFICERS DISTINGUISHED IN THE SUPPRESSION OF PIRACY.

REAR ADMIRAL ANDREW HULL FOOTE, U. S. N.
From a photograph made during the Civil War, in the
collection of F. B. C. Bradlee.

CAPT. JOHN PERCIVAL, U. S. N.
Born at Wellfleet, Mass., 1779. Died at Boston, 1862.
From a photograph made about 1850 in the collection
of F. B. C. Bradlee

REAR ADMIRAL JOSEPH SMITH, U. S. N.
Entered the service in 1809. Distinguished in 1812.
From a photograph made about 1850, in the
collection of F. B. C. Bradlee.

"THE HORRID MASSACRE OF THE UNFORTUNATE CREW OF THE SLOOP "ELIZA ANN," BY PIRATES, MARCH, 1825.

From a broadside in the collection of F. B. C. Bradlee.

visions nearly expended, no appearance of rain since the night we first landed, our thirst increasing, our strength wasting, our few clothes hanging in rags, our beards of great length and almost turned white, nothing like relief before us, no boat in sight. Think, reader, of our situation. We had marked out for each one the place for his grave. I looked at mine, and thought of my wife and family. Again we reduced the allowance of bread, but even the little which now fell to my share I could scarcely swallow. I never seemed to feel the sensation of hunger, the extreme of thirst was so overpowering. Perhaps never shall I be more reconciled to death, but my home made me want to live, although every breath seemed to increase thirst.

"Monday, 4th. Having seriously reflected on our situation, concluded to put all the shooks, &c., together and form a raft, and ascertain what weight it would carry, but here again we were disappointed, for we had not enough to carry two of us.

"Tuesday, 5th. About 10 o'clock A. M. discovered a boat drifting by on the southeast side of the island, about a mile distant. I deemed it a providential thing to us, and urged Thomas and George trying the raft for her. They reluctantly consented and set off, but it was nearly three P. M. when they came up with her. It was the same boat we had built! Where, then, was my friend Bracket and those who went with him? Every appearance was unfavorable. I hoped that a good Providence had yet preserved him. The men who went for the boat found it full of water, without oars, paddle, or sail; being in this condition, and about three miles to the leeward, the men found it impossible to tow her up, so left her, and were till eleven o'clock at night getting back with the raft. They were so exhausted that had it not been nearly calm, they could never have returned.

"Wednesday, 6th. This morning was indeed the most gloomy I had ever experienced. There appeared hardly a ray of hope that my friend Bracket could return, seeing the boat was lost. Our provisions nearly gone, our mouths parched extremely with thirst, our strength wasted, our spirits broken, and our hopes imprisoned

within the circumference of this desolate island in the
midst of an unfrequented ocean, all these things gave to
the scene around us the hue of death.   In the midst of
this dreadful despondence a sail hove in sight, bearing the
white flag.   Our hopes were raised, of course, but no
sooner raised than darkened by hearing a gun fired.   Here,
then, was another gang of pirates.   She soon, however,
came near enough to anchor, and her boat pushed off
towards us, with three men in her.   Thinking it no worse
now to die by sword than famine, I walked down immediately to meet them.   I knew them not.   A moment before the boat touched the ground, a man leaped from her
bows and caught me in his arms!   It was Nickola! saying, 'Do you now believe Nickola is your friend? yes,'
said he, 'Jameison will yet prove himself so.'   No words
can express my emotions at this moment.   This was a
friend indeed.   The reason of my not recognizing them
before was that they had cut off their beards and whiskers.   Turning to my fellow-sufferers, Nickola asked,
'Are these all that are left of you, where are the others?'
At this moment seeing David's grave.   'Are they dead,
then? ah, I suspected it.   I know what you were put
here for.'   As soon as I could recover myself, gave him
an account of Mr. Bracket and the others.   'How unfortunate,' he said, 'they must be lost, or some pirates have
taken them, but,' he continued, 'we have no time to lose,
you had better embark immediately with us, and go where
you please, we are at your service.'   The other two in the
boat with him were Frenchmen, one named Lyon, the
other Parrikete.   They affectionately embraced each of
us, then holding to my mouth the nose of a teakettle,
filled with wine, said, 'Drink plenty, no hurt you.'   I
drank as much as I judged prudent.   They then gave it
to my fellow-sufferers.   I experienced almost immediate
relief, not feeling it in my head; they had also brought
in the boat for us a dish of salt beef and potatoes, of
which we took a little.   Then sent the boat on board for
the other two men, being five in all, who came ashore, and
rejoiced enough was I to see among them Thomas Young,
one of my crew, who was detained on board the Mexican,
but who had escaped through Nickola's means; the other

a Frenchman, named John Cadedt. I now thought again
and again, with troubled emotion, of my friend Bracket's
fate. I took the last piece of paper I had and wrote with
a pencil a few lines, informing him (should he come there)
that I and the rest were safe ; that I was not mistake nin
the friend in whom I had placed so much confidence, that
he had accomplished my highest expectations, and that I
should go immediately to Trinidad, and requested him to
go there also, and apply to Mr. Isaac W. Lord, my consignee, for assistance. I put the paper into a junk bottle,
previously found on the beach, put in a stopper, and left
it, together with what little flour remained, a keg of water
brought from Nickola's vessel, and a few other things
which I thought might be of service to him. We then
repaired with our friends on board, where we were kindly
treated. She was a sloop from Jamaica, of about twelve
tons, with a cargo of rum and wine, bound to Trinidad.
I asked 'which way they intended to go !' They said 'to
Jamaica,' if agreeable to me. As I preferred Trinidad, I
told them if they would give me the Exertion's boat,
which was alongside (beside their own) and some water
and provisions, we would take chance in her, 'for perhaps,' said I, 'you will fare better at Jamaica than at
Trinidad.' After a few minutes' consultation, they said,
'you are too much exhausted to row the distance of one
hundred miles, therefore we will go and carry you ; we
consider ourselves at your service.' I expressed a wish to
take a look at the Exertion, possibly we might hear something of Mr. Bracket. Nickola said 'very wel,' so got
under way and run for her, having a light westerly wind.
He then related to me the manner of their desertion from
the pirates. As nearly as I can recollect his own words,
he said, 'A few days since the pirates took four small
vessels, I believe Spaniards ; they having but two officers
for the first two, the third fell to me as prize-master, and
having an understanding with the three Frenchmen and
Thomas, selected them for my crew, and went on board,
with orders to follow the Mexican, which I obeyed. The
fourth, the pirates took out all but one man, and bade him
also follow their vessel. Now our schooner leaked so bad
that we left her, and in her stead agreed to take this little

sloop (which we are now in), together with the one man. The night being very dark, we all agreed to desert the pirates, altered our course, and touched at St. Maria, where we landed the one man ; saw no boats there, could hear nothing from you, and agreed one and all, at the risk of our lives, to come and liberate you if you were alive, knowing as we did that you were put on this Key to perish. On our way we boarded the Exertion, thinking possibly you might have been there. On board her we found a sail and paddle.* We took one of the pirate's boats, which they had left alongside of her, which proves how we came by two boats. My friend, the circumstance I am now about to relate will astonish you. When the pirate's boat with Bolidar was sent to the before-mentioned Key, on the 19th of January, it was their intention to leave you prisoners there, where was nothing but salt water and mangroves, and no possibility of escape. This was the plan of Baltizar, their abandoned pilot, but Bolidar's heart failed him, and he objected to it ; then, after a conference, Captain Jonnia ordered you to be put on the little island from whence we have taken you. But after this was done, that night the French and Portuguese part of the Mexican's crew protested against it, so that Captain Jonnia, to satisfy them, sent his large boat to take you and your fellow-prisoners back again, taking care to select his confidential Spaniards for this errand. And will you believe me, they set off from the Mexican, and after spending about as much time as would really have taken them to come to you, they returned, and reported they had been to your island and landed, and that none of you were there, somebody having taken you off ! This all my companions here know to be true. I knew it was impossible you could have been liberated, and therefore we determined among ourselves that should an opportunity occur we would come and save your lives, as we now have.' He then expressed, as he hitherto had done (and I believe with sincerity), his disgust with the bad company which he had been in, and looked forward with anxiety to the day when he might return to his native country.

*This proved to me that Mr. Bracket had been there, these being the ones which he took from the island.

"I advised him to get on board an American vessel, whenever an opportunity offered, and come to the United States, and on his arrival direct a letter to me, repeating my earnest desire to make some return for the disinterested friendship which he had shown towards me. With the Frenchman I had but little conversation, being unacquainted with the language.

"Here ended Nickola's account. 'And now,' said the Frenchman, 'our hearts be easy.' Nickola observed he had left all and found us. I gave them my warmest tribute of gratitude, saying I looked upon them, under God, as the preservers of our lives, and promised them all the assistance my situation might ever enable me to afford. This brings me to

"Thursday evening, 7th, when, at 11 o'clock, we anchored at the creek's mouth, near the Exertion. I was anxious to board her; accordingly took with me Nickola, Thomas, George, and two others, well armed, each with a musket and cutlass. I jumped on her deck, saw a fire in the camboose, but no person there; I called aloud Mr. Bracket's name several times, saying, 'It is Captain Lincoln, don't be afraid, but show yourself,' but no answer was given. She had no masts, spars, rigging, furniture, provisions, or anything left, except her bowsprit and a few barrels of salt provisions of her cargo. Her sealing had holes cut in it, no doubt in their foolish search for money. I left her with peculiar emotions, such as I hope never again to experience, and returned to the little sloop, where we remained till

"Friday, 8th. When I had a disposition to visit the island on which we were first imprisoned. Found nothing there; saw a boat among the mangroves, near the Exertion. Returned, and got under way immediately for Trinidad. In the night, while under full sail, run aground on a sunken Key, having rocks above the water, resembling old stumps of trees; we, however, soon got off and anchored. Most of these Keys have similar rocks about them, which navigators must carefully guard against.

"Saturday, 9th. Got under way again, and stood along close in for the main island of Cuba, in order that if we should see the pirates, to take our boats and go on shore.

"Sunday, 10th. Saw the highlands of Trinidad. At night came to anchor in sight of the town, near a small Key. Next morning—

"Monday, 11th.—Got under way—saw a brig at anchor about five miles below the mouth of the harbor; we hoped to avoid her speaking us; but when we opened in sight of her discovered a boat making towards us, with a number of armed men in her. This alarmed my friends, and as we did not see the brig's ensign hoisted, they declared the boat was a pirate, and looking through the spy-glass, thought they knew some of them to be the Mexican's men! This state of things was quite alarming. They said, "we will not be taken alive by them." Immediately the boat fired a musket; the ball passed through our mainsail. My friends insisted on beating them off. I endeavored to dissuade them, believing, as I did, that the brig was a Spanish man-of-war, who had sent her boat to ascertain who we were. I thought we had better heave to. Immediately another shot came. Then they insisted on fighting and said, if I would not help them I was no friend. I reluctantly acquiesced, and handed up the guns, commenced firing upon them, and they upon us. We received several shots through the sails, but no one was hurt on either side. Our two boats had been cast adrift to make us go the faster, and we gained upon them, continuing firing until they turned from us and went for our boats, which they took in tow for the brig. Soon after this it became calm; then I saw that she had us in her power. She armed and manned two more boats for us. We now concluded, since we had scarcely ammunition, to surrender, and were towed down alongside the brig, taken on board, and were asked by the captain, who could speak English, 'what for you fire on the boat?' I told him we thought her a pirate, and did not like to be taken by them again, having already suffered too much, showing my papers. He said, 'Capt. Americana, never mind, go and take some dinner—which are your men ?' I pointed them out to him, and he ordered them the liberty of the decks; but my friend Nickola and his three associates were immediately put in irons. They were, however, afterwards taken out of irons and examined, and I understood the Frenchmen agreed to enlist, as they judged it the surest way to better their condition. Whether Nickola enlisted I do not know, but think that he did, as I understood that offer was made to him ; I, however, endeavored to explain more distinctly to the captain the benevolent efforts of these four men by whom my life had been saved, and used every argument in my power to procure their discharge. I also applied to the governor, and exerted myself with peculiar interest, dictated as I trust with heartfelt gratitude—and I ardently hope ere this Nickola is on his way to this country, where I may have an opportunity of convincing him that such an act of benevolence will not go unrewarded. Previous to my leaving Trinidad I made all the arrangements in my power with my influential friends, and doubt not that their laudable efforts will be accomplished. The sloop's cargo was taken on board the brig, after which the captain requested a certificate that I was politely treated by him, saying his name was Captain Candama, of the privateer brig Prudentee of eighteen guns. This request I complied with.

His first lieutenant told me he had sailed out of Boston, as commander for T. C. Amory, Esq., during the last war. In the course of the evening my friends were taken out of irons and examined separately, then put back again. The captain invited me to supper in his cabin, and a berth for the night, which was truly acceptable. The next morning, after breakfast, I with my people were set on shore, with the few things we had, with the promise of the Exertion's small boat in a day or two. But it was never sent me—the reason let the reader imagine. On landing at the wharf Casilda we were immediately taken by soldiers to the guard-house, which was a very filthy place ; thinking, I suppose, and even calling us pirates. Soon some friends came to see me. Mr. Cotton, who resides there, brought us some soup.   Mr. Isaac W. Lord, of Boston, my merchant, came with Captain Tate, who sent immediately to the governor, for I would not show my papers to any one else.   He came about sunset, and after examining Manuel, my Spanish fellow-prisoner, and my papers, said to me, giving me the papers, 'Captain, you are at liberty.'   I was kindly invited by Captain Matthew Rice, of schooner Galaxy, of Boston, to go on board his vessel and live with him during my stay there. This generous offer I accepted, and was treated by him with the greatest hospitality, for I was an hungered and he gave me meat, I was athirst and he gave me drink, I was naked and he clothed me, a stranger and he took me in.   He likewise took Manuel and my three men for that night.   Next day Mr. Lord rendered me all necessary assistance in making my protest.   He had heard nothing from me until my arrival.   I was greatly disappointed in not finding Mr. Bracket, and requested Mr. Lord to give him all needful aid if he should come there.   To Captain Carnes, of the schooner Hannah of Boston, I would tender my sincere thanks for his kindness in giving me a passage to Boston, which I gladly accepted.   To those gentlemen of Trinidad, and many captains of American vessels, who gave me sea clothing, &c., I offer my cordial gratitude.

"Captain Carnes sailed from Trinidad on the 20th of February.   Fearing the pirates, we kept a long distance from the land and two degrees to westward of Cape Antonio.   On our passage experienced several gales of wind, in one of which, while lying to, shipped a sea, which did considerable injury, and swept a young man overboard from the pump, named Nelson.   We never saw him again.   We arrived at Boston March 25th, and when I stepped upon the wharf, though much emaciated, I felt truly happy.

"I am fully of the opinion that these ferocious pirates are linked in with many inhabitants of Cuba, and the government in many respects appears covertly to encourage them.

"It is with heartfelt delight that, since the above narrative was written, I have learned that Mr. Bracket and his

companions are safe ; he arrived at Port d'Esprit, about
forty leagues east of Trinidad. A letter has been received from him, stating that he should proceed to Trinidad the first opportunity. It appears that after reaching
the wreck, they found a boat from the shore, taking on
board some of the Exertion's cargo, in which they proceeded to the above place. Why it was not in his power
to come to our relief will no doubt be satisfactorily dis-
closed when he may be so fortunate as once more to
return to his native country and friends.

"For many months I remained without any certain information respecting the fate of Mr. Bracket and his
companions. But in the course of the ensuing autumn,
if I recollect right, Mr. Bracket very unexpectedly paid
me a visit at Hingham, the place of my residence. We
were mutually rejoiced to see each other once more among
the living, as for a time at least each had regarded the
other as dead. He gave me an account of his adventures
and of the reasons why he did not return to us. He
told me that when they left us and put to sea, in the miserable boat which we had constructed, they went to the
Exertion, and fortunately found a better boat, of which
they took possession, and suffered the old one to float
away, and it accordingly passed our solitary island in its
random course, causing us a great deal of alarm. From
the wreck they steered among the keys to the mainland
of Cuba, and reached Principe, the town where my cargo
was sold. Here Mr. Bracket related his tale of suffering
and requested assistance to rescue the remaining prisoners
on the key. The authorities furnished him with several
soldiers, with whom he put again to sea, with the humane
intention of coming to relieve us. They had gone but a
short distance, however, when the soldiers positively refused to go any further and forced him to return with
them to Principe ; thus all his hopes of being able to
rescue us were entirely extinguished. A stranger, and
helpless as he was, it was out of his power to do anything
more, and he could only hope that we might have been
saved in some other way. Friendless, without money,
and debilitated by recent suffering, he hardly knew which
way to turn. He was desirous of reaching home, and

finally resolved to travel to the north side of Cuba. After a long and tedious journey, during which he suffered dreadfully from the hard travelling and want of necessaries and comforts, he at length arrived at Havana, from which port he took passage to Boston. Thus the reasons of his conduct were satisfactorily explained, and my uncertainty respecting his fate happily terminated.

"I felt great anxiety to learn what became of Jamieson, who, my readers will recollect, was detained on board the Spanish brig Prudentee, near Trinidad. I heard nothing from him, until I believe about eighteen months after I reached home when I received a letter from him, from Montego Bay, Jamaica, informing me that he was then residing in that island. I immediately wrote to him and invited him to come on to the United States. He accordingly came on passenger with Capt. Wilson of Cohasset, and arrived in Boston in August, 1824. Our meeting was very affecting. Trying scenes were brought up before us ; scenes gone forever, through which we had passed together, where our acquaintance was formed, and since which time we had never met. I beheld once more the preserver of my life, the instrument, under Providence, of restoring me to my home, my family and my friends, and I regarded him with no ordinary emotion. My family were delighted to see him and cordially united in giving him a warm reception. He told me that after we separated in Trinidad, he remained on board the Spanish brig. The commander asked him and his companions if they would enlist ; the Frenchmen replied that they would, but he said nothing, being determined to make his escape the very first opportunity which should present. The Spanish brig afterwards fell in with a Columbian privateer, an armed brig of eighteen guns. Being of equal force, they gave battle, and fought between three and four hours. Both parties were very much injured, and, without any considerable advantage on either side, both drew off to make repairs. The Spanish brig Prudentee put into St. Jago de Cuba. Jamieson was wounded in the action by a musket ball through his arm, and was taken on shore, with the other wounded, and placed in the hospital at St. Jago. Here he remained for a consid-

erable time, until he had nearly recovered, when he found
an opportunity of escaping and embarked for Jamaica.
He arrived in safety at Kingston, and from there traveled
barefoot over the mountains, until, very much exhausted,
he reached Montego Bay, where he had friends, and
where one of his brothers possessed some property. From
this place he afterwards wrote to me. He told me that
before he came to Massachusetts he saw the villainous
pilot of the Mexican, the infamous Baltizar, with several
other pirates, brought into Montego Bay, from whence
they were to be conveyed to Kingston to be executed.
Whether the others were part of the Mexican's crew or
not I do not know. Baltizar was an old man, and, as
Jamieson said, it was a melancholy and heart-rending
sight to see him borne to execution with those gray hairs,
which might have been venerable in virtuous old age,
now a shame and reproach to this hoary villain, for he was
full of years and old in iniquity. When Jamieson received the letter which I wrote, he immediately embarked
with Capt. Wilson and came to Boston, as I have before
observed.

"According to his own account, he was of a very respectable family in Greenock, Scotland. His father
when living, was a rich cloth merchant, but both
his father and mother had been dead many years. He was
the youngest of thirteen children, and being, as he said,
of a roving disposition, had always followed the seas.
He had received a polite education, and was of a very
gentlemanly deportment. He spoke several living languages, and was skilled in drawing and painting. He had
travelled extensively in different countries, and acquired
in consequence an excellent knowledge of their manners
and customs. His varied information (for hardly any
subject escaped him) rendered him a very entertaining
companion. His observations on the character of different nations were very liberal, marking their various traits,
their virtues and vices, with playful humorousness, quite
free from bigotry or narrow prejudice.

"He was in France during the disturbance between
France and England, when all British subjects whatever
in France were detained prisoners of war. He was one

who was thus compelled to remain a prisoner to Napoleon.
He was there at the time of Napoleon's memorable expedition to Russia, and saw the splendid troops of the
Emperor when they left delightful France to commence
their toilsome and fatal journey, and also the remnant
when they returned, broken down, dispirited, haggard and
wan, their garments hanging about them in tatters, and
hardly life enough in them to keep soul and body together.
The particulars respecting this period he could communicate with the minuteness of an eye-witness, which consequently rendered them very interesting.   During the first
part of his residence in France he was supported by re-
mittances from his father and allowed the liberty of the
city of Valenciennes, a gentleman there being bound for
his good behavior.   He thus had an opportunity of visiting and becoming acquainted with the inhabitants.   He
lived in this manner several years.   At length aroused, as
he said, by the consciousness that he was spending the
best days of his life in idleness, he formed the determina-
tion to try and make his escape from the country.   He
honorably released the gentleman who was bound for him
from his obligation, frankly telling him that he should
run away the first opportunity.   From this time he was
alternately arrested and imprisoned, and by various strata-
gems effected his escape, until he had been placed in
ninety-three different prisons.   During his wanderings he
climbed the Alps, and visited the famous passage, cut
through the solid rocks by Hannibal, which, as he said,
was of sufficient magnitude to admit a large loaded wagon
to pass through.   From his long residence in France he
had learned to speak the French language with a facility
almost equal to a native.   The charm of his conversation
and manners drew people around him, they hardly knew
how or why.

"I was in trade between Boston and Philadelphia at the
time he came to Massachusetts, and he sailed with me
several trips as my mate.   He afterwards went to Cuba,
and was subsequently engaged in the mackerel fishery out
of the port of Hingham during the warm season, and in
the winter frequently employed himself in teaching navigation to young men, for which he was eminently quali-

fied. He remained with us until his death, which took place in 1829. At this time he had been out at sea two or three days, when he was taken sick and was carried into Cape Cod, where he died, on the first day of May, 1829, and there his remains lie buried. Peace be to his ashes! They rest in a strange land, far from his kindred and his native country.

"Since his death I have met with Mr. Stewart in Philadelphia, who was commercial agent in Trinidad at the time of my capture. He informed me that the piratical schooner Mexican was afterwards chased by an English government vessel, from Jamaica, which was cruising in search of it. Being hotly pursued, the pirates deserted their vessel and fled to the mangrove bushes, on an island similar to that on which they had placed me and my crew to die. The English surrounded them, and thus they were cut off from all hope of escape. They remained there, I think, fourteen days, when, being almost entirely subdued by famine, eleven surrendered themselves and were taken. The others probably perished among the mangroves. The few who were taken were carried by the government vessel into Trinidad. Mr. Stewart said that he saw them himself, and such miserable objects that had life he never before beheld. They were in a state of starvation; their beards had grown to a frightful length, their bodies were covered with filth and vermin, and their countenances were hideous. From Trinidad they were taken to Kingston, Jamaica, and there hung. Thus there is every reason to believe that this horde of monsters was at last broken up and dispersed."

By 1824 piracy in West Indian waters had been suppressed to a great extent, and although sporadic attacks were made for some years more on attractive merchantmen, yet they were as nothing in number and frequency compared with the wholesale murder and pillage practiced with impunity a few years before.

Commodore Porter determined to take his fever-stricken squadron to recuperate in a cooler climate, and after an absence of several months returned to his station. This absence tended to revive somewhat the drooping spirits of the freebooters. There was a secret association of desperadoes with some of the merchants and custom house officers, most of the latter being natives of old Spain, intent only on making their fortunes and greedy and rapacious beyond imagination. They prevailed on the Spanish authorities, some of whose high officials, it is believed, were not above accepting bribes, to refuse the American naval forces the privilege of pursuing the pirates in Spanish territory ; but even so, the latter found themselves no longer able to arm and equip many formidable vessels.

As soon as the United States fleet returned to its former cruising ground, the little "mosquito fleet" resumed the arduous work of scouring the coasts, convoying merchant vessels, and destroying all suspected haunts of pirates.

Before the fleet left for the north, during the autumn of 1823, the barge "Gnat" returned from a most arduous cruise among the keys north of Cuba in search of piratical establishments.

While at Cayo Roman, midshipman Hunter was captured by a gang of desperadoes while on his way to buy some provisions. The pirates took him some distance away, but released him at night. Lieutenant Freelons, commanding the "Gnat," seized all the boats he could find, blockaded the island, and remained there six days without capturing any of them. He, however, managed to destroy three large row galleys, fitted with masts and sails, belonging to the pirates, together with a large quantity of arms and ammunition they had left behind in their hasty retreat.

This particular gang was organized under the leadership of one Antonio El Majorcam, a notorious freebooter, said at one time to have been an officer in the Spanish navy. He subsequently became a highwayman on shore. In August, 1824, Lieutenant Paine, in the schooner "Terrier," captured a launch with eight men just after they had plundered a French barque, which he recaptured from them off Havana. Lieutenant C. W. Skinner, commanding the schooner "Porpoise," at Matanzas, on Oct. 20th, 1824, secretly sent a boat expedition from his vessel, in command of Lieutenant Hunter, to examine the adjacent bays and

SPANISH SAILOR ABOUT 1820
From a lithograph in the collection of F. B. C. Bradlee

UNIFORMS OF U. S. NAVY ABOUT 1820
From a lithograph in the collection of F. B. C. Bradlee.

U. S. SLOOP-OF-WAR "ONTARIO"

Painted at Port Mahon, Minorca.

From the painting in possession of the Peabody Museum.

inlets, long notorious as retreats of pirates. Two days after Lieutenant Hunter returned with a piratical schooner mounting a twelve-pound brass pivot gun, a large new row galley, and ten smaller row boats ; one of these was captured with three men on board. They stated that their vessel had been taken by armed men, who had given them that boat in exchange, with a promise of returning in a few days. The next day he discovered a suspicious schooner standing to sea in chase of another vessel in sight. On his approach the schooner tacked and stood in for the shore, closely pursued by the boats. The crew abandoned the schooner and fled to the woods, where they were sought for, but unsuccessfully. The schooner proved to be a pirate mounting the usual pivot brass heavy gun and small arms.

From the number of valuable nautical instruments, trunks of clothing, rigging, and sails, three United States flags, and from the stains of blood on the articles on board, she must have robbed several vessels and murdered their crews. No papers were discovered which could lead to the identification of the vessel or vessels captured. Several articles of clothing were marked "Captain Shaw," quite a few had the initials "A. S." embroidered on them. A bag, on which was painted "Brig 'Morning Star's' Letter bag" ; a card marked "Mrs. Loris's boarding house, Charleston, So. Ca.", and several other articles, were found. The three prisoners were sent to Matanzas, together with the blood-stained relics. The schooner herself was manned and cruised as a decoy, but piracy had largely ceased in that neighborhood, and thenceforth only asserted itself on very favorable opportunities.

President James Munroe, in his message to Congress, dated December 1st, 1824,* paid high compliments to the navy in his references to their services in suppressing piracy :

"The activity, zeal and enterprise of our officers and men have continued to command approbation. All the vessels have been kept uniformly and busily employed,

---

*Messages and State Papers of James Munroe, Fifth President of the United States.

where the danger was believed to be greatest, except for short periods, when the flag officer (Commodore Porter) supposed it necessary that they should return to the United States to receive provisions, repairs and men, and for other objects essential to their health, comfort and efficiency.

"No complaints have reached the Navy Department of injury from privateers of Porto Rico or any other Spanish possessions, nor have our cruisers found any violating our rights. A few small piratical vessels and some boats have been taken, and establishments broken up, and much salutary protection afforded our commerce. The force employed, however, has been too small constantly to watch every part of a coast so extensive as that of the Gulf of Mexico, and some piratical depredations have therefore been committed, but they are of a character, though perhaps not less bloody and fatal to the sufferers, yet differing widely from those which first excited the sympathy of the public and exertions of the Federal Administration. There are few, if any, piratical vessels of large size in the neighborhood of Cuba, and none are now seen at a distance from the land. But the pirates conceal themselves, with their boats, in small creeks, bays and inlets, and finding vessels becalmed, or in a defenceless situation, assail and destroy them. When discovered, they readily and safely retreat into the country, where our forces cannot follow, and by the plunder which they have obtained, and which they sell at prices low and tempting to the population, and by the apprehensions which they are able to create in those who would otherwise give information, they remain secure, and mingle at pleasure in the business of the towns and transactions of society, and acquire all the information necessary to accomplish their purposes.

"Against such a system no naval force can afford complete security, unless aided by the cordial, unwavering and energetic co-operation which would render their lurking places on land unsafe, and make punishment the certain consequence of detection. Unless this co-operation be obtained, additional means ought to be intrusted to the Executive, to be used in such manner as experience may dictate."

Shortly after this message was read news was received from Commodore Porter that he had punished the Spanish authorities at Foxardo, Porto Rico, for their ill-concealed hostility to the American naval officers engaged in suppressing piracy. His act was disapproved by the President and his cabinet, with subsequent serious results, for after Commodore Porter was relieved, the zeal of the navy naturally received a cold douche. The pirates and their friends were not long in perceiving this, and temporarily resumed their operations, as will be seen in the following pages.

Commodore Porter's official report of his conflict with the Spanish authorities was as follows:

"United States Corvette 'John Adams',
"Passage Island, November 15th, 1824.

"Sir: I have the honor to inform you that, on my arrival at St. Thomas I was informed that Lieutenant Commandant C. T. Platt, of the United States schooner 'Beagle', who had visited Foxardo, a town on the east coast of Porto Rico, about two miles from the sea, for the purpose of making inquiries respecting a quantity of dry goods supposed to have been deposited there by pirates, was, after being recognized as an American officer by the proper authorities, there imprisoned and shamefully treated.

"Indignant at the outrages which have so repeatedly been heaped upon us by the authorities of Porto Rico, I proceeded to this place, where I left the flagship (the 'John Adams'), and, taking with me the schooners 'Grampus' and 'Beagle' and the boats of the 'John Adams', with Captain Dallas and part of his officers, seamen and marines, proceeded to the port of Foxardo, where, finding preparations were making to fire on us from the shore batteries, I sent a party of seamen and marines to spike the guns, which was done in a few minutes, as the Spaniards fled on the landing of the party.

"I then landed with 200 seamen and marines and marched to the town, spiking on the way the guns of a small battery placed for the defence of a pass on the road, and reached the town in thirty minutes after landing. I found them prepared for defence, as they had received information from St.Thomas of my intentions of visiting the place. I halted about pistol-shot from their forces drawn up on the outskirts of the town, and sent in a flag requiring the alcade, or governor, with the captain of the port, the principal offenders, to come to me to make atonement for the outrage, giving them an hour to deliberate.

"They appeared accordingly, and after begging pardon (in the presence of all the officers) of the officer who had been insulted, and expressing great penitence, I permitted them to return to the town, on their promising to respect all American officers who may visit them hereafter.

"We then returned to the vessels and left the harbor, after being at anchor about three hours. As we were getting under weigh, a number of persons appeared on the beach bearing a white flag, and having with them some bullocks and a number of horses apparently laden—no doubt a present from the authorities of the place, which they informed me they should send me. There is no doubt that our persons and our flag will be more respected hereafter than they have been by the authorities of Porto Rico.

"Every officer and man on this occasion conducted themselves in a manner to meet my entire approbation.

"I am, with great respect, your obedient servant,

"D. Porter.

"Hon. Secretary of the Navy,
      Washington City."

This report, though it was evidently in harmony with the expressed wishes of the administration, produced an order relieving Porter of his command. As usual, there were "wheels within wheels", and the question of upholding the honor of one's flag and country became inextricably mixed with politics, some, if not most of the latter being of a not very high order.

In passing it is, perhaps, not uninteresting to wonder what would happen to the unfortunate naval officer, say, in the year of grace 1924, a century after the events related above, should he undertake to resent in like manner an insult to the United States flag. He would lose his commission, that goes without saying, but he would be extraordinarily lucky if a worse fate did not befall him. Commodore Porter was court-martialed for overstepping his authority and doing that for which, in any other country, he would have been promoted and highly honored.

The commodore and his friends asserted, and it is thought not entirely without reason, that the court was "packed" with his personal and political enemies, and it must be remembered that a century ago political feeling ran high, and gentlemen, especially officers of the army and navy, were held accountable for their words. Duels were frequent, and an incident not wholly unlike Commodore Porter's case led to the famous encounter between Commodores Barron and Decatur, which resulted in the latter's death.

The result of the court-martial so deeply wounded the feelings of Commodore Porter that he immediately resigned from the navy. He afterwards entered the service of Mexico as admiral, and served with brilliant success against the Spaniards, but he resigned after the Mexicans had been relieved of external foes and returned home. Later in his life he received several appointments in the United States diplomatic service, and finally as minister to Turkey, where he died March 3d, 1843.

David Porter was born in Boston, February 1st, 1780; he was appointed midshipman in the navy April 16th, 1798; lieutenant, October 8th, 1799; master commandant, April 20th, 1806; captain, July 2d, 1812. His father, Captain David, commanded a Boston merchant ship, and was actively engaged in the Revolution, when he attained the rank of lieutenant in the Continental navy. After the peace in 1783, the elder Porter removed to Baltimore, and engaging in the West India trade, introduced his son to the naval career at the age of sixteen.

Young Porter served in the frigate " Constellation", in her famous action with the "Insurgente", in February 1799, during our war with France; his good conduct in the action and in securing the prize, caused his promotion soon after.

In January, 1800, he was wounded in an engagement with a pirate off San Domingo; in August, 1801, Lieutenant Porter was made executive officer of the schooner "Enterprise", which captured a Tripolitan cruiser of superior force.

While first lieutenant of the frigate "New York", the the flagship of the Mediterranean squadron, he commanded a boat expedition which destroyed several feluccas laden with wheat, under the batteries of Tripoli, and was again wounded.

Lieutenant Porter was then transferred to the unfortunate frigate "Philadelphia", which was captured while aground in the harbor of Tripoli, in October, 1803 ; he was eighteen months a prisoner, and on his release he was promoted to the command of the schooner "Enterprise". While in command of her, in 1806, Porter severely punished twelve Spanish gunboats that rashly attacked him while in sight of Gibraltar.   Appointed to the command of the small frigate "Essex", 32 guns, Captain Porter sailed from New York on what was to be one of the most famous cruises ever undertaken by a United States man-of-war, July 3d, 1812.

He soon made several valuable captures : H. B. M. ship sloop "Alert" of 20 guns—the first ship of war taken in our second war with Great Britain—on December 12th, the "Essex" captured the British post office packet "Nocton", with specie to the amount of $55,000 on board ; and, at the close of January, 1813, the future Commodore Porter sailed for the Pacific, where he played havoc among the British trading and whaling fleet.

Nevertheless, on March 28th, 1814, the "Essex" and her commander were captured, after a severe fight, in the neutral port of Valparaiso, by the British frigate "Phoebe", 36 guns, and sloop "Cherub", 28 guns. Captain Porter published a narrative of this remarkable cruise in 1822.   From 1815 to 1823 he was one of the navy commissioners, which office he resigned, as has been seen, to accept the command of the fleet in West Indian waters. David Porter had positive and stirring qualities, was fertile in resources, combined with great energy ; excessive, and, sometimes, not over-scrupulous ambition.   He was impressed with and boastful of his own powers, given to exaggeration in relation to himself.   Not too generous to older and superior living officers, Commodore Porter was brave, daring, and endowed with the qualities that go to make up a great naval leader.

He was the father of David D. Porter, who played such a prominent part in the naval history of the Civil war, and was, after the death of Admiral Farragut in 1870, made, in his turn, admiral of the navy, a position he held until his death in 1891; another brother, Commodore William Porter, distinguished himself on the western rivers during the war of Secession, his death in 1864 being the result of severe injuries caused by the bursting of a boiler. It cannot, however, be said that the later Porters were as popular as their father; they were too much given to self-appreciation at the expense of others; David D., especially, from having been an intimate friend of General Grant, became in his later years on "official" terms only with the latter, the result, it is said, of a back-biting letter written to Secretary of the Navy Welles by Admiral Porter while the siege of Vicksburg was in progress.

After the recall of Commodore Porter, Captain Lewis Warrington, U. S. N., succeeded to the command of the squadron, which, during 1825, consisted of the frigate "Constellation", corvette "John Adams", brigs "Hornet" and "Spark", schooners "Grampus", "Shark", "Fox", "Ferret", "Jackal", the steamer "Sea Gull", store-ship "Decoy", and the barges. The "Ferret" was capsized in a sudden squall on February 4th, 1825, off the coast of Cuba; five of her crew were drowned and the vessel sunk. Turning back a few months, before the events related above had taken place, the Salem *Gazette* for January 23d, 1824, reported the following act of piracy:

"Capt. Labonisse arrived at New York, 22 days from Domingo City, informs that a small schooner was fitted out at that place, to go in quest of the pirates who robbed the brigantine 'William Henry' of Salem.*

"The governor furnished men, arms, ammunition and money. After being out 12 days, the schooner returned with 18 pirates, a considerable quantity of hides, coffee and indigo, and some cash, found on the island of Saona, 25

*The only brigantine "William Henry" to be found in the Salem Ship Register was an old vessel of 166 tons, built at Kingston, Mass., in 1784. Registered at Salem, July 15th, 1790; William Gray, Jr., owner; Thomas West, master.

leagues to windward of St. Domingo, and it was expected they (the pirates) would receive the punishment due their crimes."

The same paper for April 1st, 1824, contains an exciting tale of marine highway robbery:

"The brig 'Echo', Blanchard, of Portland, Maine, 25 days from St. Croix, has arrived at N. Y. Capt. Blanchard reports that on the 17th inst., in lat. 31.50, long. 73, he saw a vessel at the eastward, bearing down upon the 'Echo', which had all sail set she could carry. At midnight the strange vessel passed the stern of the 'Echo', put about and stood towards her. It was soon found that she outsailed the 'Echo', and at 1 o'clock A. M. she came within pistol shot, fired two muskets into her, and ordered the captain to come to and send his boat on board, which being done, the boat soon returned, full of armed men, to the number of about fifteen.

"When the boat came alongside, they demanded of the captain his papers. They inquired as to the longitude they were in, and demanded if there was any money on board. The 'Echo's' crew were then driven into the forecastle, and the pirates began breaking open all the chests in the cabin, and all in the brig, taking away all the clothes they could find. Three trunks belonging to the cargo were also broken and plundered. They likewise took away the new foresail, which was bent, a new jib, two steering sails, etc., a quantity of spare rigging, blocks, etc. Much more they destroyed. They further took a spare topmast, several other spars, and would have taken the cargo had it not been for a squall which came on and obliged them to take to their own ship, which they did, keeping a small boat and oars.

"Two of the 'Echo's' crew were kept on board the pirate while the plundering was going on. They described the vessel as a full-rigged brig, mounting 30 6-pounders and a long 18 amidships. The decks were full of men, apparently Spaniards for the most part."

A few months later the Salem Gazette again recorded an act of piracy, as follows:

"September 20th, 1824.

"N. Y. papers of Sept. 8th contain an account of the

recapture of the brig 'Henry', of Hartford (Conn.), from the pirates, by a launch fitted out for the purpose by Capt. Graham, R. N., of H. B. M. frigate 'Icarus', and the capture of two piratical vessels of Cayo Blanco, in the Bay of Honda. The pirates all escaped but six, who were shot in the attempt. The pirates, it is stated, had previously captured 12 vessels, burnt them to the water's edge, and murdered their crews."

On the 4th of March, 1825, Lieutenant Sloat, in command of the schooner "Grampus", heard of a piratical sloop in the vicinity of the island of St. Thomas. He fitted out a merchant sloop, with a lieutenant, a midshipman (Andrew Hull Foote, of whom mention will be made later), and 23 men, in pursuit. The pirate, not suspecting the real character of this vessel, came alongside and opened fire. Sloat and his men returned shot for shot with a twelve-pound carronade (a type of gun very successful at short range), and after a hot fight of some forty-five minutes, the pirates beached their craft to escape by land. Two of them were killed, and, strange to relate, ten more were captured by the Spanish soldiers after they had landed. The notorious pirate chief Cofrecina was amongst those captured, all of whom were executed by the terrible "garrote" method in Porto Rico.

Midshipman Andrew Hull Foote, who was to have such a distinguished career in the Civil war, then a young man of sixteen (he received his midshipman's warrant in 1822), behaved in a particularly gallant and brilliant manner in this engagement. He was born at New Haven, Connecticut, September 12th, 1806, and was the son of Governor S. A. Foote ; owing to his distinguished services in the long and hard contest of the West India squadron against the pirates, Midshipman Foote was advanced to the grade of lieutenant, May 27th, 1830. In those days the navy was small, and there was no retired list for the senior officers ; the result being that in the junior grades promotion was practically stagnant, to the great detriment of the service, and so it was not until December 19th, 1852, that Foote, the future hero of the Civil war, attained the rank of commander. While stationed at the naval asylum, 1841-43, he prevailed upon many of the inmates to give up their spirit rations ; being one of the first to introduce the principle of total abstinence from intoxicating drinks in the navy, and continued this effort in the "Cumberland" in 1843-45, besides delivering every Sunday an extemporaneous sermon to the crew.   In 1849-52, in command of the brig "Perry", he was on the African coast, successfully engaged in suppressing the slave trade, and published a book on the subject, "Africa and the American Flag."   Although Admiral Foote possessed sterling qualities and the highest professional attainments, it is to be doubted whether he was a cheerful companion among a few officers cooped up for months on a small vessel.   This feeling cropped out in a diary kept by one of the "Perry's" officers while she was on the African coast, and it is not to be wondered that the commissioned force rather complained that their commander, with his strict Puritanical notions, his habit of preaching, and his strong dislike of alcoholic liquors at a time when drinking was common, did not add to the gayety of a long voyage.

During the gloomy "secession" winter of 1860-61, Commander Foote was executive officer at the Brooklyn navy yard; he was an intimate friend from boyhood of Hon. Gideon Welles, soon to be Secretary of the Navy in President Lincoln's administration, and the future admiral performed a service of inestimable value to the country by warning Mr. Welles of certain officers of the navy who, he was sure, would not be faithful to their oath, and giving him, also, his professional estimate of many other officers.

In July, 1861, Foote was promoted to be full captain (then the highest rank by law in the navy) ; two months later he was made flag officer—at that period a mere temporary grade—of the flotilla fitting out on the western rivers.   He sailed from Cairo, Illinois, on February 4th, 1862, with seven gunboats, four of them ironclads, to attack Fort Henry on the Tennessee river.   Without waiting for the co-operation of General Grant, he attacked the fort and compelled its surrender, and without the help of Flag Officer Foote and the navy, the army under General Grant could not, a few days later, have captured Fort Donelson.

Foote was severely wounded in the ankle at the latter battle, which injury compelled him to go east on sick leave a few weeks later. He was made a rear admiral and the head of one of the bureaus in the navy department on July 31, 1862. It was also the intention of the administration to have given Admiral Foote the command of the South Atlantic blockading squadron in place of Admiral Du Pont, but the former's health had been shattered, and he died in New York City on June 26th, 1863, after a short illness.

In March, 1825, Lieutenant W. W. McKean (afterwards commodore and well known for convoying home, in 1860, the first Japanese embassy to this country), with the steam-galliot "Sea Gull" and barge "Gallinipper", took command of an expedition, in co-operation with the boats of H. B. M. frigate "Dartmouth", to search a certain key reported to be a base of piratical operations. They soon found a schooner secreted behind trees. A brief but spirited action ensued, which resulted in a complete victory; eight pirates were killed and nineteen were captured, their schooner was also taken after she had been run ashore.

Her armament consisted of two brass six-pounders, five swivel blunderbusses, and arms, etc., for a crew of 35 men. She pretended to carry Spanish papers, but these were discovered to be false. Cases of American goods were found on board the schooner and on shore. Another small topsail schooner was captured by the expedition, but her crew escaped. In 1828 the United States West India squadron was commanded by Flag Officer Charles G. Ridgeley (for his gallant services during the war with the Barbary corsairs this officer had received the congressional gold medal of honor), and consisted of the following vessels: Sloop-of-war "Natchez", flagship, 18 guns, master commandant Budd; sloop-of-war "Erie", 18 guns, master commandant Turner; sloop-of-war "Hornet", 18 guns, master commandant Claxton; sloop-of-war "Falmouth", 18 guns, master commandant Morgan; schooner "Grampus", 12 guns, Lieutenant Latimer; and schooner "Shark", 12 guns, Lieutenant Adams.

It was found necessary to keep a squadron in these

waters, with a view to prevent piracy, for some years, and although sporadic outbreaks took place from time to time, there was no comprehensive revival of the free-booters' "trade." The same system of marine police was continued, and with the more or less active co-operation of the Spanish authorities, the marine highwaymen became fewer and far between, until by the early 1830's it was difficult to find any more, and merchant vessels bound to the West Indies had a reasonable chance of arriving at their destination without being attacked.

The war on the West India pirates is one of the bright pages in the history of the United States navy. In this, as well as other operations, our men were uniformly successful, and although often outnumbered in individual encounters, bravery, good discipline and good marksmanship (for which our sailors have always been renowned) won the day.

The course pursued by President Munroe and his administration, resulting in the court martial of Flag Officer David Porter for resenting the insult to his officers by the Spanish authorities, naturally encouraged the pirates. Our officers felt that energetic measures on their part might not be upheld by their government, so they naturally became extremely cautious, and the result was manifested in renewed sporadic outbreaks of piracy.

The Salem *Register* for March 19th, 1829, contained the following gruesome tale of murder and robbery on the high seas :

"PIRACY.

"We gave in our last paper a condensed account of the horrible piracy and murder committed on board the brig 'Attentive' of Boston. A more particular account of the bloody affair is given in the following statement, made under oath by the second officer of the brig, who was the only person left alive (and his escape was most providential) to furnish the horrid recital:

"The Notarial Certificate sets forth the testimony of Alfred Hill, who stated 'that he was second mate of the brig 'Attentive', Capt. Caleb W. Grozier, of Boston, which vessel sailed hence on Sunday, February 22d inst., bound to New York, from Matanzas, having on board the following named persons, viz: Caleb Grozier, master ; Joseph Jordan, first mate ; this appearer, Alfred Hill, second mate ; John Robinson, Joseph Blaseday, and Potter, seamen ; and cook, a black man, name unknown. That off Point Yaco, was boarded and brought to by a piratical schooner, about 60 or 70 tons burthen, full of men armed with cutlasses, and having on board two large guns, who ordered the boat to be lowered and sent on board the schooner, which was done, having on board Capt. Grozier and two men, Joseph Blaseday and John Robinson ; that as soon as the boat got alongside of the schooner a number of her men jumped on board, took out the two seamen, and immediately shoved alongside of the brig and boarded her, and ordered all hands, except the captain, into the fore peak. After shutting the scuttle over, they waited about ten minutes, and ordered all hands on deck again. That at this time he, the said Alfred Hill, was stowed away among the cargo, for the purpose of secreting himself ; that they were called on deck separately ; that he then heard a heavy groan from the captain, and heard him distinctly repeat these words, 'Lord have mercy on my soul,' and heard a scuffling on deck and groans of the people ; that after the noise had ceased they commenced searching, as he supposes, for money ; that at 4 o'clock in the afternoon they knocked out her bow port, when she immediately began to fill with water ; hearing a noise on deck at the time, he supposed that the pirates had not left her, and was afraid to go upon deck ; that having discovered the noise to proceed from the flapping of the sails, after having remained below till twilight, he went upon deck and got some blankets, with which he endeavored to stop up the bow port, but found it of no use, as the force of the sea washed them in again ; that he then filled the topsails, to endeavor if possible, to get her back into the harbor. That about three miles and a half from the shore she sunk, and with the assistance of a plank, he succeeded in getting ashore about 4 o'clock the following morning, and continued walking along shore as far as he could ; that he then went to a house, where they gave him an order to go to Mr. Roberts' ferry, where he dined. That from thence he went to the plantation of Mr. Echevarria, where he slept last night, from whence he this morning came to town. That the brig was overhauled and boarded between 12 and 1 o'clock of the day of their leaving port, and that the pirates left her, as he supposes, between 4 and 5 o'clock in the afternoon. That after coming on deck, he discovered marks of blood near the rails, and pieces of watches, &c., and wearing apparel strewed about the cabin and deck. That he has no doubt, from the noise he heard, and the appearance of blood, that the captain and crew were murdered."

"The 'Attentive' was cleared for Matanzas on the 4th of December last. The following list of her officers and crew is taken from the Custom House files:

Capt. Grozier, aged 58, of Boston, a native of Truro; Jeremiah Jordan, 1st mate, a native of Canton, Mass., residence in Medford; A. Hill, of Portsmouth, 2d do., aged 17; Joseph Blasdel, of do., aged 21; Stephen Potter, of Thomaston, aged 25; John Robertson, a native of the Netherlands, aged 39; Andrew Liahman, a native of Alexandria, aged 43; John Price, cook, of N. York (black), 33.

"There is a great reason to fear that the officers and crew of the brig "New Priscilla", of Salem, have shared an equally deplorable fate, although many persons entertain hopes that they may have escaped in the boats, which were not seen on board the vessel when she was fallen in with. The 'New Priscilla' was last from Charleston, S. C., bound to Matanzas, and was commanded by Capt. Charles Hart, an enterprising, resolute man, and worthy citizen. He likewise was owner of a part of the vessel. A letter from Capt. Weston, who has arrived at Charleston from Havana, says he has no doubt that Capt. Hart and his crew were all cut off.

"The captain of an English sloop informed Capt. Watson, who arrived at Charleston, S. C., on the 7th inst., from Havana, 3d inst., that the same day the brig 'New Priscilla', of Salem, was seen on the Bank, he saw a ship lying to, in company with a small vessel, and that several other vessels were in sight, some of which probably fell into the hands of the pirates."

STEAM SLOOP-OF-WAR "REGENT"

Built in 1840-41 by Brown & Bell, New York, for the Spanish Government, for use in Cuban waters

From a lithograph in the Collection of F. B. C. Bradlee

SCHOONER "FALMOUTH"

Built about 1856, and was at one time rigged as a brig. She landed several "cargoes" of slaves
at various points on the southern coast in the late 50's

From a sketch in the collection of F. B. C. Bradlee

"From a slip from the Charleston Courier we learn that the Governor General of Cuba has issued a proclamation offering a reward of $5000 for the capture of the piratical schooner (which had captured the brig 'Attentive' and murdered her crew), together with all or two-thirds of the crew—$2000 for the schooner alone, and $250 for each and every one of her crew.

"The American merchants and masters of vessels in Havana chartered a vessel to go in pursuit of the pirate."

A few months later the New York Shipping and Commercial List, the largest and most influential mercantile and financial paper published in the United States at that time—its files from the beginning, 1808, up to 1860, are a mine of valuable information relating to the commercial history of our country—reported the following serious cases of piracy, and most of the newspapers published in the seaports, denounced in scathing editorials the lax policy pursued by the past administrations. President Munroe had gone out of office on March 4th, 1825, and had been succeeded by President John Quincy Adams, who was never a friend to an efficient army or navy. But when Andrew Jackson—"old Hickory"—became chief magistrate, March 4th, 1829, he issued orders that "The seas should be swept of the marine highwaymen, if the navy had to be doubled."

"Oct. 21, 1829.

"Ship 'Globe', Macy, at the Cape de Verdes, from Buenos Ayres, was robbed of $1200, clothes, etc., by a piratical schooner, 17th June, lat. 6 N., long. 22 W."

"Dec. 16, 1829.

"Ship 'Candace', Lindsey, from Marblehead, Mass., for Sumatra, returned to Marblehead, 12th inst., having been robbed of all her specie, about $20,000, on the 13th of November, lat. 9 N., long. 24 W., by an hermaphrodite piratical brig."

The "Candace" was a large, important ship in her day. Her captain, Nathaniel Lindsey, Jr., was equally well known, and as they both hailed from Essex County, Massachusetts, an extended account of this occurrence, taken from various sources, will be found not uninteresting. It may be stated that it is more than likely that every soul on the "Candace" would have been murdered but for the pluck of Capt. Lindsey.

"Salem Gazette, Dec. 15, 1829.

"Marblehead, Dec. 12—Arr. ship 'Candace', Lindsey, from Marblehead 20th Oct. for Sumatra.   On 13th Nov., lat. 9 N, lon. 24 W. (a little S. of Cape de Verde Islands), fell in with a piratical hermaphrodite brig, which boarded and robbed them of all their specie ($19,850), 7 bales of dry goods, the principal part of the officers' clothing, watches, provisions, etc.   The officers and crew of the piratical vessel were Spanish and Portuguese, and about 40 in number, had a long brass 32-pounder amidships, and two small guns.   They confined the officers in the cabin and the crew in the forecastle, under a guard, while they plundered the vessel.   They boarded the 'Candace' about 3 P. M., and left her about 7, at which time another vessel was in sight, which they stood for.   They used no violence to the crew nor injured the vessel in any respect. The 'C.' had 5 boxes of opium which they declined taking, and said they would make them a present of it.

"The 'Candace', a fine full-rigged ship of 428 tons, was owned by Messrs. Bixby and Valentine of Marblehead and Boston, and was commanded by Capt. Nath'l Lindsey, Jr., of Marblehead.   The property on board of her was insured only to the amount of $14,000.   The Boston Courier states that Capt. Lindsey, in case the pirates had proceeded to murder, had everything prepared to blow up the ship."

The Salem Gazette, in an editorial inspired by the "Candace" outrage, said, in its issue of Dec. 18th : "The robbery of the ship 'Candace', Capt. Lindsey, mentioned in our last, is a fact calculated to alarm our East India merchants, and it is to be hoped that it will awaken the attention of the Federal government as well as those of the sovereign states.

"Other outward bound Indiamen have been chased by suspicious-looking vessels, near the line, who reconnoitre them, and, if they appear to be well armed, usually make off.   There can be no doubt that these vessels are Brazilian Guineamen on their way to the coast for a cargo of slaves. Slavers are generally fast sailing craft, manned with a motley mixture of all nations, of unprincipled characters and piratical dispositions ; and already exiled from the society of honest men, and desperadoes by profession, they are reckless of consequence. If they chance to meet any unarmed vessel, with specie, they have no objection to making her a prize.

"They are well armed and full of men, so that resistance in case of such an attempt would be useless. The crime once committed, they are off in a moment—they paint their sides of a different stripe, and if the same ship should meet again it would be impossible for her to identify them. Such dangerous freebooters ought to be looked after. Two or three small vessels cruising between Brazil and the opposite coast would be sufficient to keep them in check, and would aid in suppressing the diabolical traffic in sinews and freedom."

An absolutely true and unexaggerated account of this unpleasant experience, as published in "Old Marblehead Sea Captains," by Benjamin J. Lindsey (Captain Lindsey's nephew), is as follows. It was originally printed in the Marblehead *Messenger* for January 21st, 1881 :

"The ship 'Candace', Capt. Nathaniel Lindsey, Jr., of Marblehead, master, sailed from Marblehead for the coast of Sumatra in October, 1829, supplied with 20,000 hard dollars to purchase a cargo of pepper. Samuel Graves of Marblehead was the chief officer.*

"While in the track where Indiamen cross the equator, Nov. 18, 1829, she was chased many hours by a pirate brig, overtaken and robbed. The particulars of the affair we have gleaned from various sources, but principally from a graphic account by Capt. Graves, which he kindly furnished us in writing.

"The 'Candace' was in latitude 9 N., longitude 24 W., and 28 days out of port. The night preceding the piracy was one of those warm, still nights so common in the tropics. The ship was becalmed and rocked lazily on the long and regular swell. The cabin windows being open, Capt. Lindsey heard at times during the night, in the dis-

*Samuel Graves was afterwards one of the best known of Marblehead's many "deep water" shipmasters.

tance astern, the creaking of a heavy boom, as of some big vessel close behind. This was his first intimation of the pirates' approach.

"At daybreak a large hermaphrodite brig was discovered astern and gaining on the 'Candace'. Suspicion was at once aroused, and every sail that would draw was ordered to be set. Still the chaser gained, and at ten o'clock ran up a large red flag and fired a shot which dropped about half a mile astern.

"The officers and crew of the pursued ship strained every nerve to obtain some slight advantage which might allow them to escape, and many were the ominous glances at the dark-hulled brig which all the while crept nearer and nearer to them, and was now seen to be full of men.

"At that time Spanish vessels, fitted out at Havana for a slaving voyage, in accordance with Spanish laws, then proceeded along the coast of Cuba, where more men and guns were clandestinely taken on board, and then sailed for the equator in the track of Indiamen, knowing they took specie to purchase their return cargoes. These slavers often robbed every vessel they met with on their voyage, and were guilty of the most shocking cruelty and barbarity known to man. The stories of piratical murders were household words, and every mariner's heart sank at the dreadful prospect of encountering one of these robbers of the sea.

"The feelings of those on board the 'Candace' at the inevitable fate which apparently awaited them can be better imagined than described. They had no reason to expect that they would form any exception in the long wake of blood and horror which usually marked a pirate's course, and as they saw that escape was getting to be hopeless, each man prepared himself for the worst.

"That the chase was in dead earnest was easy to be seen. At intervals there were heavy squalls, which obliged it to take in all sail and put the vessel before the wind. When the squall abated, the next instant all sail would be set again and the pursuit of the ship resumed.

"At noon another shot was fired, which fell about two hundred yards astern. At 2.45 a third passed over the fore-yard of the 'Candace' and dropped a quarter of a mile ahead. It was then discovered that the brig was full of men and was armed with a large gun in the waist mounted on a pivot, besides four long brass nines.*

"The armament of the 'Candace' consisted only of two four-pound cannons, five or six muskets and as many pistols. Her crew numbered but sixteen men and boys. She was therefore totally unprepared to cope with her adversary, and it was felt that resistance would avail nothing. 'Had we been prepared to combat the enemy,' writes Capt. Graves, 'no braver or better man walked the deck of a ship than Capt. Lindsey, nor would have defended his ship with more stability.'

"The 'Candace' was hove to, and the pirate, with her men to quarters, also hove to, and ordered the boat of the 'Candace' to come to them. The mate and four men proceeded to the pirate craft, but when within a few yards of her were met by their boat and ordered to return with them at once.

"After boarding the 'Candace' the pirates questioned the captain sharply, and getting what information they desired, returned to their brig. Immediately two boats, full of Spaniards and Portuguese, ferocious-looking fellows, armed to the teeth with pistols and daggers, left the pirate craft and boarded the ship. There were thirty in all, and by the aid of an interpreter they at once ordered the officers into the cabin and the sailors into the forecastle, and stationed a sentry at each place.

"It was agreed between the captain and the mate that in case a massacre was begun, one of them should fire into a barrel of gunpowder in the hold and explode the ship. It was thought to be a better fate to kill all in one general ruin.

"Soon the cabin swarmed with the miscreants, who demanded the money or the lives of the officers. Regretting his inability to defend his ship, Capt. Lindsey very reluctantly gave up the money, which was quickly removed to the pirate vessel by another set of men, while the first lot consulted together on the deck as to whether or not the vessel had better be destroyed.

"Mr. Graves, who had some slight acquaintance with

*"Nines," meaning cannon throwing a nine-pound shot.

the Spanish language, overheard their conversation, where-in some of them thought it advisable to supply themselves with provisions from the 'Candace' (which was done), and then take the prisoners on deck, one at a time, and shoot them, and set fire to the ship.   Others proposed another plan.

"While this discussion was going on, they ordered the second mate on deck.   The hearts of the other officers beat quick, and each took a swift resolution to sell his life as dearly as possible.   Having no doubt but that the pirates were about to slay their first victim, officer Graves seized his pistol, quickly dropped from the cabin to the hold, and leveled the weapon at the powder barrel.   Just then a voice from above shouted, 'Stop! they have not killed him.'   It was a timely warning, for in another second the occupants of the cabin and the pirates on deck would have perished together, 'in one red burial blent.'

"However, the conversation still having a murderous tone, it was felt that danger was imminent.   The chief mate went between decks, determined to defend himself at all hazards, but five of the pirates dropped on him unawares from the after hatch, overpowered him, took away his weapons, and pointing a knife at his breast, demanded his watch and money.   The first he handed them, but the latter being the proceeds of a former voyage to India, he did not give up.   They made a search and were near the money several times, but did not get it.

"One of the most singular circumstances connected with the whole affair, and one to which it is not improba-ble all on board the 'Candace' owed their lives, is thus narrated by Capt. Lindsey :

" 'Our supercargo, having a brother an actor, he took with him theatrical dresses to wear ashore among the natives, an opportunity offering.   He went to his room, dressed himself in a full black silk gown and a square white cravat, turned down the broad sides of an old-fash-ioned military hat (with a low crown), and thus imitated a Spanish padre.

" 'He seated himself in his room, looking very serious, counting a string of beads around his neck (saying his prayers, of course).   When seen by the pirates, they crossed themselves and turned away with a hideous look.'

"The supercargo thus lost nothing, although he had considerable gold in his possession.

"The conversation of the pirates, which was long and animated, took up time and brought night nearer, which proved to be a favorable circumstance. A heavy squall arose, with rain, thunder and lightning. Suddenly and with much confusion, the pirates took to their boats and pulled for their brig, it may be not caring to be separated any longer from the precious money which had been transferred to the vessel, and which, perhaps, they were not quite certain was in safe hands; but this is all conjecture.

"The 'Candace' had been heading east, but immediately wore around to the west, very cautiously getting everything in readiness, without attracting the attention of the pirates, whom it was feared might even yet change their minds and return. At last all sail was cracked on and the good ship leaped across the waves, every man breathing freer as they widened the distance between themselves and the pirate craft. Darkness shut in and hope revived. In the morning the brig had disappeared.

"Capt. Lindsey, who was a diligent reader of the Scriptures, after retiring to his stateroom that night, took down his Bible, according to his usual custom. He opened the book at random at the one hundred and twenty-fourth psalm, which so wonderfully fitted itself to circumstances that it seemed almost like a divine message to those on board and made a lasting impression on his mind. The reader will do well to turn to it.

"On a stormy day in December the people of Marblehead were surprised at seeing a ship under full sail heading for the harbor, and surprise gave way to excitement when it was discovered that it was the 'Candace', which was supposed to be in another quarter of the globe. The news quickly spread, and hundreds hastened to the wharves to ascertain the meaning of the unlooked-for return. As the story was told, it may be imagined that interest was not in any degree lessened.

"The 'Candace' was the property of Bigsbee and Valentine of Boston and Marblehead, and a few days later sailed for Boston.

"The pirate craft was afterwards thought to be the Spanish brig 'Macrinarian', commanded by Mansel Alcantra, a Spaniard who had committed many outrages on the high seas. He is supposed to have been responsible for the tragical loss of the Boston ship "Topaz" She was formerly a Liverpool packet, but while on her way from Calcutta to Boston, in 1829, under command of Captain Brewster, she was destroyed by pirates in the vicinity of St. Helena, and every one on board was murdered. Suspicion strongly indicated that Alcantra had done the foul deed.

"A letter from Havana, July 12th, received at Baltimore, states that the brigantine 'Mauzanarez', which robbed the 'Candace' of Marblehead, has been sent into Sierra Leone with a cargo of slaves and sold, and the captain and crew set at liberty, the captors being ignorant of their character."

We are indebted to the Marblehead *Register*, a paper published in Marblehead from 1830 to 1832, for the following interesting tales of piracy. In those days Marblehead was, from a commercial point of view, a much more important town than it is to-day. Nearly all its inhabitants were connected with the sea in one way or another, so that the *Register* literally teemed with marine news. It was a surprisingly high-class newspaper, and one learns with regret that Mr. Blaney, the editor, after a two years' heroic struggle against adverse circumstances, was obliged to suspend publication for lack of financial support.

"June 12th, 1830.
"The U. S. corvette 'Vincennes', Wm. B. Finch, Esqre., commander, arrived at Boston day before yesterday from St. Helena, having been only 33 days on her voyage from that island. Through Capt. Finch the following particulars of an act of piracy are learned:

"On the 12th of May (1830), lat. 7.28, lon. 18.30, the 'Vincennes' boarded the French brigantine 'Eliza', Capt. Pihon, 47 days from Bordeaux, bound to Bourbon. The 'Eliza' had fallen in with the brig 'St. Helena' in the East India Company's employ, on the 24th of April, lat. 3.3 N., lon. 9.24 W., from St. Helena, bound to Sierra Leone, and learned that she had been overtaken by a piratical vessel on the 6th of April, in S. lat. 2, W. lon. 11.30. A desperate gang boarded the 'St. Helena', and after having bound the captain (Harrison) and a passenger (Dr. Waddell), and thrown them into the sea, murdered also the mate and eight seamen and rifled the vessel. The pirate was a 3 masted schooner, mounting ten guns, and one on a pivot. He had a crew of about 70 men, principally blacks. Capt. Pihon rendered every assistance in his power to enable the 'St. Helena' in her destitute state to reach Sierra Leone. He was requested by the survivors of the crew to give publicity to the misfortune of the vessel."

"Marblehead Register,
    July 3d, 1830.

"Piracy—The 'Repeater', at Baltimore, in 30 days from the coast of Africa, gives the following intelligence : 'On the 19th of May was boarded by a boat from H. B. M. sloop-of-war 'Medina', who informed Capt. Rose that a despatch vessel, bound to Sierra Leone, was boarded a few days previous by a pirate, and the crew treated in the most horrible manner, tying the captain and first officer back to back and throwing them into the sea, and so continued until twelve others had shared the same fate. After remaining thirty hours, plundering and destroying all that was on board, they cut away the masts and fired several shots through the hull. Five of the crew during the time were concealed below deck, and thus escaped a watery grave—they afterwards rigged jury masts, and fortunately reached their destined port.'

"On 20th May, off Cape Vergo, was spoken by an English armed vessel, who ordered the 'R.' to send a boat on board, which was refused on account of leaking badly. After some conversation, permitted to proceed, and desired that the 'R.' should keep a good lookout, as several pirates were on the coast."

"Marblehead Register,
    July 17th, 1830.

"Extract of a letter from an officer of a Salem ship at Havana, dated June 21 :
"There is an English sloop-of-war here having caught

the villain that robbed the 'Candace'* of Marblehead. The sloop-of-war chased him from Cape Antonio to the Isle of Pines before succeeding in taking him. A beautiful schooner arrived here this afternoon—a Guineaman. After having landed 150 slaves, he was overhauled by the Englishman and brought in the news. The English seem to catch everything, but the Americans, if they look out as sharply, are less fortunate."

"Another letter states that the American Vice Consul (at Havana) has taken measures to inform the British commander respecting the robbery of the 'Candace', and it is supposed he will take the crew on board and carry them to Jamaica, leaving the vessel at Havana."

"Aug. 7th, 1830.

"A letter from Havana, July 12, received at Baltimore, states that the brig 'Manzanarez', which robbed the 'Candace' of Boston, had been sent into Sierra Leone, with a cargo of slaves, and sold, and the captain and crew set at liberty, the captors being ignorant of their real character."

"Marblehead Register,
        "September 3d, 1831.

"Capt. Fabens, of the brig 'Richmond'† of Salem, arrived at Norfolk (Va.), from the former port, states that on the 20th inst., in lat. 37, lon. 74.25, saw a vessel of a suspicious character, a clipper built brig of about 200 tons, with five or six guns on each side. She passed close to leeward of the 'Richmond' and ran close across the stern, seemingly with an intention of reconnoitering them, after which she stood to the E. about 2 leagues and hove round and stretched to the westward in pursuit of a ship supposed to be a New York and Charleston packet."

"Marblehead Register, Sept. 18th, 1830.

"Havana—By the schooner 'Rockland', at Philadelphia, the editors of the Baltimore American have received a letter from their attentive correspondent at Havana, under date of August 21, which says :

*The writer of this letter was evidently misinformed, as it has been seen that the "Candace" was brought into port by her crew.

†According to the Salem Ship Register, the "Richmond" was a brig of 153 tons, built in Salem in 1825, and owned and commanded by Wm. Fabens, Jr.

"The brig 'Sultana', Smith, of Baltimore, which arrived here from Liverpool on the 14th inst., was chased on the south side of the Island of Cuba by a schooner under Buenos Ayres colors.

"She is known to be a privateer fitted out at Omoa, under a commission of Central America, in July.   She is a small gaff topsail schooner, with a brass eight-pounder on a pivot, and a crew of forty-four men, French, Italians, Creoles of St. Domingo, English, and a few Indians of Central America, commanded by a Spaniard of this island named Vallanueva, and well known in the Colombian service.

"The vessel is named the 'General Morazan', after the President of the Republic.   *There is little doubt that the above vessel is a pirate.*   The colors of Central America are exactly similar to those of Buenos Ayres, except that in the union the former has a rising sun and one or two volcanic mountains.   Most of the Spanish, American and British cruisers on this station are informed of the circumstances.' "

"October 9th, 1830.

"Brig 'Sabbatas', Capt. Howard, at New York from Cette, was boarded off St. Michaels, Western Islands, by a British frigate, the boarding officer of which informed Capt. H. that they had captured a piratical brig which had captured a Sardinian brig, and sent her into St. Michaels; they supposed the piratical brig was one of Don Miguel's squadron.   The British frigate was then in search of the rest of Don M.'s fleet."

Basil Lubbock, in his wonderfully interesting work on the old-time British sailing ships, "The Blackwall Frigates" (James Brown and Son, Glasgow, 1922), says of the latter day pirates :

"In the nineteenth century the true pirate had generally served an apprenticeship in a slaver, and his ship was always a heeler, usually built in Baltimore or Havana for the slave trade.   It was only the most daring ruffian who dared show his colors—the black flag with the skull and crossbones—and he almost invariably sneaked down on his prey with some little known ensign at his peak.

"The following notices, taken from the shipping papers of the year 1838,* will give a good idea of his usual methods:

'20th June, in 35° N., 70° W., the Thule was brought to by a brig carrying a red and white flag; deck covered with men, most of whom were black; weather heavy; cargo not tempting enough.

'25th June, in 34° N., 67° W., the William Miles was boarded by a piratical schooner about 150 tons, under Brazilian and Portuguese colours, with 50 or 60 men on board. Took two casks of provisions.

'4th July, in 36° N., 47° W., the Ceylon (American brig) was boarded by a piratical schooner under Portuguese colours; wine, water and provisions taken.

'5th July, in 38° N., 44° W., the Catherine Elizabeth was boarded by a schooner under Spanish colours; appeared to have 50 or 60 men. Took a cask of beef and one of pork.

'The Azores packet, five days from Teneriffe, was boarded by a piratical brig full of men, which took from her a chain cable, hawsers, etc.

'Eliza Locke, o' Dublin, was chased off Madeira by a suspicious schooner for two days in May.

'29th July, an American schooner was boarded off Cay West by a piratical schooner and plundered of 400 dollars worth of articles.

'5th July, in 39° N., 34° W., the Isabella was boarded by a Spanish brig and robbed of spare sails, cordage, canvas and twine.

"It is noticeable from these reports that the corsair only left traces of his path where he had met with ships from which there was nothing worth taking beyond provisions and bosun's stores. Who knows how many 'missing ships' the above buccaneers could have accounted for?

"Perhaps the best known pirate of the thirties was Benito de Soto, a villain whose history is worth noticing. Benito de Soto was a Portuguese. In 1827 he shipped before the mast in a large brigantine at Buenos Ayres.

---

*In the first pages of this book the author mentioned the case of the brig "Mexican" of Salem, as the very last vessel attacked by pirates in the Atlantic (1832). He was not then aware of the above quotation.

This vessel, named the 'Defensar de Pedro', sailed for the coast of Africa to load slaves. Like all slavers, she carried a large crew of dagoes; the mate, a notorious ruffian, made friends with de Soto on the run across, and between them they hatched a plot to seize the ship on her arrival at the slave depot. The 'Defensar de Pedro' hove to about ten miles from the African shore, and as soon as the captain had left the ship to see the slave agent, de Soto and the mate took possession of her; 22 of the crew joined them, but the remaining 18 refused. These men were immediately driven into a boat, which was capsized in an attempt to make a landing through the surf, and every one of the honest 18 drowned.

"The ship was then headed out to sea; the new pirates lost no time in breaking into the spirit room, and by sunset every man aboard had drunk himself into a stupor except Bonito. This superior ruffian immediately took advantage of this to put a pistol to the head of his helpless confederate, the mate, and daring the drunken crew to interfere, promptly shot him dead.

"The whole thing was carried through in the true piratical spirit. The drunken crew at once declared that de Soto was just the sort of captain they wanted, and without any more ado he took command.

"It appears that the ship had already got her cargo of "black ivory" on board, for Benito de Soto is next heard of in the West Indies, where he sold the slaves at very good prices.

"He remained cruising in West Indian waters for some time and plundered a quantity of ships, most of which he scuttled after battening their crews down below.

"Having exhausted this cruising ground, he next took up a position in the South Atlantic, right in the route of the traffic to the East.

"In a very short while his raking brigantine, which had been renamed the 'Black Joke', had become the scourge of those seas.

"Indeed, so great was the terror of Benito and his 'Black Joke' in those seas by 1832 that homeward bound Indiamen began to make up convoys of themselves at St. Helena before heading north.

"Early in that year a whole fleet of ships was held up there through fear of the pirate.

"At last a convoy of eight ships was made up which started off homeward, with the Indiaman 'Susan', of 600 tons, as their flagship. Unfortunately one of these vessels, a barque, the 'Morning Star', of Scarborough, homeward bound from Ceylon, with 25 invalid soldiers and a few passengers, was an extraordinary slow sailer. By the third day all the ships had gone ahead except the 'Susan', which, in order to keep back to the 'Morning Star's' pace, had to reduce sails to topsails and foresail.

"This progress was at last too slow for the 'Susan', and bidding good-bye to the barque, she also went ahead.

"At 11 A. M. on the second day after parting with the 'Morning Star', the 'Susan' sighted a large brigantine, crowded with men and showing a heavy long tom* amidships. The pirate immediately bore down upon the Indiaman, and clearing his long gun for action, hoisted the skull and crossbones at the main.

"The 'Susan' was only a small Indiaman of 600 tons and eight guns, nevertheless the sight of her four starboard and broadside guns run out made Benito de Soto sheer off into her wake. Here he dodged about for over two hours, hesitating whether to attack or not ; finally he sailed off in the direction he had appeared from. It was a lucky escape, for by some oversight the 'Susan' had no powder on board, though tons of shot.

"Meanwhile the 'Morning Star' was jogging along in the wake of the 'Susan'. On the 21st February, when abreast of Ascension, a sail was sighted at daylight on the western horizon. Her hull was fast disappearing from sight when suddenly she altered her course and bore down upon the barque. The action was a suspicious one, especially when a pirate was known to be in the vicinity, and Captain Sauley of the 'Morning Star' immediately called all hands and crowded sail to get away.

"The stranger proved to be a long black brigantine with raking masts. 'The Black Joke' was whispered round the decks with bated breath.

---

*"Long tom", the nickname by which sailors referred to a heavy pivot brass cannon, usually a 24 or 32-pounder.

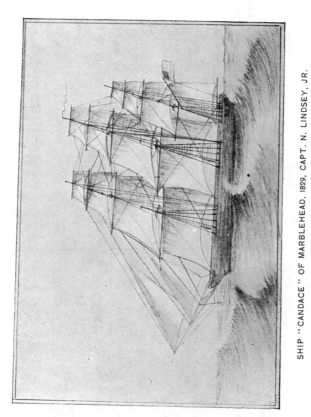

SHIP "CANDACE" OF MARBLEHEAD, 1829, CAPT. N. LINDSEY, JR.

From a drawing in the collection of F. B. C. Bradlee

PIRATE BRIGANTINE "BLACK JOKE" SINKING THE INDIAMAN "MORNING STAR," FEBRUARY 21, 1832

From an engraving in Hanney's "Freebooters of the Sea."

"The pirate, as she rapidly overhauled the slow-sailing 'Morning Star', hoisted British colours and fired a gun for the barque to back her topsail, but Captain Sauley kept on ; thereupon the Colombian colours replaced the British on the pirate. He was now so close to the barque that his decks could be seen crowded with men. Benito de Soto himself could be made out standing by the mainmast —a head and shoulders taller than his crew. Suddenly he sprang to the long gun and fired it. It was loaded with canister, which cut up the rigging of the 'Morning Star' and wounded many of her crew.

"Captain Sauley held a hasty conference with his officers and passengers. It was decided to surrender; the colours were thereupon struck and the topsail backed.

"The 'Black Joke', with her long tom trained on to the deck of the barque, now ranged up to within 40 yards, and de Soto in stentorian tones ordered Captain Sauley aboard the brigantine with his papers. A courageous passenger, however, volunteered to go to try and make terms with the pirate. But he and his boat's crew returned to the barque, bleeding and exhausted, having been cruelly knocked about and beaten by the pirates. He brought the following arrogant message: 'Tell your captain that Benito de Soto will deal with him alone. If he does not come I'll blow him out of the water.' At this Captain Sauley went aboard the 'Black Joke', taking his second mate and three soldiers with him, besides the boat's crew.

"Benito de Soto, cutlass in hand, silently motioned the wretched skipper to approach. Then, as he stood in front of him uncertain what to do, the pirate suddenly raised his cutlass and roared out, 'Thus does Benito de Soto reward those who disobey him.' The blow fell in full sight of the terrified people on the deck of the 'Morning Star.' The poor skipper was cleft to the chin bone and fell dead without a sound at the pirate's feet. A shout of horror echoed across from the barque, at which Sauley's second mate, who had been motioned forward, turned quickly in his tracks, only to be struck down and killed by Brabazon, de Soto's chief officer.

"The pirates, like wild beasts, having tasted blood,

wanted more.   The long gun was trained on the deck of the 'Morning Star', and as the ladies ran screaming below a shower of grape rattled about their ears.   A boat of armed cut-throats next boarded the barque, but no resistance was offered, so Major Lobic and his sick soldiers were first stripped of their clothes and then thrown into the hold, a sick officer named Gibson dying from the brutal treatment shown to him.

"The ladies were fastened into the fo'c'sle, and looting commenced.   All this time de Soto stood calm and composed at his vantage post by the mainmast of the 'Black Joke', directing operations with the voice of a tiger. Stores, instruments and cargo, including seven packages of jewelry, were transferred to the pirate, and the cabins were looted of every vestige of clothing.

Then the hatches were battened down, and, with the steward to wait upon them, the pirates settled down to a regular buccaneering carousal.   The wretched women were brought out of the fo'c'sle, and their screams rang out over the sea.   It was a scene of awful savagery.

"Fortunately the pirates became so drunk that they forgot de Soto's bloodthirsty orders to butcher every soul aboard.   However, they first locked the women in the fo'c'sle again, and then cut the rigging to pieces, sawed the masts in two, bored holes in the ship's bottom, and, satisfied that she would sink, tumbled into their boats and returned to the 'Black Joke', which immediately filled her topsail and went off after another victim.

"Meanwhile on the 'Morning Star' there was not a sound to be heard.   For long those below had been shutting their ears to the screams of their women and the drunken yells of the pirates, and now they suddenly realized that the pirate had sheered off, but at the same time they also realized their horrible fate if they failed to break their way out of the hold, for in the semi-gloom it was noticed that the ship was slowly filling with water. The women, though they succeeded in forcing their way out of the fo'c'sle, did not dare show themselves on deck for some hours, being half crazed with fear.   And it was only after some desperate struggles that the men succeeded in bursting a hatch open.

"Rushing on deck, they found that it was nearing sunset. The vessel lay rolling sluggishly, an utter wreck. Forward the women were discovered huddled together in a state of collapse. Aft the compass had disappeared, whilst, almost more serious still, not a bit of food or drop of water remained.

"The pumps were quickly manned and the leaks plugged. Fortunately for the unhappy survivors, a ship hove in sight next day, and with her assistance the 'Morning Star' actually succeeded in getting home, where her arrival in the Thames created a great sensation.

"In the meantime Benito de Soto, on learning that the crew and passengers of the 'Morning Star' had not been butchered in accordance with his orders, put back again to look for her, but failing to find her concluded that she had gone to the bottom, and thereupon resumed his cruising.

"He is next reported as being thwarted in his attack on an outward bound Indiaman by a sudden storm. The story is well told by one of the Indiaman's passengers, and as it presents a good picture of the times, I herewith give it in full:

" 'The gong had just sounded 8 bells, as Captain M. entered the cuddy, "care on his brow and pensive thoughtfulness." So unusual was the aspect he wore that all remarked it; in general his was the face of cheerfulness, not only seeming happy, but imparting happiness to all around.

"What has chased the smiles from thy face ?" said one of the young writers; a youth much given to Byron and open-neck cloths. "Why looks our Caesar with an angry frown? But poetry apart, what is the matter?"

"Why, the fact is, we are chased !" replied the captain. "Chased! Chased!! Chased!!!" was echoed from mouth to mouth in various tones of doubt, alarm and admiration.

"Yes, however extraordinary it may seem to this good company," continued our commander, "I have no doubt that such is the fact; for the vessel which was seen this morning right astern and which has maintained an equal distance during the day is coming up with us hand over hand. I am quite sure, therefore, that she is after no

good ; she's a wicked-looking craft; at 1 bell we shall
beat to quarters."

"We had left the Downs a few days after the arrival
of the 'Morning Star', and with our heads and hearts
full of that atrocious affair, rushed on the poop. The
melancholy catastrophe alluded to had been a constant
theme at the cuddy table, and many a face showed signs
of anxiety at the news just conveyed to us. On ascending the poop assurance became doubly sure, for, certain
enough, there was the beautiful little craft overhauling
us in most gallant style. She was a long, dark-looking
vessel, low in the water, but having very tall masts, with
sails white as the driven snow.

"The drum had now beat to quarters, and all was for
the time bustle and preparation. Sailors clearing the
guns, handing up ammunition, and distributing pistols and
cutlasses. Soldiers mustering on the quarter deck prior
to taking their station on the poop—we had 200 on board.
Women in the waist, with anxious faces, and children
staring with wondering eyes. Writers, cadets and assistant surgeons in heterogeneous medley. The latter, as
soon as the news had been confirmed, descended to their
various cabins and reappeared in martial attire. One
young gentleman had his 'toasting knife stuck through
the pocket-hole of his inexpressibles—a second Monk-
barns ; another came on exulting, his full dressed shako
placed jauntingly on his head as a Bond Street beau
wears his castor ; a third, with pistols in his sash, his
swallow-tailed coat boasting of sawdust, his sword dangling between his legs in all the extricacies of novelty—he
was truly a martial figure, ready to seek for reputation
even at the cannon's mouth.

"Writers had their Joe Mateon and assistant surgeons
their instruments. It was a stirring sight, and yet, withal,
ridiculous.

"But, now, the stranger quickly approached us, and
quietness was ordered. The moment was an interesting
one. A deep silence reigned throughout the vessel, save
now and then the dash of the water against the ship's
side, and here and there the half-suppressed ejaculation of
some impatient son of Neptune.

"Our enemy, for so we had learned to designate the stranger, came gradually up in our wake. No light, no sound issued from her, and when about a cable's length from us she luffed to the wind, as if to pass us to windward; but the voice of the captain, who hailed her with the usual salute, 'Ship ahoy!' made her apparently alter her purpose, though she answered not, for, shifting her helm, she darted to leeward of us.

"Again the trumpet sent forth its summons, but still there was no answer, and the vessel was now about a pistol shot from our larboard quarter.

"Once more, what ship's that? Answer, or I'll send a broadside into you," was uttered in a voice of thunder from the trumpet by our captain.

"Still all was silent, and many a heart beat with quicker pulsation.

"On a sudden we observed her lower studding sails taken in by some invisible agency; for all this time we had not seen a single human being, nor did we hear the slightest voice, although we had listened with painful attention.

"Matters began to assume a very serious aspect. Delay was dangerous. It was a critical moment, for we had an advantage of position not to be thrown away. Two main-deck guns were fired across her bow. The next moment our enemy's starboard ports were hauled up and we could plainly discern every gun, with a lantern over it, as they were run out.

"Still we hesitated with our broadside, and about a minute afterwards our enemy's guns disappeared as suddenly as they had been run out. We heard the order given to her helmsman. She altered her course, and in a few seconds was astern of us.

"We gazed at each other in silent astonishment, but presently all was explained. Our attention had been so taken up by the stranger that we had not thought of the weather, which had been threatening some time, and for which reason we were under snug sail. But, during our short acquaintance, the wind had been gradually increasing, and two minutes after the pirate had dropped astern it blew a perfect hurricane, accompanied by heavy rain.

"We had just time to observe our friend scudding before it under bare poles, and we saw him no more.

"After this audacious attempt, Benito de Soto steered north, with the intention of running into Corunna to refit and dispose of plunder.   Off the Spanish coast he captured a local brig, and after plundering her, sank her, with all on board except one man, whom he retained to pilot the 'Black Joke' into Corunna.   As the pirate neared the harbor, with this man at the helm, de Soto said to him:

" 'Is this the entrance?'

"The reply was in the affirmative.

" 'Very well, my man,' went on the pirate captain, 'you have done well, I am obliged to you,' and drawing a pistol from his belt, he shot the wretched man dead.

"At Corunna the pirate managed to sell his plunder without arousing suspicion, and obtaining ship's papers under a false name, shaped a course for Cadiz.   But the weather coming on, he missed stays one dark night close inshore and took the ground.   All hands, however, managed to reach the shore safely in the boats, and de Soto, nothing daunted by his misfortune, coolly arranged that they should march overland to Cadiz, represent themselves as shipwrecked mariners, and sell the wreck for what it would fetch.   At Cadiz, however, the authorities were more on the alert than at Corunna, and arrested six of the pirates on suspicion that they were not what they represented themselves to be.   They were not quite quick enough, however, de Soto and the rest of the pirate crew getting clean away.   The pirate captain made his way to Gibraltar, where some of the invalid soldiers out of the 'Morning Star', on their way to Malta, happened to recognize him in spite of the fact that he wore a white hat of the best English quality, silk stockings, white trousers, and blue frock-coat.   He was thereupon arrested, and in his possession were found clothes, charts, nautical instruments and weapons taken from the 'Morning Star'.   This was enough to convict him, but under his pillow at the inn where he was stopping the maid servant discovered the pocket-book and diary of Captain Sauley, which settled matters.

"He was tried before Sir George Don, Governor of Gibraltar, and sentenced to death. The British authorities sent him across to Cadiz to be executed along with the pirates captured there. A gallows was erected at the water's edge. He was conveyed there in a cart, which held his coffin. He met his death with iron fortitude. He actually arranged the noose round his own neck, and finding the loop came a little too high, calmly jumped on to the coffin and settled it comfortably round his neck, as cool and unconcerned as if it had only been a neckcloth. Then, after taking a final look round, he gazed for a moment steadfastly out to sea. As the wheels of the tumbril began to revolve, he cried out, 'Adios todos!' (farewell all), and threw himself forward in order to hasten the end.

"Thus died Benito de Soto, the last of the more notable pirates, and a true example of the old-time sea rover.

"Curiously enough, in the autumn of the very year that finished Benito de Soto's career, a man of the same name was also taken for piracy. This man was the mate of the pirate schooner 'Pinta', which brought disaster to the brig 'Mexican', of Salem, on the 20th of September, 1832."*

In the following pages the author has, with much trouble, compiled from the files of the New York Shipping and Commercial List a complete list of vessels of every nation attacked by pirates from 1824 to 1832.

Oct. 20, 1824.

The polacre brig "Union", under English colors, from Gibraltar to Vera Cruz, ran ashore on the N. E. point of the harbor of Neuvitas and bilged—crew captured and cargo plundered by the pirates.

Brig "Albert", Phillips, of New York, from Cadiz to Havana, captured by a Colombian pirate off Stirup Key; was cast away on the 11th Sept. near Abaco. Vessel a total loss.

Nov. 17, 1824.

The brig "Laura Ann", Shaw, of New York, from Montevideo for Havana, with jerked beef, has been cap-

*The account of this act of piracy will be found on pp. 8-11.

tured and burnt by pirates, on the coast of Cuba, and all
on board murdered, with the exception of one man.
Dec. 11, 1824.

Schooners "Ann", Ryan, and "Rainbow", Davis, from
Jamaica for North Carolina, have both been plundered by
a piratical schooner.
Dec. 18, 1824.

The French ship "Calypso", captured by pirates near
Cape St. Philip, Cuba, has been recaptured by the U.
States schooner "Terrier", and was proceeding for Thomp-
son's Island (now Key West), 16th ult.
Dec. 22, 1824.

The Spanish corvette "Alvea", from Corunna for Havana, was captured 1st ult. by the Colombian schooner
"Aquilla", commanded by a famous pirate, and taken
into Port Cavello.
Jan. 12, 1825.

The brig "Edward", Dillingham, from Bordeaux for
Havana, was captured by pirates near the coast of Cuba,
11th Oct. last—not known where she was carried. Part
of her crew escaped in one of her boats.
Jan. 15, 1825.

Spanish brig "Maceas", from Gibara, Cuba, for Cadiz,
with a cargo of tobacco, was captured on the 3d ult. by
the pirate schooner "Centella", formerly a Colombian
privateer.
Jan. 26, 1825.

The wreck of the French ship "Jerome Maximillien",
Marre, which sailed from this port (New York) early in
December for Port au Prince, drifted ashore at Turks
Island, about 30th ult.—no person on board. She is
supposed to have been plundered by pirates and her crew
murdered.

Ship "Louisa", Hopkins, from Providence for New
Orleans, has put into Savannah—having seen a pirate off
the Hole in the Wall.
Feb. 9, 1825.

Brig "Betsey", Hilton, from Wiscasset (Maine), for
Matanzas, with lumber, has been totally lost on the
double-headed Shot Keys, as is stated by a sailor named

Collins, who belonged to her, and who also states that all the crew except himself were murdered by pirates after the shipwreck.

March 12, 1825.

Schooner "Mobile", Prescott, from Baltimore for Porto Rico, put into Jacquemel about the middle of February, having been chased by two piratical boats, and threw over her deck load.

March 19, 1825.

Brig "Alexander", Linzee, of Boston, at Rio Janeiro, was fired upon and robbed of sundry articles by a schooner of about 75 tons, in lat. 7 N. long. 21 W.

May 18, 1825.

Schooner "Planter", Eldridge, from this port (New York), for Neuvitas, was captured by a pirate about March 10th. Captain and crew supposed to be murdered.

May 21, 1825.

Schooner "Alert", Eldredge, of Yarmouth, has put into Antigua, in distress, having been robbed by a pirate in lat. 17, lon. 58.

June 4, 1825.

Brig "Edward", Ferguson, from Havana for this port (New York), was captured by a pirate on the 17th of February last. A passenger and two of the crew were landed on an island on the coast of Cuba. The remainder supposed to have been murdered, and the vessel de· stroyed.

Sept. 7, 1825.

Spanish brig "Carmen", from Barcelona and Cadiz for Havana, with government stores, was captured on June 28, off Baracoa, by the pirate "Zulene".

Oct. 22, 1825.

Spanish ship "Catalina del Commercio", of Barcelona, from Cuba, was captured by a pirate on Aug. 4. Crew sent into Cadiz.

Nov. 12, 1825.

Dutch ship "Augustine", Granswald, from Campeachy for Havana, was captured by a Colombian pirate on 29th ult.

Jan. 25, 1826.

Schooner "Gen. Warren", Morris, of Cohasset, from Boston for Tampico, put into Charleston 13th inst.—part of her crew having landed at the double-headed Shot Keys, where they were supposed to be detained by pirates.

April 12, 1826.

Schooner "Hope and Susan", Chase, from Marseilles for Havana, has been captured by the piratical Colombian privateer "Constantia", and sent into Carthagena.

August 9, 1826.

Brig "Henry", Green, from Boston, arrived at Rio Grande early in May—was robbed by a pirate a little south of the equator.

March 31, 1827.

Brig "Falcon", Somers, of Gloucester, Mass., had been robbed in the Archipelago, by Greek pirates, and would have to proceed to Smyrna for provisions.

May 2, 1827.

Brig "Ann", of and from Salem,* for river La Plata, was spoken about the middle of March, having been robbed of sails, rigging, provisions, etc., by a piratical schooner near the Equator.

Dec. 1, 1827.

Brig "Bolivar" Clark, of and from Marblehead, Mass., to Mobile, Oct. 12th, was chased by an armed schooner, supposed to be a pirate; part of the brig's cargo was thrown overboard to avoid capture.

Dec. 5, 1827.

Brig "Cherub", Loring, from Boston, was taken by a pirate, Sept. 5th, two miles from the island of Ceriga, and plundered of all her cargo, sails, rigging, etc.

Dec. 26, 1827.

Brig "Rob Roy" was plundered by Greeks, between the islands of Tino and Micani, of about 40 cases of opium and 10 cases of indigo, with all the clothing and money of the officers.

---

*The brig "Ann" referred to is probably the vessel built at Pembroke in 1815, 204 tons. On July 21st, 1821, she was owned by Henry Prince and Henry Prince, Jr.; Charles Millet, master.

Brig "Phoebe Ann", of Portsmouth, N.H., from Trieste for Smyrna, was taken by the Greeks to Napoli de Malvaiza, and there robbed of all the cargo she had.

Dec. 27, 1828.

Schooner "Carroll", Swain, from Marblehead, Mass., for St. Andrews Bay, East Florida, was plundered at sea by pirates about Nov. 3d, and on the 18th went ashore on St. Rose Island—threw overboard part of her cargo, and got into the bay about 40 miles from Pensacola, where she lay in five feet of water, 27th ult.

Aug. 9, 1828.

Brigantine "Fox", at Rio de Janeiro, of and from Gloucester, Mass., was robbed by an armed schooner, under Mexican colors, in lat. 34 N., long. 34, of part of her cargo, spare sails, clothes, money, watches, etc.

Oct. 11, 1828.

Schooner "Industry", Hunter, at Guadaloupe, from Newbern, N. C., was plundered by a piratical schooner, 17th Aug., lat. 28.14, of her chain cable, rigging, stores, clothes, etc.

Nov. 1, 1828.

Bremen brig "London Packet", Wessels, arrived at Laguira, 7th Oct. In lat. of Madeira was boarded by a piratical schooner and robbed of property to the amount of $7000.

March 14, 1829.

Brig "America", Crabtree, of Sullivan, Maine, at St. Barts, 7th Feb., was robbed of various articles to the amount of $200 by a schooner under French colors, lat. 26, long. 64.

March 18, 1829.

Brig "New Priscilla", of Salem, was seen, 14th Feb., near Dog Keys; no person on board, having been captured by a pirate; crew supposed to be murdered.

Brig "Atlantic", Grover, of Boston, which sailed from Havana 21st Feb., was captured by a pirate, and all hands murdered except one, who was secreted, and the vessel scuttled.

March 21, 1829.

Brig "Fawn", of Salem,* was robbed near the line, on her passage to India, last June, by a schooner under Buenos Ayrian colors, of sundry articles of cargo, amounting to $1500.

Brig "Triton", of Waldoborough, Maine, at St. Croix, 26th Feb., was robbed of provisions, boat, clothing, etc., in lat. 26, long. 69.

Oct. 7, 1829.

Schooner "Perry", Hoodless, at Newburyport from Barracoa, was robbed of part of her cargo, on her outward passage, by a piratical schooner, lat. 30, long. 69.

Oct. 9, 1830.

Brig "Orbit", Woodbury, of and for this port (N. Y.), from the Coast of Africa, was fallen in with, 11th Sept., lat. 13.10 N., long. 45.42 W., in the possession of a piratical crew, who had boarded her, murdered the captain and mates, and were supposed to be heading for St. Thomas.

Sept. 28, 1831.

SUPPOSED PIRACY.

The brig "Wade", on 29th Sept., 1830, in lat. 37 N., long. 59 1-2 W., six days out from New York, boarded the barque "Henry", without any other name or letters on her stern, with masts all gone by the board, part of an English Jack made fast to one of the poop rails, cabin ceiling and transom tore to pieces, as if in search of money, furniture thrown down the run, forecastle empty. Saw a rug in the cabin which appeared to be stained with blood; water casks all stove; cargo, rum and sugar; appeared tight, and only to have been abandoned about three weeks; coppered to the bends.

*The "Fawn" referred to was a brig of 168 tons, built at Quincy, Mass., in 1816. In 1826 Robert Brookhouse, Josiah Lovett, Jr., of Beverly, were her owners, and Emery Johnson, master.

No less a person than Richard Henry Dana, in his "Two Years Before the Mast", relates that the vessel he was in, the brig "Pilgrim", of and from Boston, bound to the coast of California, was chased by a supposed piratical craft, "September 22d (1834), when, upon coming on deck at seven bells in the morning, we found the other watch aloft throwing water upon the sails; and, looking astern, we saw a small clipper-built brig, with a black hull, heading directly after us.

"We went to work immediately and put all the canvas upon the brig which we could get upon her, rigging out oars for extra studding sail, yards, and continued wetting down the sails with buckets of water whipped up to the mast-head, until about nine o'clock, when there came on a drizzling rain. The vessel continued in pursuit, changing her course as we changed ours, to keep before the wind.

"The captain, who watched her with his glass, said she was armed and full of men, and showed no colors. We continued running dead before the wind, knowing that we sailed better so, and that clippers are fastest on the wind. We had also another advantage. The wind was light, and we spread more canvas than she did, . . . while she, being a hermaphrodite brig, had only a gaff topsail aft. . . . All hands remained on deck throughout the day, and we got our firearms in order, but we were too few to have done anything with her if she had proved to be what we feared.

"Fortunately there was no moon, and the night which followed was exceedingly dark, so that, by putting out our lights on board and altering our course four points, we hoped to get out of her reach. We removed the light in the binnacle, and steered by the stars, and kept perfect silence through the night. At daybreak there was no sign of anything in the horizon, and we kept the vessel off to her course."

Among the many well known American sea captains in the palmy days of our merchant marine probably the best remembered is Capt. Samuel Samuels, who for many years commanded the equally well known New York and Liverpool packet ship "Dreadnought." This craft holds the record for the fastest transatlantic passage ever accomplished by a sailing vessel, she having, on two voyages in 1859, sighted the Irish coast within ten days of her departure from Sandy Hook.*

Captain Samuels' adventures all over the world as a sailor are contained in a most interesting volume, "From the Forecastle to the Cabin," now out of print and not easy to obtain. When a mere boy, Samuels came near being captured by pirates in the Gulf of Mexico, while on a voyage from Liverpool to Galveston, Texas, in the British brig "Emily". The exact date of the occurrence cannot be given, for the only fault with Captain Samuels' book is that he rarely gives the dates of events, but as nearly as can be reckoned, his narrow escape from being captured by the freebooters took place in 1837.

"The vessel came down on us like a meteor. Before we got on deck she was close aboard on our starboard beam. Peter told me to look at her carefully. ('Peter' was a middle-aged man, a sailor on the 'Emily', who had taken a great fancy to young Samuels ; he appears, nevertheless, to have been a 'hard ticket', and, as will be seen further on, had at one time been himself a pirate.)

"She was a two top-sail schooner ; that is, she had a square fore and main top-sail, with top-gallant sails over. When these square sails were furled, the yards on deck, and the masts housed, the fore and aft sails would equal single reefs. This rig is now obsolete ; though, if I were going to build a large sailing yacht, I would rig her in this way. She would be the most rakish and saucy-looking craft afloat. The stranger had a long swivel [cannon] amidships and a smaller one mounted forward of the foremast. She was painted black, had a flush deck, and four quarter boats. No flag was flying. We were hailed in good English, though he who hailed us looked like a Spaniard.

'What ship is that ?' he asked. 'Where are you from, and where are you bound ?'

"We replied to all these interrogations. Our captain was too much astonished at her extraordinary speed and

*See "The 'Dreadnought' of Newburyport," by F. B. C. Bradlee, 2d edition, Essex Institute, Salem, Mass., 1921.

BRIGANTINE "OHIO," BUILT AT MARIETTA. OHIO, IN 1847

Was at one time in the slave trade

From an original painting in the Peabody Museum, Salem

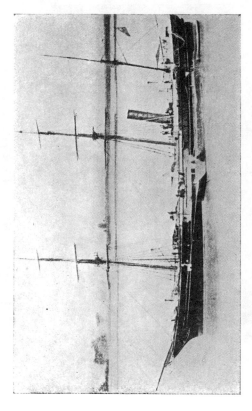

CONFEDERATE STATES STEAMER "McREA"

Formerly the slaver and pirate "Marquis de la Habana." The only "steam pirate" known to history.
From a photograph taken at Baton Rouge, La., in 1861.

From the Collection of F. B. C. Bradlee.

appearance to ask any questions. There was no name on her stern, and only three men were to be seen on deck. Captain Gillette asked the mate what he made her out. He replied that she was a mystery, and that he did not like her looks, as she appeared like neither a war-ship nor a merchantman.

"At ten o'clock the wind moderated enough to let us set all light sails, including the starboard studding sails. At noon we sighted the mysterious stranger again right ahead. At 1 P. M. a heavy squall was coming down on us. Then we took in the studding-sails, and royal. The main top-gallant studding-sail fouled over the brace block, and I went aloft to clear it. While I was on the yard the squall struck us with terrific force. Everything had to be let go by the run to save the masts. The studding-sail blew to ribbons in my hands. The top-sail halyards had been let go, and down I went with the yard. I had secured myself on the foot-rope near the brace block. This I did to save myself from being knocked off by the slapping of the top-gallant sheet. It was marvellous that I was not thrown from the yard when it came down on the cap. The squall was soon over, but it took the rest of the day to repair the split sails.

"About four o'clock the stranger hove to till we passed her, when she trimmed her canvas and was alongside again like magic.

"What does your cargo consist of ?" he asked.

"Coal, salt, crates, and iron," we replied.

"She starboarded her helm and hauled to the southward, but before dark was ahead of us again. By this time all hands showed uneasiness, but said nothing. Supper was announced, but no one had any appetite. We all sat on the forecastle, straining our eyes into the darkness to see if we could discern the schooner. The captain came forward at eleven o'clock to join the mate, who had been sitting forward among us all the evening.

"Mr. Crawford," he said, "let us trim the yards and haul up four points to the southward. I don't like that craft. She was right ahead when last seen. We had better give her the slip during the night."

"Peter now joined in and said, 'If you don't want

them to board us, we had better keep our course. They have their eye on us, and if we attempt to avoid them they may suppose we are not bound for Galveston, and that our cargo is not of such small value as we told them. Once on board of us they will show their true character, and before daylight we shall all have walked the plank and the 'Emily' will be sunk five thousand fathoms deep. None of us will be left to tell the tale. I have been on these waters before, Captain Gillette, and know these crafts, and what I am talking about.'

"Peter's words were ominous. They sent a thrill of horror through us all. They sounded like the death sentence pronounced by a judge in deep, solemn tones, to a prisoner whose hours are numbered.

"The course was not changed. Silence pervaded the whole crew. The night was very dark. Suddenly Peter nudged me and motioned me to follow him aft. When abreast of the gangway he whispered in my ear, 'Boy, be a man. Don't tremble so. Your teeth chatter as if you had the ague. Slip down below and bring up a pannikin of rum ; you know where it is stowed. You need courage to carry out what you will have to undertake before sunrise. By that time there will be no more of the 'Emily' or her crew, except you and me. Get the rum, and then hear the rest.'

"I groped my way down the after hatch and into the store-room and got the rum. I begged him not to take too much, as I knew his desperate character when in liquor.

'Don't fear,' he said, 'I never take too much in serious times. Now drink a little yourself; it will brace you up. Put the cup where we can get it again, and let us walk the deck where we can be seen but not heard. Much of my life you have heard me relate, from boyhood to manhood. The rest you shall hear now. My first criminal act, when I was a mere child, led on by others, landed me and them in the galleys, whence we escaped after murdering the guard. All except me were taken and guillotined. I was too small to have a hand in the murder. At the trial my plea of ignorance of an evil intent saved me from the extreme penalty of the law, but I was sent on

board a French man-of-war, from which I escaped after
many years of service. Then I found myself in the Spanish navy, and after the battle of Trafalgar I shipped in a
slaver.

"We were on our way from the Congo, bound to San
Domingo, with four hundred slaves stored in the hold.
The prospects were good for a profitable voyage. When we
were off Porto Rico a schooner, just like the one you have
seen this morning, came up and hailed us. It was just
getting dark, and she passed ahead. When the next day
was breaking she hailed us to heave to, and brought her
guns to bear. In a moment we were grappled and boarded. Part of our crew at once attacked our officers, and,
with the pirates who had boarded us, made short work of
those who showed any resistance. We who had done this
were allowed to join the pirate crew, as we had proved
ourselves worthy of them. If we had acted otherwise
we would have been slain also.

"An officer with a prize crew took charge of our schooner after we had been sent aboard the pirate, and took the
slaver into Havana, where she and her cargo were sold.
I stayed with the pirates three years, but their life did
not suit me, and I made my escape during a battle with
two English ships-of-war which had discovered our
stronghold in the Bay of San Lorenzo.

"'Now, boy,' Peter continued, 'to save ourselves we
must join these pirates, who will board us about daybreak. You take your position behind Mr. Crawford, and
as soon as they board strike him with the knife between
the shoulders.'

"At these instructions my knees began to give way.
Peter seized me, or I should have fallen. The story he
told me was all very well until it became my turn to be
an actor. But a nip of rum, administered by him, set me
all right. He said it would be better to kill the mate
than to be killed myself, and our crew would all be
slaughtered anyway. He called it justifiable self-defence,
and said that after we had joined the pirates he would
find a way for us to escape. He so worked on my imagination that I really felt I was going to do an excusable
deed. The knife he gave me was his favorite one it had a

very long blade incased in a wooden sheath, instead of
the leather usually used for sheath-knives. I agreed to do
as he bade me, and took my place behind the mate. Peter
took his place near the captain. It had just struck seven
bells. There had been scarcely a word spoken forward
during the night. The sound of the bells fell upon me
like a funeral knell. Tears began to run down my cheeks.
Mr. Crawford had always been good to me; why should
I kill him? Everybody had treated me well on board. I
thought of home, and the plans I had laid for the future;
now my aspirations and hopes would all be ruined in the
next half hour. A horror of the situation seized me. I
slipped off the bitts upon which I had been sitting and
walked aft. Peter followed me. He said ;

" 'You had better take a little more rum. I don't think
the cook will serve us with coffee this morning. It is
chilly for you after the long night's watch. I see that
you have a slight attack of ague.'

" 'No, Peter, I don't want to drink ; I am not cold.
But I would rather be killed than commit murder in such
cold blood.'

"But his pleadings, his love for me, and the review of
his friendship, had their effect. The demon that seduced
our great mother was whispering in my ear. I again did
as he told me, and stationed myself behind the mate.

"The silence was broken by the captain saying he
wished it was daylight.

" 'It will be here soon enough,' I heard Peter say. "I
see it breaking in the east, and before the sun is up all
will be over.'

"The day was indeed breaking, and night was furling
her black flag. The light mounted slowly towards the
zenith, and as our eyes were strained to catch a glimpse
of the mysterious craft, we saw her shoot out of the darkness, heading across our bow to the northward. We
looked in that direction and saw a large West India merchantman about four miles on our starboard beam. She
was running before the wind, with studding-sails set on
both sides, and was evidently Dutch from her build.

" 'She is doomed,' Peter said, 'and we are safe. Those
poor fellows will never muster round the grog-pail again.

Presently you will see the schooner make her heave to.'

"The words were scarcely spoken when we saw the smoke from her Long Tom. The signal was unheeded, and a shot brought down her foremast, which took the maintopmast with it. This crippled her so that in less than an hour she was out of sight astern.

"While in Amsterdam, years after, my curiosity led me to ascertain what ships were lost during the year in which the above incident occurred and I learned that the ship 'Crown Prince William', from Rotterdam, bound for Curacoa, was never heard from.

"We felt ourselves safe for the time being, but changed our course, fearing that after she had pillaged and sunk the ship, she might overtake and destroy us, to avoid being reported. We did not consider ourselves out of danger until we entered the harbor of Galveston."

The case of the disappearance of the British-Australian packet ship "Madagascar" was not, strictly speaking, due to piracy in the old sense of the term; yet the loss of this fine vessel resulted from a deeply laid plot, and it is interesting to include this thrilling sea tale, one of the most audacious in the criminal annals of the ocean. It is reproduced by the kind permission of Basil Lubbock, Esq., author, and Messrs. James Brown and Son, Glasgow, publishers of that wonderful book of marine history, "The Blackwall Frigates"; supplemented somewhat by a letter from the secretary of Lloyd's, London, to the author.

It must be remembered that soon after the discovery of gold in Australia, in the early 1850's, the population was of a very "mixed" character; ship's crews were exceedingly hard to get, and captains took what there was without asking questions, being only too glad to fill their forecastles for the home run.

"In July, 1853, she (the 'Madagascar') lay in Port Phillip (Australia), with the Blue Peter flying, a full complement of passengers, and 68,390 ounces of gold dust on board. Just as she was about to sail, Melbourne detectives hurried on board and arrested two of her passengers for being concerned in the McIvor Gold Escort robbery, which had been the latest piece of robbery under arms to excite the colony.

"The passengers were tried, and though a great deal of gold dust was found in their baggage on the 'Madagascar', the crime could not be brought home to them.   After being delayed a month by this affair, the 'Madagascar' sailed.   And when time passed and she did not arrive, all sorts of rumors began to circulate in order to account for her disappearance, but the most general belief was that she had been captured by a number of desperadoes, who, it was said, had taken passage in her for that very purpose.

"Years afterwards the following story went the round of the colonies.   A woman in New Zealand, being on her death-bed, sent for a clergyman and said that she had been a nurse on the ill-fated 'Madagascar'.   According to her the crew and several of the passengers mutinied when the ship was in the South Atlantic.   Captain Harris and his officers were all killed, and the rest of the passengers, with the exception of some of the young women, were locked up below.   The boats were then lowered, and the gold and young women put into them.   Finally the mutineers followed, having set fire to the ship and left their prisoners to burn.

"However, they soon paid for their crimes with their own lives, for only one of the boats, containing six men and five women (the narrator amongst them), succeeded in reaching the coast of Brazil, and even this boat was capsized in the surf, and its cargo of stolen gold dust lost overboard.

"The sufferings of its crew had been severe enough on the sea, but on land they grew more terrible day by day.   At last a small settlement was reached.   But this proved a death trap, for yellow fever was raging.   In a very short time only two of the mutineers and this woman remained alive.   They, after more hardships and privations, at last reached civilization.   Then the two scoundrels, after having dragged the woman with them through every kind of iniquity, eventually deserted her.   One of them disappeared entirely, but the other, according to her, was hanged in San Francisco for murder.

"The woman described herself as having been a nurse on board the 'Madagascar', and this may have been possible, as there was a Mrs. de Carteret with her children on board. . . .

"The nurse's story can never be proved; but it is likely enough, for before the 'Madagascar' sailed there were many sinister rumors in Melbourne concerning the objects and antecedents of her crew and many of her passengers."

According to a letter from the secretary of Lloyd's to the author, the "Madagascar" was not finally posted as "missing" until June 21st, 1854, nearly a year after the date of her sailing from Melbourne.

This celebrated tragedy of the sea forms the basis for one of Mr. Clark Russell's best marine novels, "The Tale of the Ten"; in it he has slightly altered the facts, and, of course, the names; the story also ends well, but otherwise the tale is largely as related above.

The last actual case of piracy was one quite as picturesque, and perhaps more curious than any related before in this little book, and certainly may be said to have been modern and up-to-date, as the piratical vessel in question was a steamer. As far as the author can trace, it is the only case of a "steam pirate". In February, 1860, General Miramon, who was then the principal representative of the Mexican so-called "Clerical and Conservative" party, with a company of followers, chartered at Havana the steamer "Marquis de la Habana",* which was the property of a Spanish Havana firm and had made one or more voyages as a slaver.

General Miramon's plan was that he and his "friends" were to be landed at Vera Cruz, where they hoped to bring about a revolution, a common occurrence in modern Mexico. The "Marquis de la Habana" was a wooden propeller of about 600 tons and carrying one or two old-fashioned 32-pounders and a modern brass-rifled pivot 24-pounder. Unfortunately for Miramon, when his steamer appeared off Vera Cruz and refused to show the flag of any civilized country, the United States fleet, then cruising off the Mexican and Central American coasts, on the watch to prevent the landing of Walker and his band of

*The "Marquis de la Habana" is not to be confused with another steamer "Habana", which, prior to the Civil war, plied regularly between New Orleans and Havana, and became the well known Confederate cruiser "Sumter".

filibusters, also stopped Miramon and his gang from going
ashore.

Here was a quandary for the Mexican "general" and
his friends ; they had very little or no money, the "Marquis de la Habana's" charter had only been partially settled,
and the rank and file of the proposed landing party were
clamoring for the liberal pay promised them.   However,
Miramon, or some other fertile brain among his followers,
soon hit on the following scheme, which, if successful
(and it might easily have been), would have filled all
their pockets with gold, and at a moderate amount of
risk.

The plan was as follows :   What could be easier than
to stop one of the homeward-bound California "treasure"
steamers, plunder the ship and her passengers, then put
on all steam, run the "Marquis de la Habana" ashore on
some unfrequented spot on either the Central or South
American coasts, and all hands could scatter, each for
himself.   It must be remembered that this was years before the building of the first trans-continental railroad,
and the principal means of communication between California and the east was by steamer from San Francisco to
Panama, thence by rail across the Isthmus to Aspinwall,
whence one of "Commodore" Vanderbilt's big side-
wheelers in eight or nine days more landed the traveller
in New York.

Neither were there, in 1860, many ocean cables to give
the alarm, so that the pirates could be traced and overtaken.   Moreover it did not take long for Miramon's followers, composed for the most part of the refuse of the
world that then hung about Cuban and Central American
ports, to fall in with the scheme.

Unfortunately for them, however, the proverb, "There's
many a slip 'twixt the cup and the lip", proved but too
true.

Somehow, and in some way, very likely by treachery.
news of the bold plot reached the ears of Commander
Jarvis, commanding the U. S. (sailing) sloop-of-war
"Saratoga",* and he immediately set forth in search of

*The "Saratoga" was originally built at the Portsmouth
Navy Yard as a frigate, but in 1860 had been recently cut down to
a sloop-of-war.

the miscreants, and as they were supposed to be not far off and the wind was light, the "Saratoga" was taken in tow by the steamer "Indianola". Sure enough, in a few hours, on March 6th, the "Marquis de la Habana" and a schooner were found anchored side by side off Point Anton Lizardo. Upon the approach of the "Saratoga", Miramon's vessels attempted to escape, but were soon overtaken, and in answer to Commander Jarvis' order to surrender, the "Marquis de la Habana" fired twice from her pivot gun. The "Saratoga" now gave them a broadside, upon which a general contest ensued, and Miramon was soon forced to surrender, but not before some twenty men were killed and wounded. Many of the Mexicans escaped ashore in small boats while the fight was going on. It was said that Miramon had the Spanish flag hoisted and was captured with it flying above him.

A prize crew was now put on board the "Marquis de la Habana", and Lieutenant R. T. Chapman was ordered to take her to New Orleans and turn her over to the U. S. marshal there "as being a pirate on the high seas".

It has been impossible to find out what became of Miramon, whether or not he was indicted; if so, perhaps the breaking out of the Civil war put an end to his troubles. At any rate, he afterwards became prominent as one of Emperor Maximilian's staunchest supporters during his short reign in Mexico, and was executed with him at Queratero in 1867. The "Marquis de la Habana" was taken into the Confederate navy as the "McRae". She was fitted out as a commerce destroyer, and it was hoped would be a companion ship to the "Sumter", "Alabama", etc.

The Union fleet, however, proved too vigilant, and the "McRae" was never able to reach the open sea. She took part in the battle of New Orleans in April, 1862, under the command of Lieutenant Thomas B. Huger, C. S. N., who was mortally wounded, like the "McRae" herself, which sank the next day from injuries received in the battle.

That the danger from pirates in the Gulf of Mexico as late as 1861 was not altogether unfounded is proved by the following despatch from Hon. Isaac Toucey, Secretary of the Navy in President Buchanan's cabinet, to Lieutenant Charles Thomas, commanding the U. S. S. "Falmouth", stationed at Aspinwall :

"Navy Department, Washington City,
          "January 19th, 1861.
"Sir :

"It is rumored that a piratical expedition is on foot to proceed to the Isthmus for the purpose of seizing the California steamers with their treasure ; that a schooner has already been chartered to convey the expedition to Aspinwall, where they will be clandestinely landed and make their attack after the treasure shall have been put on board the steamer.   There may not be foundation for this rumor.   You will, however, be vigilant, and, if necessary, be prompt to use all means at your command for the protection of the California steamers and their treasure, or other property of citizens of the United States.

          "I am, respectfully,
               "Your obedient servant,
                    "I. Toucey,
                         "Secretary of the Navy."
"Lieutenant Charles Thomas,
     "Commanding U. S. Storeship 'Falmouth',
          "Aspinwall, New Grenada."

The coast of New England, in fact, the whole Atlantic coast line, is full of traditions of pirates.   A most peculiar one is the legend of the shrieking woman of Marblehead, which is a ghost story connected with that part of the town known as Oakum Bay.

A piratical cruiser, having captured a Spanish vessel about the middle of the seventeenth century, brought her into Marblehead harbor, which was then the site of a few humble dwellings.   The male inhabitants were all absent on their fishing voyages.   The pirates brought their prisoners ashore, carried them at the dead of night into a retired glen, and there murdered them.

Among the captives was an English female passenger. The women of Marblehead heard her dying outcries, as they rose through the midnight air, and reverberated far and wide along the silent shores.   She was heard to exclaim, "O, mercy! Lord Jesus Christ save me! Lord

Jesus Christ save me!" Her body was buried by the pirates on the spot. The same piercing voice is believed to be heard, at intervals more or less often, almost every year, on clear moonlight nights. There is something, it is said, so wild, mysterious, and evidently super-human in the sound, as to strike a chill of dread into the hearts of all who listen to it.

The writer of an article on this subject in the old Marblehead Register of April 3d, 1830, declared that "there are not wanting at the present day persons of unimpeachable veracity and known respectability who still continue to firmly believe the tradition, and to assert that they themselves have been auditors of the sounds described, which they declare were of such an unearthly nature as to preclude the idea of imposition or deception.

No less a person than the late Judge Joseph Story, who died in 1845, a native of Marblehead, and who became one of the most prominent constitutional lawyers in the country, about the last person who would be taken in by ghost stories, averred that "he had heard those ill-omened shrieks again and again in the still hours of the night." A perusal of the old records reveal the fact that about 1700 the whole coast of Essex County, Massachusetts, was infested with pirates, and in Gloucester particularly there were the famous John Phillips and John Quelch, who were hung in 1704 for their piratical activities.

At the Point of Pines, on the shore line between Lynn and Revere, there has ever been a romance that pirate gold is supposed to be safely hidden somewhere on that point of land. According to tradition, a great chest of gold is buried at the root of a tree, the chest being covered by a large flat stone. This treasure chest is supposed to have been placed there by the same pirate crew of which tradition also says that they had their retreat in what has since been always known as Pirate's Glen, in one of the wildest and loneliest spots in Saugus.

Not far from the Point of Pines was once the old half-way house known as "The Blew Ankor," a tavern much patronized by travellers. Here it was that a party was formed to search for the treasure, and David Kunksshamooshaw, a wizard with a divining rod, located the spot where the treasure was buried, and the party by the light of their lanterns, began to dig. Soon their shovels struck a rock, and with a level it was partially razed, and there were those who claimed they saw an old chest beneath it. Then a mighty wind arose, and coming on the back of the wind was a hatless giant on a charger, shouting, 'By my blood, what do ye here? Filching my gold, hard earned upon the sea by danger and fire. But the devil will save his own, I wot. Avoyant ye, or bear a pirate's malediction."

So stunned were the diggers that they backed away from the spot, the stone sank into the chest, and the searchers ran for their lives. At various times in the centuries gone by, the Saugus river was the scene of mysterious fortune parties, it being claimed that this little stream quite often afforded an opportunity of hiding when the pirates were too hard pressed.

The particular story which has lasted the longest and has interest even now is that connected with Dungeon rock in the great Lynn Woods reservation, which is visited by thousands every year. According to tradition, the pirates at one time brought a beautiful woman to the woods, coming up the Saugus river, seeking a post in the rocks and crags from the tops of which a good view of the ocean was obtained. They found such an outlook, and here they built a hut, dug a well and made a garden, and the woman lived, died and was buried there.

Three of the pirates in this particular escapade were captured and died on the gibbet in England. The fourth, Thomas Veale, escaped to the cavern, where he is supposed to have hidden his booty. He worked the remainder of his life as a shoemaker or cordwainer, only coming down into the village for food.

Then came the earthquake of 1658, and the shock of the great convulsion of nature split to its foundation the rock in which the cavern was located, blocking the entrance and enclosing Veale in a frightful rocky tomb. The cliff has ever since been known as the Dungeon rock.

Hiram Marble, in 1854, began a search of Dungeon rock cavern for the pirate gold, and for thirty years up to the time of his death continued an unsuccessful search.

His son continued his efforts, and tons of rocks were moved by them in the course of time, but with no results.

Now and again comes the tale of someone searching for treasure gold in the sands of Gloucester or along the Ipswich-Newburyport dunes, but never yet has there come a story of the discovery of any of these mysterious chests, lined with gold and precious jewels, which were supposed to be the particular property of pirates at large. In the seventeenth century it is certain that the Isles of Shoals, off Portsmouth, N. H., were the resort of pirates with such names as Dixy Bull, Low and Argall (a licensed and titled buccaneer), who left the traces of their own lawlessness in the manner of life of the islanders. It was a convenient place in which to refit or obtain fresh provisions without the asking of troublesome questions.* The pirates could expect little booty from the fishermen, but they often picked them up at sea to replenish their crews.

In the year 1689 two noted buccaneers, Thomas Hawkins and Thomas Pound, cruised on the coast of New England, committing many depredations. The Bay Colony determined on their capture, and dispatched an armed sloop called the "Mary", Samuel Pease, commander, which put to sea in October of that year. Hearing the pirates had been cruising at the mouth of Buzzard's Bay, Captain Pease made all sail in that direction. The "Mary" overhauled the outlaw off Wood's Hole. Pease ran down to her, hailed, and ordered her to heave to. The freebooter ran up a blood red flag in defiance, when the "Mary" fired a shot athwart her forefoot, and again hailed, with a demand to strike her colors. Pound, who stood upon his quarter-deck, answered the hail with, "Come on, you dogs, and I will strike you." Waving his sword, his men poured a volley into the "Mary", and the action for some time raged fiercely, no quarter being expected. Captain Pease at length carried his adversary by boarding, receiving wounds in the hand to hand conflict of which he died.

In 1723 the sloop "Dolphin", of Cape Ann, was taken on the Banks by Phillips, a noted pirate. The able-bodied

*"Massachusetts Colonial Records", vol. IV, part 2, p. 449.

of the "Dolphin" were forced to join the pirate crew. Among the luckless fishermen was John Fillmore of Ipswich. Phillips, to quiet their scruples, promised on his honor to set them at liberty at the end of three months. Finding no other hope of escape, for of course the liar and pirate never meant to keep his word, Fillmore, with the help of Edward Cheesman and an Indian, seizing his opportunity, killed three of the chief pirates, including Phillips, on the spot. The rest of the crew, made up in part of pressed men, submitted, and the captured vessel was brought into Boston by the conquerors on the 3d of May, 1724. John Fillmore, the quasi pirate, was the great-grandfather of Millard Fillmore, thirteenth President of the United States.

It is affirmed on the authority of Charles Chauncy that Low once captured some fishermen from the "Shoals". Disappointed, perhaps, in his expectation of booty, he first caused the captives to be barbarously flogged, and afterward required each of them three times to curse Parson Mather or be hanged. The prisoners did not reject the alternative.

No doubt these pirates had heard of the sermons Cotton Mather was in the habit of preaching before the execution of many of their confederates. In his time it was the custom to march condemned prisoners under a strong guard to some church on the Sabbath preceding the day on which they were to suffer. There, marshaled in the broad aisle, they listened to a discourse on the enormity of their crimes and the torments that awaited them in the other world, this being the manner in which the old divines administered the consolations of religion to such desperate malefactors.

New England could contribute a thick volume to the annals of piracy in the New World from the records of a hundred years subsequent to her settlement. The name of Kidd was long a bugbear with which to terrify wayward children into obedience, and the search for his treasure continues, as we have seen, to this day. Bradish, Bellamy and Quelch sailed these seas like true followers

SCHOONER YACHT "WANDERER"

Built at Long Island, N. Y., in 1857.   A celebrated slaver

From a sketch in the collection of F. B. C. Bradlee

SCHOONER YACHT AND SLAVER "WANDERER"

From a model in the collection of F. B. C. Bradlee

of those dreaded rovers who swept the English coasts and sent their defiance to the king himself:

"Go tell the King of England, go tell him thus from me,
Though he reigns king o'er all the land, I will reign
        king at sea."

They have still the ghost of a pirate on Appledore,* one of Kidd's men. There has consequently been much seeking after treasure. The face of the spectre is "pale and very dreadful" to behold; and its neck, it is averred, shows the livid mark of the hangman's noose. It answers to the name of "Old Bab". Once no islander could be found hardy enough to venture on Appledore after night-fall.

In 1700 Rear Admiral Benbow was lying at Piscataqua, with nine of Kidd's pirates on board for transportation to England. Robert Bradenham, Kidd's surgeon, says the Earl of Bellomont, was the "obstinatest and most hardened of 'em all." In the year 1726 the pirates William Fly, Samuel Cole, and Henry Greenville were taken and put to death at Boston, after having been well preached to in Old Brattle Street by Dr. Colman. Fly, the captain, like a truculent knave, refused to come into church, and on the way to execution bore himself with great bravado. He jumped briskly into the cart, with a nosegay in his hands, smiling and bowing to the spectators as he passed along, with real or affected unconcern. At the gallows he showed the same obstinacy until his face was covered.†

The various legends relative to the corsairs, and the secreting of their ill-gotten gains among these rocks, would of themselves occupy a lengthy chapter; and the recital of the fearful sights and sounds which have con-

*Appledore is one of the islands forming the group called the Isles of Shoals. They lie ten miles off Portsmouth, N. H.

†After execution the bodies of the pirates were taken to the little island in Boston harbor known as Nix's Mate, on which there is a monument. Fly was hung in chains, and the other two buried on the beach. The total disappearance of this island before the encroachments of the sea is the foundation of a legend. Bird Island, in the same harbor, on which pirates have been executed, has also disappeared. It formerly contained a considerable area.

fronted such as were hardy enough to seek for treasure would satisfy the most inveterate marvel-monger in the land. Among others to whom it is said these islands were known was the celebrated Captain Teach, or Blackbeard as he was often called. He is supposed to have buried immense treasure here, some of which, like Haley's ingots, has been dug up and appropriated by the islanders. On one of his cruises, while lying off the Scottish coast waiting for a rich trader, he was boarded by a stranger, who came off in a small boat from the shore. The new-comer demanded to be led before the pirate chief, in whose cabin he remained some time shut up. At length Teach appeared on deck with the stranger, whom he introduced to the crew as a comrade. The vessel they were expecting soon came in sight, and after a bloody conflict became the prize of Blackbeard. It was determined by the corsair to man and arm the captured vessel. The unknown had fought with undaunted bravery and address during the battle. He was given the command of the prize.

The stranger Scot was not long in gaining the bad eminence of being as good a pirate as his renowned commander. His crew thought him invincible and followed where he led. At last, after his appetite for wealth had been satisfied by the rich booty of the Southern seas, he arrived on the coast of his native land. His boat was manned and landed him upon the beach near an humble dwelling, whence he soon returned, bearing in his arms the lifeless form of a woman.

The pirate ship immediately set sail for America, and in due time dropped her anchor in the road of the Isles of Shoals. Here the crew passed their time in secreting their riches and in carousal. The commander's portion was buried on an island apart from the rest. He roamed over the isles with his beautiful companion, forgetful, it would seem, of his fearful trade, until one morning a sail was seen standing in for the islands. All was now activity on board the pirate; but before getting under way the outlaw carried the maiden to the island where he had buried his treasure, and made her take a fearful oath to guard the spot from mortals until his return, were it not 'til doomsday. He then put to sea.

The strange sail proved to be a warlike vessel in search of freebooters. A long and desperate battle ensued, in which the cruiser at last silenced her adversary's guns. The vessels were grappled for a last struggle, when a terrific explosion strewed the sea with the fragments of both. Stung to madness by defeat, knowing that if taken alive the gibbet awaited him, the rover had fired the magazine, involving friend and foe in a common fate.

A few mangled wretches succeeded in reaching the islands, only to perish miserably, one by one, from cold and hunger. The pirate's mistress remained true to her oath to the last, or until she also succumbed to want and exposure. By report, she has been seen more than once on White Island—a tall, shapely figure, wrapped in a long sea-cloak, her head and neck uncovered, except by a profusion of golden hair. Her face is described as exquisitely rounded, but pale and still as marble. She takes her stand on the verge of a low, projecting point, gazing fixedly out upon the ocean in an attitude of intense expectation. A former race of fishermen avouched that her ghost was doomed to haunt those rocks until the last trump shall sound, and that the ancient graves to be found on the islands were tenanted by Blackbeard's men.*

In the autobiography of the late Rear Admiral B. F. Sands, U. S. N., "From Reefer to Rear Admiral", he states that in 1838 he was employed on coast survey work, as were in turn all naval officers at that period, and "Whilst walking along the shore near Babylon (Long Island, N. Y.), as our work progressed, Mr. Renard and I were on one occasion amusing ourselves skipping flat pebbles into the sea, watching them as they glanced from ripple to ripple on the water, when just as I was about to launch one I felt it was unusually heavy, and curiosity made me examine it. After some little rubbing I found it to be a Spanish dollar of date 1700. The edge was

---

*A somewhat more authentic naval conflict occurred during the war of 1812 with Great Britain, when the American privateer, "Governor Plummer," was captured near Jeffrey's Ledge by a British cruiser, the "Sir John Sherbrooke." The American had previously made many captures. Off Newfoundland she sustained a hard fight with a vessel of twelve guns, sent out to take her. She also beat off six barges sent on the same errand.

almost sharpened by friction on the sandy beaches. The discovery prevented the throwing of pebbles that had not been weighed and examined. That, particular find was placed *dans ma poche* as a lucky piece, but unluckily it went, with a quantity of other silver, some years later, into the pocket of a burglar who helped himself to what I had.

"On returning to camp with it that afternoon, it was held to be one of Captain Kidd's dollars, and the sight of it revived many stories of search for the pirate's hidden treasure, as it was claimed that this neighborhood was one of his favorite resorts.

"One old fisherman told me of his grappling a bag of money with his tongs whilst fishing for oysters off the inlet; that feeling something heavy and knowing that shell-fish could not be so weighty, he became excited as it was hauled near to the surface, and, finding its weight diminishing, he quickened his movement, and giving a vigorous jerk into the boat, found remaining in the teeth of his tongs only the tied end of an old canvas bag and two or three Spanish dollars.

"He concluded that he had first gotten hold of a sack of Kidd's treasure, which had been thrown overboard upon approaching the coast in a boat in bad weather. He marked the place by bearings, and frequently repeated his search, but without the slightest success.

"In this connection I will here relate an incident which occurred to Mr. Renard (Admiral Sand's chief in coast survey work) the following season. There was wild excitement in the papers of the day about a discovery of some of Kidd's treasure on the beach near Babylon by a countryman, who was walking along the beach after a gale, which was a common custom on this coast, in the hopes of picking up driftings from the sea.

"He saw on a sand-hill half blown away by the gale some pieces of old canvas, which, upon inspection, proved to be bags with money scattered about, to secure which he hurried home, and, bringing a cart, carried off his *treasure* trove. Some of the neighbors got wind of it, and the whole region was up and out on the search, with no greater success than a few old silver dollars and canvas bags, which, however, but served to keep up the excitement for some months afterwards.

"Mr. Renard, seeing the news in the papers, at once recognized from the description given that we had gone over the place in our survey; so hiring a buggy he started for the locality, and, sure enough, it was that very hill upon which I had erected a signal for our survey. The hill having been partly blown away, showed where the treasure deposit was made, which was within three feet of the hole dug for the signal staff, which lay there upon the top of the hill.

"In his letter to me telling of the fact, Mr. Renard expressed his wonder that I had not placed my signal pole three feet nearer the hidden treasure, it being said that the lucky finder had carried away in his cart some *fifteen thousand dollars*.

" . . . My detail this season (1839) was for the Atlantic coast of New Jersey below Long Branch, the latter part of the coast having been apportioned to my old friend and chief, Mr. Renard.

"This part of the coast about Barnegat had gained a bad reputation, because of the frequent recurrence of wrecks there and the robberies and murders accompanying them. The wrecks were usually caused by false lights shown by the natives to lure vessels to their destruction, when the whole neighborhood would turn out in force, robbing and maltreating the victims of their treachery without pity, their conduct bringing upon the inhabitants the odious name of Barnegat Pirates.

"It was, therefore, deemed advisable for our two parties to keep together as much as possible, at least when near the most dangerous part of the coast, that we might have mutual protection in our numbers, not expecting to be treated as welcome visitors for many reasons.

" . . . Our experience, however, was quite different from our anticipations, the people there keeping aloof from us altogether and in no wise troubling us."

The inhabitants of Block Island, in the eighteenth century, also had an unenviable reputation as "wreckers", which has even been celebrated in a poem by Whittier. It is, nevertheless, but fair to say that the historian of

Block Island, Rev. S. T. Livermore, after careful and prolonged researches, denies emphatically the cruel allegations as regards the islanders:

"All this barbarous work is here charged upon a little population of as pure morals as ever adorned any part of Puritan New England. Let no one suppose that the poet (Whittier) was aware of misrepresentation and injustice to the islanders. He, like others, doubtless supposed that the piracy once common about Block Island was carried on by the inhabitants. But that was not the case. Pirates from abroad, near the beginning of the eighteenth century, infested the island, and as they sallied forth from this point upon our own and foreign vessels, they gave a reputation, probably, to the island which in nowise belonged to the descendants of the Pilgrims."*

The pirate vessels "Ranger" and "Fortune" were headed for Block Island when captured by the colonial cruiser "Greyhound" in 1723. Twenty-six of the members of their crews were executed on Gravelly Point, at Newport, R. I., July 19th, 1723."†

As late as 1740 the Rhode Island General Assembly voted an appropriation of £13 13s. "for victuals and drink to the pirates at Block Island and their guards"; and from the fact of keeping pirates as prisoners on the island, many abroad doubtless heard frequent mention of "Block Island pirates," without distinguishing them from the native citizens of the island. But in all these cases the pirates appear to have been foreigners to the island, lodging there only temporarily.

In 1861, during the Civil war, Captain William Harwar Parker, C. S. N., was on duty at various places on the North Carolina coast. He says: "I used to hold long conversations with a pilot I met at the mouth of the Neuse river. He had passed his life on the sound (Pamlico), and was a real old-fashioned fellow, a believer in signs and tokens. He told me of his many attempts to find the money buried by Teach the pirate. Teach frequented Pamlico Sound and used to lie at an island in it

*"History of Block Island," by Rev. S. T. Livermore, A. M.
†"Colonial Records of Rhode Island," Vol. IV, pp. 329-331.

from which he could watch Hatteras and Ocracoke Inlets.

"I visited this island and every square foot of earth on it had had a spade in it in the search for Teach's money. Everybody hereabouts believed that Teach had buried a large amount of money *somewhere* on the shore of the sound. This pilot told me he had sometimes seen lights on the shore, which lights indicated the spot where the money was buried. The great point was to get to the place before the light was extinguished.

"He said he had several times jumped into a boat and pulled for one, but unfortunately the light always disappeared before he could reach the shore.

"Such was the tale that was told to me
   By that shattered and battered son of the sea."*

And so nearly the whole eastern coast line of the United States might be gone over. Much of it has traditions of pirate's hidden treasure, but it is to be doubted whether even a small proportion has been found in spite of the many persistent efforts to do so.

From the "Compromise" of 1850 until the breaking out, in 1861, of the Civil war, the group of public men in the Southern States known as "fire-eaters" and often called "the Slave Power" by the northern press, while diligently striving to enlarge the field of their political power, were also mindful of a corresponding increase in the number of their human working tools. Many of these politicians openly urged upon their constituents the re-opening of the African slave trade in order to meet this want, and, according to them, bring to the South unending prosperity.

While it was evident that the spirit of the age would not permit of a legalized trade in African negroes, nevertheless the result of this ceaseless agitation was that a large illicit foreign slave traffic sprang up, mainly under the American flag, and in vessels built, owned and equipped in American ports.

The North will, also, have to assume equal blame with the South in this nefarious business, for, while it must be

*"Recollections of a Naval Officer," by Capt. William Harwar Parker, C. S. N.

acknowledged that the smuggling in of negroes at certain points of the southern coast was comparatively easy, and, public opinion in that section being largely in its favor, the risk, even if the slavers were detected, was not great, still it must be admitted that a majority of the vessels employed in this trade, their owners and masters, all belonged in New England.

Since the abolition of the foreign slave trade in 1808, the bringing in of African negroes to the United States constituted a case of piracy according to the federal laws, and so the story of the last few shiploads of blacks brought to our shores is not, it would seem, out of place in this little volume. It may astonish some of our readers to know that as late as 1862 a native of the State of Maine was hung in the city of New York for piracy, the result of his being caught red-handed in a bold attempt to slip in a large cargo of negroes. The New York *Herald,* in the summer of 1860, published an estimate that "from thirty to forty slavers are fitted out every year, in New York, Boston, Bristol, R. I., Portland, Me., and other eastern ports ; but New York and Boston are the favorite places, from the fact that the operations of the traders can be carried on with less risk of detection. Comparatively a limited number are captured on the coast of Africa, and those that are so captured are taken by British cruisers, while but few fall into the hands of the United States squadron.

A New York correspondent of the Charleston, S. C., *Mercury,* said, in its issue of Aug. 15th, 1860, "That it is no exaggeration to state that a dozen or twenty slavers leave New York annually. These facts have recently come to my knowledge . . . It is not possible for any one person to know the whole extent of the business, but some things cannot be kept secret and are well known to many. . . . I know of two ladies, now attracting adoration at a fashionable watering place, who invested in a little venture of this kind not long ago, and, as a result, have augmented their bank accounts—one to the extent of $23,000, and the other $16,000. The headquarters of the traffic in this city (New York), are mainly in South,

William, Broad and Water streets.   Two vessels are now
fitting out here for the business."

A few days later the New York *Herald* claimed to have
"information that no less than six vessels have left New
York for the African coast within the past fortnight, all
of which expect to have negroes for their return cargoes."

Among these latter day slavers the best known and the
one standing out most prominently in the public eye was
the schooner "Wanderer."   She had, it was said, been originally designed and intended for a yacht, and was built at
Setauket, Long Island,by James Rowland, in 1857, largely
on the plan of the famous "America", the cup defender,
although the "Wanderer" was somewhat larger, measuring 260 tons register, 105 feet in length, 26 feet beam.
June, 1857, saw the launch of the future slaver, and
shortly after she is said to have made a trip from New
Orleans to New York in nine days.   Since the days of the
"Red Rover", that weird roamer of the seas, it is doubtful
if any vessel so vividly aroused public interest as the so-
called yacht"Wanderer", for it may be stated that there is
grave reason to doubt if she ever quite deserved the innocent prefix to her name.

When she first arrived in New York harbor she was
looked on as a model yacht, but very soon her mysterious
proceedings attracted the attention of U. S. Marshal Isaiah
Rynders, who was snubbed by many persons for what they
considered his officious meddling in arresting her.   The
"Wanderer" was then lost sight of for several months
(the schooner's whole career is naturally shrouded in obscurity), when she suddenly turned up in a southern port,
having landed a large and valuable cargo of slaves at
an obscure part of the Georgia coast.*

Such were the profits arising from this illicit traffic that
a vessel often paid for itself twice over in one voyage.
It was estimated that there were then about forty American
vessels engaged in the foreign slave trade.   These, it was
calculated,shipped 600 negroes each from theAfrican coast,
of whom 500 were landed at the port of destination.   Al-

*When the author passed some time at Mobile, Ala., in 1914, sev-
eral old and uncouth negroes were pointed out to him as having
been landed near Mobile by the "Wanderer."

lowing $3000 for each vessel for brokerage and commission from the port whence she sailed ; $4000 on each vessel for officers and men, $15 a head for the purchase of negroes on the African coast, and $42 to secure the landing of each negro at the port of delivery, the whole cost came up to $1,467,000. Twenty thousand negroes, at $500 each, would produce $10,000,000, a clear profit of $9,524,000, or upon two voyages a year, more than $17,000,000.

While on the African coast the "Wanderer" fell in with a British cruiser, and with characteristic coolness the slaver's captain hoisted the New York Yacht Club flag, and entertained the British officers in lavish style, responding to the toast given by one of these officers in honor of the club, in a speech of considerable ability and impudence. Little did the jolly mariners of England dream that they were accessories before the fact to an infamous violation of the laws of God and man. After her African voyage, the "Wanderer" again changed hands and was bought by a Mr. Lamar of Georgia, who entered, it was said, into an agreement to re-sell her to one "Captain" Martin.

About the middle of October, 1859, Martin "stole" the "Wanderer", so it was pretended, and went to sea without papers, intending to go to Africa for another freight of human beings. Lamar, the owner, pursued a little way in a steamboat, but undoubtedly by preconcert without success, for the so-called "theft" had probably been arranged between the owner and the "thief" as an easy and shrewd way of getting the schooner to sea without the trouble and risk of custom house preliminaries, and of securing to the owner a pretext for reclaiming her without even the trifling cost of a sham purchase should she fall into hands unfriendly to her.

The crew, it seems from subsequent events, knew nothing of her destination till they were out at sea, and most of them went on unwillingly after learning it.

On Nov. 22d, 1859, when near the Canaries, the captain taking four men with him in a boat, boarded a French vessel which they had met to obtain a supply of provisions. The rest of the crew seized the opportunity to escape, set all sail and steered for Boston, where they arrived on Dec. 24th, bringing also with them two Portuguese women, whom the captain had decoyed on board at one of the Azores and carried off with the intention of exchanging them in Africa for negroes.

On their arrival at Boston the crew of the "Wanderer" surrendered the vessel to the United States authorities, and legal proceedings were begun against her as a slaver. She was also libelled by the crew for their wages, and by persons who had furnished her with supplies for their respective dues. Lamar, on hearing of the arrival of his ship, made formal demand for her, offering in support of his claim the copy of an indictment in the United States Circuit Court for the district of Georgia against the late master for piratically running away with her. After a long hearing and an appeal by counsel for the government, the "Wanderer" was restored to Lamar, on his giving bond for $5940 to abide the final decision of the court in her case.

The Boston *Transcript* for March 5th, 1860, contained the following account of the court proceedings :

" 'Wanderer'.—This notorious vessel is now riding at anchor in the stream, ready for the sea, the admiration of all who behold her tasteful model and beautiful proportions. The 'Wanderer' has been surrendered to her owner, Mr. Lamar, of Savannah, under a bond of $5000, to abide by the decision of the court in her case, which is soon to be tried. In the meantime she is in the hands of Capt. C. R. Moore, one of our most experienced and worthy shipmasters, who takes her to Savannah. She is cleared by E. D. Brigham and Co."

The "Wanderer" returned to Savannah, but her career afterwards, as has been mentioned, was a good deal of a mystery, and naturally so. It has been stated that during the early months of the Civil war she was armed and became part of the "Georgia State Navy," which was to protect the coast of this "sovereign state from the incursions of the Yankees."

Still another account has it that the "Wanderer" was used as a revenue cutter at Pensacola and was afterwards in the cocoanut trade between the southern ports of the

United States and the West Indies, and that eventually she was wrecked on Cape Henry. Her owner, while she was a slaver, Lamar, was killed in the last battle of the Civil war, at Columbus, Ga., April 16th, 1865.

By 1859 the maritime commerce of Salem had sensibly declined, overshadowed as it was by New York and Boston. The foreign trade indeed had almost ceased to exist, and, therefore, one could hardly imagine a worst place to fit out a vessel for a slaving voyage. Secrecy, the prime necessity and of the first importance for carrying on such operations was practically impossible in a small seaport where everyone knew each other and which was notoriously full of marine "loafers." Yet in that same year the New York and Boston papers reported that there were two vessels in Salem fitting out for the slave trade. As may be imagined, these articles created quite a sensation, which resulted in a semi-humorous editorial in the Salem *Register* of August 11th, 1859.

"SLAVERS FITTING OUT AT SALEM.

"The New York Times has the following special despatch, dated Boston, Aug. 7: 'There are at this time two vessels fitting out at Salem, in this State, for the slave trade on the coast of Africa. The principals in the affair are a Spanish firm in New York; and the pecuniary equipment of the vessels has just been forwarded, in the form of nearly $20,000 in hard specie. If the government really wishes to stop this infamous trade, it must look North as well as South, and to these small New England ports, as well as New York and New Orleans. There will be no difficulty in identifying the craft at Salem, and this is not the first instance in the last three months.'

Immediately upon the receipt of the above startling information, we despatched, after the most approved fashion of the New York and Boston press, a corps of special reporters to every quarter of the city, with explicit instructions to burrow in every dock and explore every cove, inlet, outlet, mill stream, sluice-way, and brook, leading in or out of, or any wise connected with the waters of the harbor, and to ferret out the infernal slaver, or perish in the attempt. The most keen-sighted of the experts was furnished with a pair of seven league boots, and the way he streaked it down town, notebook in pocket and pencil whittled to the sharpest kind of a point, in hand, was a caution to the Custom House loafers, who were balancing themselves on the hind legs of their chairs, enjoying their siesta and dreaming of their next quarter day. His progress was a sight to behold.

Since the days of John Gilpin, with the exception of the ever memorable 'gallopade' of President Polk and Secretary (now President) Buchanan through the streets of Salem in 1847, urged on by the forty oath power of Marshal Barnes—no such specimen of go-aheadtiveness has been manifested as was exhibited by our Corypheus of reporters on this occasion. . . .

The first approach to discovery was made at Phillips wharf, where our reporter was 'sure he'd got 'em.' His attention was rivetted on this locality from the moment that he saw several twig-looking vessels apparently 'well found', and about which there was no little bustle. Ever and anon, from a distance, he saw large quantities of round, shining black bodies hoisted up from the vessel's hold and dumped in great haste into freight cars on the wharf alongside. . . .

Imagine his 'feelinks', then, when he found what he had supposed to be darkies in the act of landing to be nothing more than lumps of good, honest, Pennsylvania anthracite! Somewhat sobered by this rebuff, his drooping spirits were revived by soon seeing another sight. . . .

At Webb's wharf, sure enough, were some mysterious looking craft which certainly required overhauling. Sundry long, low, black-looking hulls, partially dismantled, apparently a little the worse for wear. . . . these sorry looking old hulls, we say, afforded to our reporter ample grounds for suspicion, and thither he hurried, but also only to find . . . that, vulgarly speaking, he had smelled a 'mice' of the largest kind. . . .

But, seriously, somebody has been 'sold'. There are some half a dozen of the regular African traders lying at the wharves, although not one . . . is justly liable to suspicion. When a vessel does fit away at Salem for the slave trade, we venture to predict that it will not escape

the lynx-eyed observation of the *habitues* of the wharves.
. . ."

In spite of the preceding article, there was at this time
in the slave trade a vessel which had been wholly or partially owned in Salem—the celebrated clipper ship "Nightingale." Nor must mention be omitted of the brig "Mary
Pauline", 172 tons, built at Hartford, Connecticut, in
1833. Under the name of "Lalla Rooke" this vessel had
been a well known slaver, but unfortunately no record of
her as such can be found. In 1843 she was registered
from Salem, Henry E. Jenks, Charles Hoffman, Osgood
Dunlap, owners; Neal P. Heweson, master. During the
year 1845 the "Mary Pauline" was lost at sea while on a
voyage to Africa.

The "Nightingale" (named for Jenny Lind, the celebrated Swedish singer, and her figurehead was a beauti-
fully made bust of her), was built at Portsmouth, N. H.,
by Samuel Hanscom, in 1851. She was 174 feet long,
36 feet beam, and registered 1066 tons. For some weeks
before she was launched the following advertisement appeared in the Boston papers: "For London direct from
Commercial wharf. The new clipper ship 'Nightingale'
will positively sail Aug. 1, for the purpose of conveying
visitors to the Crystal Palace (the First World's Fair)
Exhibition in London, and back to the United States. The
vessel has been built and fitted up expressly for this ex-
cursion and affords exceptional accommodations."

The "Nightingale" arrived at Boston, from Portsmouth,
July 19th, 1851, under command of Captain Yeaton, and
he and Hon. Ichabod Goodwin of Portsmouth remained
agents of the vessel until Oct. 18th, when she was registered in the name of Sampson and Tappan of Boston.

Captain Arthur H. Clark, author of the "Clipper Ship
Era", to whom the author is indebted for a portion of the
facts relating to the "Nightingale", says : "That in addition to her elaborate passenger fittings for carrying tour-
ists to the London World Fair, the ship carried a mechanic's lien of $31,500, which Sampson and Tappan were
obliged to liquidate, in addition to the $43,500 they paid
for the 'Nightingale', but as it turned out, she was a
cheap ship at that, and made a large sum of money for
her owners."

THE CELEBRATED CLIPPER SHIP AND SLAVER "NIGHTINGALE"

Built at Portsmouth, N. H., 1850

From a print in the collection of F. B. C. Bradlee

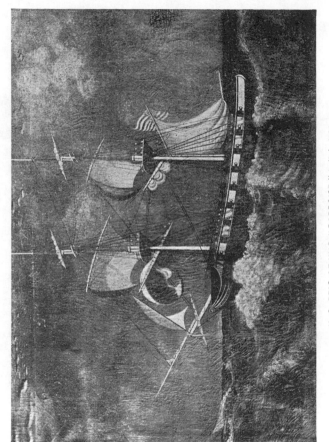

U. S. BRIG OF WAR "PORPOISE," built in 1836

From the original painting in the collection of F. B. C. Bradlee

Just before she left Boston on her first voyage, the Boston *Traveller* mentioned the "Nightingale" as follows: "Naval architecture in perfection of model can go no further. . . . Thoroughly bolted and coppered throughout, well found in boats and tackle, cabin containing ten staterooms, instead of berths, ladies' cabin with eight staterooms, water tank holding 4500 gallons of water, and accommodations for 250 passengers."

Sampson and Tappan ran her in the Australian and California trades,where freights were in the early 50's very high, until 1859, when the "Nightingale" changed hands, and a part of her later career, when a slaver, is necessarily somewhat obscure, as her owners during that period would obviously shun publicity.

Captain Clark says of her: "She was sold to a firm in Salem (it may be stated, however, that the "Nightingale" was never registered from Salem, but that does not in the least prevent her having been owned in that city), who sent her to Rio Janeiro, intending to run her in the coffee trade, but she was sold to a Brazilian, who used her as a slaver, and she landed a cargo of Africans on the coast of Brazil prior to her capture by a United States man-of-war.

"Assuming this story to be correct, it would appear that when the 'Nightingale' became the property of a Brazilian she was legally under the Brazilian flag, but it by no means follows that she did not obtain a United States register, which was a valuable asset. Nothing could be more simple, and, as a matter of fact, it is exactly what it appears did happen. Bowen (her legal captain at this period) was made the dummy owner, consignee, and captain, and is so registered in the American Lloyds, while one Cortina was the real captain, who represented the actual owners, which accounts for his presence on board the 'Nightingale' when she was captured."* It is a fact worth noting that the "Nightingale" was registered

---

*A common trick practiced by slaving ships at this period, especially those under the American flag, was to carry two crews and two sets of officers, American and foreign, generally Spanish or Portuguese. If captured by an American man-of-war, it would be claimed that the ship, officers and crew were foreign, the Americans being merely passengers; if captured by the British, the opposite claim would be made.

as belonging to the port of New York; nevertheless, Bowen does not seem to have considered it necessary to paint out "Boston," which was on her stern when captured.

The Salem *Gazette* for June 18th, 1861, relates the capture of the "Nightingale" as follows, and its account of the ship's career before her seizure varies considerably from that of Captain Clark's, yet bears every mark of accuracy. This knotty question is left for our readers to decide for themselves.

"Capture of a Slaver: The slave ship 'Nightingale' was brought into New York on Saturday, in charge of Lieut. J. J. Guthrie, U. S. N., and a prize crew from the U. S. sloop-of-war 'Saratoga'. The 'Nightingale' was captured April 23d (1861), off Kabenda, W. C. A., by the 'Saratoga', having on board 950 negroes. She was taken into Monrovia, where the cargo was put on shore, and 272 men, 97 women, 340 boys, and 92 girls, making a total of 801, 160 having died on the passage from Kabenda. The 'Nightingale' is a clipper ship of 1100 tons burthen, built at Portsmouth, N. H., and intended for the Transatlantic or Australian passenger trade, but as her builders did not fulfill their contract, she passed into other hands. She sailed from New York Sept. 13th, 1860, with a load of grain for Liverpool, and arrived there Oct. 6th, where she discharged cargo, and was up for the East Indies. She sailed from Liverpool Dec. 2d, and on the 14th of January, 1861, anchored at the island of St. Thomas (W. C. A.). On the 22d of January she was boarded off Congo by H. B. M. 'Archer' and the U. S. S. 'Mystic', when she proceeded up the Congo river and remained there until the 1st of April, when she was fallen in with by the 'Saratoga' and boarded, and her papers found all right. She was allowed to proceed, but on the 23d of April was captured as above. The captain (Francis Bowen), the Spanish supercargo, and the cabin servant made their escape from the vessel the night previous to her sailing from Kabenda, a portion of the crew having previously escaped in the boats. Those that did not escape were transferred to the 'Saratoga' and shipped for the service."

In the "Life of Commodore George Hamilton Perkins, U. S. N.", by Carroll Storrs Alden, is another account of the "Nightingale's" earlier career as a slaver, which formed part of a letter written home by the Commodore, then Acting Master, of the U. S. steamer "Sumter":

"April 15, 1860. The clipper ship 'Nightingale', of Salem, shipped a cargo of 2000 negroes and has gone clear with them. If she gets them to Havana they will bring, on an average, $600 apiece; so you can calculate how much money will be made on her. The 'Nightingale' is a powerful clipper, and is the property of her captain, Bowen, who is called the Prince of Slavers. The first time I was up the Congo the 'Sumter' went up fifteen miles after a slaver under his command, called the 'Sultana'. We found the barque 'Sultana' and the brig 'Kibby', with their slave decks all laid and everything ready for cargo.

"We examined both ships and detained one for three days; then our captain let her go, declaring against every proof that there was nothing in the ship but what was in her manifest. Of course these ships at once filled up with slaves and calmly sailed off—there was no escape about it.

"With the money Bowen made from the sale of those slaves he has purchased the 'Nightingale', one of the fastest clippers known. When I saw Bowen in command of the 'Sultana' he was living very luxuriously; everything in his cabin had elegance, and everything about his career was as nearly as possible like that of the romantic pirates and slave captains who are introduced into novels. Our vessels cruise very little now after slavers. The captains think it useless under existing laws."

It is understood that Captain Bowen, the owner of the "Nightingale", above referred to, unlike Captain Gordon and most of the other latter-day slavers, kept the fortune he had made, and when there was no longer a profitable market for slaves, turned his attention to hotel keeping in Aspinwall, Central America, and was flourishing there when last heard of.

After her seizure the "Nightingale" was condemned and sold as a prize in New York and was bought by the government for $13,000. She was placed in charge of Acting Master D. B. Horn, and attached to the South Atlantic blockading squadron. Two light guns were mounted on her, but she served as a coal ship. From 1861 to 1864 she served alternately as a coal ship, ordnance ship, and a dispatch boat, and in 1864 was ordered to New York for repairs.

At the end of the war the "Nightingale" was again employed in the China and California trades, and in 1871 on a voyage from New York to San Francisco, she put into the Falkland Islands, leaky, with her crew in a state of mutiny, one of whom had stabbed her chief mate to death. In 1876 the old ship again changed hands at the Merchants Exchange in San Francisco, for $11,000. Her purchaser, George Howes, loaded her with oil and sent her to New York, where she was sold for $15,000 to Norwegian owners, and all further trace of her disappears.

In the early 1840's a company of shipbuilders, several of them being Essex County men, left New England and settled at Marietta, Ohio, where they engaged in the business of building western river steamboats. Between whiles they also constructed several square-rigged vessels, which were floated [towed] down the Ohio and Mississippi rivers and proved to be good sea-boats, even if they were put together thousands of miles from salt water. One of these rather unique craft, the brig "Ohio," 143 tons, built at Marietta in 1847, and for many years owned and registered in Salem, was, while on a trading voyage to the west coast of Africa, in 1848, very strongly suspected of being a slaver.

The late Rear Admiral Benjamin F. Sands, U. S. N., in his memoirs, "From Reefer to Rear Admiral," refers as follows to the "Ohio" (pp. 195-196): "The 26th of November (1848) saw us off the coast in company with the schooner (brig) 'Ohio', upon which suspicion had fallen as being a 'slaver'.

"Our captain used to sit all day with the darkies on shore, listening to their tales of the slave-dealers, and under their information believed that every vessel flying the 'stars and stripes' was engaged in aiding and abetting the slave-dealers.

"It was now suspected that the 'Ohio' was to carry the famed adventurer and slave-dealer, Captain Theodore Canot (whose career, so successful in his nefarious business, which made him for many years a prominent man on that coast) from the Colony to Gallinas, where he had a 'factory' full of slaves.

"I went on board and examined her papers and hold, but found nothing to excite suspicion except the fact, which the captain admitted, that he was to take Canot as a passenger and drop him at Gallinas en route to Sierra Leone. He explained he had no right to question his passenger as to his business.

"Captain Gordon said that he would watch him, and if he landed that old slave-trader at Gallinas he would seize the vessel as a prize and send her to the States. So off we went on another wild goose chase.

"The 'Ohio' was built at Marietta in February, and came out to this coast as a trader. On the night of the 28th of November, in a squall, we lost sight of the 'Ohio', which we were watching, but in the morning sighted a stranger, a saucy-looking schooner, and fired a shot to make her 'heave to' or show her flag. . . . We armed a couple of boats about nine o'clock and I was off in pursuit in the first cutter, the doctor having charge of the gig. . . .

"I took possession of her . . . and found a Brazilian flag in the rigging. I found, however, that she had everything in readiness for her occupation as a slaver ; the slave deck was laid, coppers in place, some forty or fifty water casks filled, etc., etc. . . . So we lost sight of Canot, who soon afterwards, finding the English and American governments in earnest, gave up the slave traffic and *reformed*. A narrative of his eventful career was published from his own notes in 1854 by Brantz Mayer."

At this time the future Rear Admiral Sands was serving in the West African squadron as executive officer of the U. S. brig "Porpoise", 12 guns, in charge of Commander Gordon. This vessel (built at the Boston Navy Yard in 1836) afterwards achieved the melancholy distinction of being one of the few U. S. men-of-war put down as "missing."

On September 21st, 1854, she and the sloop-of-war "Vincennes" left Hong Kong to survey certain islands in the Malay Archipelago; a few days later a severe gale came up, and the "Porpoise" was never heard of. She probably capsized, as did the U. S. brig "Somers", off Vera Cruz during the Mexican war. There existed a strong prejudice against these brigs in the navy, as they were considered crank and top-heavy. The picture of the "Porpoise" reproduced in this book is from the original oil painting of her in the author's collection.

The first *schooner* "Porpoise", which saw so much service against the West Indian pirates, is often confused with her namesake mentioned above, but was a totally different vessel. She was bought by the Navy Department at Portsmouth, N. H., in 1820, measured 198 tons, and carried 12 guns.

Soon after the "Nightingale's" capture by the U. S. S. "Saratoga", previously mentioned, several of her officers, together with others connected with the slave trade, were indicted for piracy (then a capital offence), according to the following article reproduced from the New York *Illustrated News* for March 15th, 1862. Captain Gordon, mentioned in the article, had been found guilty and hung, of whom more will be said further on, and that seems to have satisfied the "ends of justice," for all the other slavers had their cases placed on file.

"The following persons are indicted for serving in the slave trade: Samuel B. Hayens, first mate of the 'Nightingale'; Bradley Winslow, second mate of the same vessel; William H. Byrnes, master of the barque 'W. L. Kibby'; Morgan Fredericks, first mate of the 'Cora' ; Erastus H. Booth, master of the 'Buckeye'; George Garnett, first mate of the same vessel; Henry C. Crawford, master of the ship 'City of Norfolk' ; William Warren, first mate, and David Hall, second mate of the 'Erie', under command of the late Captain Gordon.

"Should any of these men be found guilty of the capital offence and sentenced to death, will they be hung ? To make an exception in favor of either would be to admit that Gordon was unjustly executed, and to execute them all would be regarded as an outrage on humanity.   This is one of those cases in which a horror of capital punishment induces a jury to acquit. Perhaps the lilliputian Dracas, who cry 'Death! Death!' will reflect a little."

Although the United States had been the nation to found Liberia, the state for freed negroes, our government had shown gross negligence in enforcing the laws against the slave trade.

From 1808, when the importation of slaves became illegal, till 1842, this country did practically nothing to suppress it; for the next seventeen or eighteen years, although American ships of war were sent regularly to the African coast, the perfunctory efforts accomplished but little.

On the other hand, Great Britain and other European countries, particularly France, had exhibited considerable vigilance in seizing vessels of their respective nations engaged in the nefarious business.

Vice-Admiral Jurien de la Graviere, the well known French naval commander, in his "La Marine D'Autrefois," says that when he first entered the navy (1829), some of the French men-of-war had serving on board many members of the crews of ex-slavers, whose penalty on being caught was a three years' term of service in the navy.

As has been stated before, the decade following 1850 saw a great increase in the illicit slave trade to the United States. According to Stephen A. Douglas, more slaves were imported in 1859 than in any year previous, not excluding the time when the traffic was legal; he estimated the number to be not less than 15,000. Most of our naval officers ordered to the African coast, well aware of the sentiment prevailing in governmental circles in Washington, were not over zealous in their patrol duty and would send in a prize only when the proofs were scarcely less than absolute. Even in these few cases the offending captains and their ships were released on bond, and the trials were long postponed. Whenever a man was convicted, the executive found some reason for not carrying out the sentence.

It was not until Mr. Lincoln was inaugurated that uncompromising suppression of the slave trade began and that an offender (Captain Gordon, previously mentioned), suffered the full penalty—hanging.

Meanwhile, during the fifties, since the United States often embarrassed the American offenders and France and Great Britain vigorously prosecuted all those flying her flag, the misery attending the slave traffic became intensified. Traders could not afford to wait for a favorable tide or calm, but when a speck appeared on the horizon suspected to be the sail of a man-of-war, would crowd the negroes into canoes and proceed to loading. When the canoes were caught in the surf, some of the blacks were drowned and others were devoured by sharks. This meant a money loss, but the shipmaster could afford it if he secured a moderate sized cargo and succeeded in escaping. That the slaves might be shipped at an hour's notice they were herded together in barracoons at various points on the shore. Small pox and contagious fevers frequently broke out, whereupon the sick would often be poisoned, drowned, or shot, that the epidemic might be checked.

Troubles as bad or worse followed when the negroes were crowded between decks on ships, where death from the exhaustion of fresh water, as well as from epidemics, frequently occurred. To maintain the supply of slaves on the coast, to be traded for and shipped, the fiercer tribes kept up a constant warfare; they made frequent raids, destroying villages, and bringing back hundreds of men, women and children. In exchange for slaves they received guns, merchandise of various kinds, and cheap rum.

The last demoralized the whole coast, and to the blacks of all kinds was irresistible. Although President Buchanan's administration, like the preceding ones, was remiss in dealing with this problem, Congress had become aroused by the cruelties and gross violations of law reported, and required that a more vigorous policy be instituted.

In 1859, in place of three or four heavy sailing frigates, ill adapted for the service, several small steamers were sent out. These were the "Sumter", "Mystic", and "Crusader", propellers of about 500 tons each, and carry-

ing a few light guns. The Navy Department had purchased them especially for this service from the merchant
marine, where they had been known as the "Atlanta",
"Memphis", and "Southern Star".

Of all the American naval officers stationed on the West
African coast during the last years of the nefarious slave
traffic, probably the most zealous was Commander, afterwards Rear Admiral, Andrew Hull Foote, previously
mentioned in connection with his services against the West
Indian pirates. Before Foote's time it had been the custom
for the men-of-war to stand in near the coast and attempt
to catch the slavers in the act of embarking their living
cargoes. He, however, thought that by cruising one
hundred or more miles off shore, there was as much, if
not more chance to capture the "traders", as they called
themselves, where they least suspected danger.

Suiting the action to the word, Commander Foote, then
in charge of the brig-of-war "Perry", changed his cruising
ground, at the same time disguising as far as was possible
his vessel, so that she appeared to be a merchantman.

His plan soon met with success, for on June 6th, 1850,
he captured the full-rigged ship "Martha", of New York,
one of the largest slavers on the coast. Commander Foote
sent her back to the United States, in charge of a prize
crew, and the "Martha" was seized and condemned, a feat
hitherto very difficult of accomplishment, for the slavers
generally were furnished with two sets of papers, one of
them Brazilian, and when close pressed the American
documents were thrown overboard, as was done in this
case, but they were picked up before they were even
soaked through.

Is is doubtful, however, if Commander Foote's zeal was
smiled upon in high quarters, for soon afterwards he was
recalled on some pretext, but he has left a most interesting
record of his experiences in "Africa and the American
Flag" (New York, 1854), a book which really did a great
deal towards opening the eyes of the complacent public
to the abominable traffic going on under the Stars and
Stripes. Those who wish to read of the enormities and
barbarous cruelty of the last years of the slave trade cannot do better than read this volume ; the subject is large,

so large that all the author has attempted to do is to mention a few of the best known latter day slavers, a complete list of these so-called "traders", if obtainable, would, of itself, fill a small sized-book.

Among the many "deep water" sea captains hailing from Marblehead in the last half of the nineteenth century perhaps one of the best known was Captain Michael Gregory, one of four brothers, all of whom were shipmasters. Captain "Mike", as the former was generally called, sailed for a firm named Napier, Johnson & Co., of New York, who had built for him the extreme clipper ship "Sunny South", 703 tons register. She was always considered one of the prettiest ships ever launched, and was the only sailing vessel built by the celebrated George Steers, the designer of the yacht "America", U. S. steam frigate "Niagara", and the Collins line steamer "Adriatic".

The "Sunny South" was built for the China trade and launched at Williamsburg, Sept. 7th, 1854. It is a singular fact that while this ship was well known to possess great speed when in company with other clippers, yet she never made a passage worthy of being recorded, neither was she a successful ship financially.

In 1859 the "Sunny South" was sold at Havana and her name was changed to "Emanuela". Havana and Rio Janeiro were well known as the two principal ports where slavers were bought, sold and fitted out. The next we hear of the "Emanuela" was on August 10, 1860, when she was seized by H. B. M. S. "Brisk" in the Mozambique channel, flying the Chilian flag, and with a cargo of 850 slaves packed on board.

Her chase and capture was described as follows : "At 11.30 A. M. on the 10th of August last, as H. B. M. 'Brisk', Captain De Horsey, bearing the flag of Rear Admiral the Hon. Sir Henry Keppel, K. C. B., was running to the northward in the Mozambique Channel, a sail was reported as seen from the masthead. Steam was got up without delay and sail made in chase.

"It being hazy, the stranger was shortly lost sight of. When the weather had partially cleared the stranger was reported four points on the starboard bow, and the ship's

THE SLAVER "SUNNY SOUTH," alias "EMANUELA"

Surrendering to H. M. S. "BRISK"

From a wood cut in The Illustrated London News

BARQUE "ISLA DE CUBA"

Formerly the ship "Tonquin" of Boston. A slaver of 1858-59.

From a sketch in the collection of F. B. C. Bradlee

course altered in that direction. We were now going 11 1-2 knots, and the captain, feeling that it must be something out of the common that would alter bearings at that distance in so short a time, proceeded himself with his glass to the foretopmast head, officers mounting the rigging.

"That a general excitement prevailed was evident from the manner in which our sails were trimmed, taken in, and set again. Hottentots and landsmen, who on other occasions only looked at ropes, now laid hold of them with a will. The captain's order from the masthead to keep away two points showed that he had observed something suspicious—in fact he had noticed a sudden alteration of the chase, and pronounced her to be a long, rakish-looking ship, too large to be a slaver, but thought there was something very suspicious in the sudden alteration of her course, her crowd of sail, . . .

"On closing under her lee, and when within a cable's length, a white package was thrown from her side into the sea, and the experienced then exclaimed, 'A slaver, and there goes her papers!' A few minutes more, and we sheered up alongside to leeward of as beautiful model of a ship as ever was seen. . . . It was an anxious five minutes to those on the 'Brisk' while our boats were away. A small white British ensign run up at her peak showed that she was a prize, and a voice hailed us, 'Eight hundred and fifty slaves on board!'"

The Boston *Advertiser* for March 20th, 1856, contained the following article:

"The 'Falmouth', a new little fore and aft schooner of 200 tons, was seized by the U. S. marshal at New York, suspected of being a slaver. The crew were Spanish and could not speak a word of English. The 'Falmouth' was fitted up with all the appurtenances of a regular slaver; her ownership remains a mystery."

According to the "History of the American Slave Trade," by John R. Spears, the "Falmouth" (which he describes as a brig, but the same vessel mentioned in the *Advertiser* is evidently meant, moreover the picture of her proves conclusively that her rig was that of a schooner), made three voyages as a slaver, from 1856 to 1861; she was caught each time, but at the U. S. marshal's sale was as often "bid in" and continued on the "even tenor of her ways." The last time the "Falmouth" was seized her owners are given as George H. Leinas and William Watts.

Once a vessel became a slaver it would seem that it was hard for her to shake off her bad name, even though she might have been for years engaged in lawful trade. An interesting case in question was that of the brig "C. H. Jordan". This peculiarly built craft was a very old vessel, large for her rig (she measured between 400 and 500 tons register), originally built in and belonging to Barcelona, Spain. In 1859 she was picked up, a derelict, off St. Thomas, by a Provincetown whaler, and brought into Provincetown.

She had no flag or papers. Everything by which she could be identified had been destroyed. There were slave shackles on board, lumber for slave-decks, a large number of water casks, and all the fittings of a slaver; she was seized and condemned as such by the U. S. authorities, and sold at auction to Mr. Charles W. Adams, a Boston sbip broker. He in turn sold one-quarter interest in the "Jordan" to Captain John D. Whidden of Marblehead— at the time the present lines are being written Captain Whidden, who now lives in California, is believed to be the very last survivor of the old-time Marblehead "deep water" shipmasters.* As the brig was Captain Whidden's first command, he naturally took great interest in and was very proud of her.

During his ownership and command of the "C. H. Jordan" she was engaged in the lumber trade between the United States and South American ports, and in his interesting book, "Ocean Life", Captain Whidden says that, in spite of her bluff bows, she often made fourteen or more knots while under full sail and with a favorable wind. He (Whidden) had always had his curiosity aroused by a large bloodstain on the brig's cabin floor and by several imbedded bullets in the panels of one of the staterooms.

On one occasion, while the "Jordan" was undergoing repairs at Montevideo, a former member of her crew rec-

*Capt. Whidden has since died.

ognized her and told Captain Whidden her tragic history. She had made two successful voyages from Africa, bringing slaves to Cuba and landing them on the south side of the island near the Isle of Pines. While on her third trip to the African coast, having $30,000 in specie on board, the brig's crew mutinied after reaching the coast, shooting and killing the captain and mates through the skylight, while they were sitting in the cabin. Running the vessel down across the "trades" until in the vicinity of St. Thomas, they destroyed everything on board by which she could be identified, and taking to the boats, landed at the latter port, describing themselves as shipwrecked seamen.

Most of them then proceeded to Havana, and having plenty of money, indulged freely in liquor, over-talked themselves, were arrested, tried, and executed for murder.

Another slaver whose career was famous was the brig "Echo", built at Baltimore in 1854; she measured 230 tons register, and was rated 1 1-2. After several successful negro-smuggling voyages, she was finally seized, brought into Charleston, S. C., and condemned.

When the Civil war broke out the "Echo" was fitted out as a privateer and re-named "Jefferson Davis", receiving from the President of the Confederate States her commission to "sink, burn and destroy" ships of the United States.

She was commanded by Captain Louis M. Coxetter, Lieutenants Postell and Stewart, Surgeon Babcock, Captain of Marines Sanfrau, four prize masters, and a crew of seventy men. Her armament consisted of four waist guns, two eighteen pounders, two twelve pounders, and a pivot eighteen pounder. Although the "Jefferson Davis" had but a short career, she caused much damage to our merchant marine, capturing and burning no less than eight vessels, until August 16th, 1861, when attempting to enter the harbor of St. Augustine, Fla., in a gale, she struck on the bar and became a total loss.

In Frank Leslie's Illustrated Weekly for June 23d, 1860, there is the following interesting account of the capture, red-handed, of various slavers:

"CAPTURE OF THE SLAVE VESSELS AND THEIR CARGOES.

"Our cruisers have been very successful of late in the search after the slavers which infest the Cuban coast, and have already captured three vessels with over one thousand five hundred negroes. The prizes were all taken to Key West and their cargoes landed. Such an accession to the population of that place caused the authorities no little trouble to provide suitable accommodations for them. But by activity and energy, and by calling forth every available resource, in a few days all were comfortably though roughly housed.

"On the morning of the 9th of May, while the U.S. steam sloop 'Wyandotte' was on her course for the south side of Cuba, a bark was discovered standing in shore with all sail set to a light breeze. Chase was immediately commenced and continued for four hours, when the wind dying away and the steamer gaining rapidly on the bark, the latter, mistaking the 'Wyandotte' for a Spanish coasting steamer, tacked and boldly stood out from land. About eleven A. M., the 'Wyandotte' being within speaking distance of the bark, Captain Stanley hailed her in Spanish, asking what vessel it was, and received in reply, 'American', spoken in good English. He then ordered her to show her colors, which she did by hoisting the American flag. An officer was then sent on board, and she was found to be the American bark 'Williams', Captain Simms, apparently engaged in lawful trade, as there were no visible signs of negroes being on board. But on lifting the tarpaulins with which the hatches were covered, the woolly heads of a number of negroes were immediately thrust up in bold relief to the light, causing the boarding party, in the excitement of the moment, to give three cheers, which was answered by those on board the 'Wyandotte'. Lieutenants Read and Eggleston and a prize crew of nineteen sailors and marines were then placed on board, and the officers, crew and passengers of the bark taken on board the 'Wyandotte' and the prize towed to Key West.

"The poor Africans were conveyed from the bark in

carts and taken at once to their temporary quarters, where every care was taken to provide for their cleanliness and comfort.

"The number of Africans originally taken on board the 'Williams' at the Congo River is variously stated. The American captain says there were only six hundred and sixty-four received, while other and perhaps more correct accounts state the number to have been seven hundred and fifty. If this be true, the mortality among them has been very great, for there were but five hundred and forty-six Africans on board when captured, thus leaving two hundred and four to be accounted for. To this latter number must be added the six found dead on board (said to have been killed by the crew in preserving silence and preventing detection before being boarded by captors), and the thirty-three who died on the passage to Key West —making a total of two hundred and forty-three deaths.

"The treatment they received on board this vessel bears no comparison with that given to those on board the 'Wildfire'. The vessel was found to be in a filthy condition and the living freight uncared for.

"The prisoners have been confined in jail, and are undergoing an examination before Commissioner Bethel."

Among other well-known slavers at this period were the barque "Wildfire"; Spanish barque "Cora", formerly the clipper ship "Gazelle", condemned and sold in China in the early 1850's; barque "Isla de Cuba". Quite by accident the author has discovered that the last named vessel is believed to have been the ship "Tonquin", at one time partially owned by his great-grandfather, Josiah Bradlee of Boston. In 1850 the "Tonquin" had been sent out to San Francisco with a cargo of small portable houses, made in sections for rapid erection in the mining districts. She went into the harbor of San Francisco on a full tide, there were then very few, if any, reliable charts of the coast of California; the tide fell, the "Tonquin" grounded on her own anchors, was badly damaged, condemned and sold, and eventually became a slaver.

In its last days the slave smuggling trade became a highly organized modern business; in fact John R. Spears, in his "American Slave Trade", quotes (pp. 197-198) a letter from the notorious Charles A. L. Lamar, owner of the previously mentioned "Wanderer", to Thomas Barrett of Augusta, Georgia, May 24th, 1858, in which he explains his plans for the formation of a stock company which was to employ a steamer instead of sailing vessels :

"I have in contemplation, if I can raise the necessary amount of money, the fitting out of an expedition to go to the coast of Africa for a cargo of African apprentices, *to be bound for the term of their natural lives,* and would like your co-operation. No subscription will be received for a less amount than $5,000. The amount to be raised is $300,000. I will take $20,000 of the stock myself.

"I propose to purchase the 'Vigo',* an iron screw steamer of 1750 tons, now in Liverpool, for sale at £30,000 cash. She cost £75,000. G. B. Lamar can give you a description of her. . . .

"She is as good as new, save her boilers, and they can be used for several months. If I can buy her I will put six Paixhan guns on deck and man her with as good men as can be found in the South. The fighting men will all be stockholders and *gentlemen,* some of whom are known to you, if not personally, by reputation.

"My estimate runs thus :

Steamer, $150,000; repairs, guns, small arms, coal,
   etc., $50,000, ... $200,000
Supplies, $25,000;   money for purchase of cargo,
   $75,000, ...   100,000
                                                _____
                                                $300,000

" . . . The 'Vigo' can bring 2000 with ease and comfort, and I apprehend no difficulty or risk, save shipwreck, and that you can insure against. I can get one of the first lieutenants in the navy to go out in command . . . but I would not propose to fight ; for the 'Vigo' can steam 11 knots, which would put us out of the way of any of the cruisers."

*The "Vigo" was originally built by Laird Bros. of Liverpool in 1855 for the French Franco-American line. When they failed in 1858 she had been bought by the well-known Inman line running from Liverpool to New York.

Although this charming scheme did not materialize, it is known that other steamers were employed in the slave trade, for the Boston *Transcript* for February 17th, 1860 contained the following news item concerning them:

"Havana correspondents report two steamers, named the 'Marquis de la Habana'* and the 'Democrata', about to sail for the Congo river. They belong to Marby, Bustamente and Co., and have been fitted up openly. . . . If they succeed, the number of steam slavers will be increased forthwith. . . ."

After the Civil war broke out the smuggling of negroes into the United States naturally came to an end, although a few cargoes of blacks were brought to the island of Cuba by the following American vessels:

1861—Barque "Storm King" of Baltimore, 650 slaves.

1862—Ship "Ocilla" of Mystic, Conn.

1864—Ship "Huntress" of New York.

The last gasp of the abominable, illicit slave traffic may be said to have taken place when Captain Nathaniel Gordon, of Portland, Maine, the well known commander of slave ships, was tried and executed in New York City. His indictment has already been referred to, but as he was the only slaver who ever suffered the death penalty, and his execution meant the end of an ignoble traffic which disgraced the United States, it deserves to be chronicled with some degree of minuteness.

The story of his trial is taken from the now rare files of the old New York Illustrated News.

The "Erie", Captain Gordon's vessel, was a small full-rigged ship of 476 tons, built at Warren, R. I., in 1849, but registered from the port of New York.

---

*The steamer "Marquis de la Habana", as previously mentioned, was chartered later in 1860 by the Mexican General Miramon and a party of his followers to convey them to Vera Cruz, where they hoped to stir up one of the many revolutions common to that country. The scheme was a failure, and to recoup themselves these villains were about to seize one of the California gold steamers when their plot was nipped in the bud by Commander Jarvis in the U. S. S. "Saratoga." The "Marquis de la Habana" therefore became the only steam pirate of which there is any record. She afterwards was taken into the Confederate navy as the "McRae", and is not to be confounded with another steamer "Habana" that before the Civil war plied between New Orleans and Havana and was changed into the well-known Confederate cruiser "Sumter", commanded by Captain Raphael Semmes, C. S. N.

"March 8, 1862.

"Execution of Captain Nathaniel Gordon, the Slaver.

"Captain Nathaniel Gordon, the convicted slaver, a native of Portland, Maine, was a man of slender build, about five feet six inches in height, of dark complexion, with dark whiskers and penetrating eyes, and at the time of his death was about thirty-five years of age. From his youth up he had been a sailor, in various capacities, beginning as a cabin boy, and working himself up to the position of captain. His mother is still living, and is an exemplary member of the Presbyterian Church in the city of Portland.

"He made four voyages to the coast of Africa, for negroes to be sold as slaves. Two of these voyages were successful, the negroes having been landed on the Island of Cuba. A third voyage was only partially successful, the negroes having been landed at a Brazilian port.

"His fourth voyage as a slaver was on board the ship 'Erie', with which he, his two mates and crew, were captured on the African coast, off the Congo River, by the United States steam sloop of war 'Mohican', of the African squadron. When the 'Erie' was boarded the United States officers found a cargo of 967 negroes, consisting of men, women and children.

"Immediately after the capture a prize crew was put on board the 'Erie', under command of a lieutenant and a midshipman, and the ship was headed for Monrovia. On the passage thither three hundred of the negroes died and were buried at sea. On their arrival at Monrovia the negroes were duly handed over to the agent of the United States government at that point, and set free under the civilizing influences and institutions of the Liberian Republic.

"The crew of the 'Erie' was taken on board the 'Mohican' to fill the places of the United States sailors who had been transferred to the prize ship 'Erie', and Capt. Gordon, with his two mates, were sent on to New York by the 'Erie' after landing the negroes as stated.

"The 'Erie' had previously been to Liverpool, from which port she took a cargo to Havana, Cuba. There she changed hands, and there Captain Gordon took charge of her and superintended her fitting out for the slave voyage in which she was engaged at the time of her capture.

"About the time of the arrival of the 'Erie' at this port with the prisoners, the rebellion broke out, and, as it was progressing, the lieutenant prize master turned out to be a secessionist, and, in order to identify himself more fully with the cause of the Confederacy, left for the South. This step on the part of the lieutenant bereft the government of the necessary testimony for the trial of Gordon.

"The U. S. marshal, preparatory to the trial of Captain Gordon, struck a panel of jurors from Columbia county. To this panel Gordon, through his counsel, objected, on the ground that the clerk of the U. S. Circuit Court had not served the marshal with a certified copy, in accordance with the statute, and the court sustained the objection. Had Gordon submitted himself to a trial at that time, his acquittal would have been certain, as the government had not the evidence to convict him.

The trial was postponed, and when Gordon again came into court a new jury had been impanneled, which he nearly exhausted by the pre-emptory challenges, and a number for cause, before a jury for the trial had been selected. This jury the marshal kept together until the trial was concluded.

"Previous, however, to the last trial, the ships of the African squadron had been ordered home by the Secretary of the Navy, and the marshal boarded each of them at New York, Philadelphia, Boston, and Portsmouth, N. H., respectively.

"On board the 'Michigan', at Boston, he found four sailors who had belonged to the crew of the 'Erie' at the time of her capture, and they were brought on to this city as witnesses, and on their testimony Gordon was convicted.

"When first arrested, Gordon was lodged in Eldridge street jail, and he was possessed of about $5,000. On one occasion he paid the sum of $50 for the fond privilege of a parole to enable him to live with his family in Brooklyn for a few days.

"Since the President's respite the prisoner has been fed at the private expense of the marshal.

"A handbill having reference to the execution of Capt. Gordon was seen posted about the streets on Thursday morning. It was worded as follows, and purported to have been signed by Mayor Opdyke, which was not the case :

'Citizens of New York come to the rescue! Shall a judicial murder be committed in your midst, and no protesting voices be raised against it ? Captain Nathaniel Gordon is sentenced to be executed for a crime which has virtually been a dead letter for forty years.'

"Then followed a call for a meeting at the Exchange, at 3 o'clock P. M., of all in favor of a commutation of the death penalty. On learning the fact, Inspector Carpenter* telegraphed to all the police captains to send out men to tear down the posters and to arrest any who might be found putting any of them up.

"At an early hour in the forenoon of Thursday, Mr. Murray received the following letter protesting against the execution of Gordon :

'New York, Feb. 19, 1862.

'Sir : If you have any regard for yourself, your family, or your reputation, you will not hang that man Gordon, for it will be nothing short of murder, and the stigma of it will stick while you live. Resign sooner, by all means, a thousand times over. Do not commit murder. Cut your right arm off first. Yours respectfully,

Wm. Noble.

"Gordon was almost constantly attended during his imprisonment by his wife and child. Mrs. Gordon has been permitted to remain with him whenever she chose, and her attendance has been unremitting. She is a native of Nova Scotia, about twenty-five years of age, slight but well built, and of much personal beauty.

"She has resided in Brooklyn during most of the period of her husband's imprisonment, in the family of a sea captain, who has interested himself somewhat for the comfort of Gordon himself. Mrs. Gordon has visited Washington several times, it is said, and for the last time

*One of the high officials of the New York Metropolitan police.

no longer than last Friday. Her pecuniary means are
derived exclusively from benevolent persons, who have
supplied her with what she pressingly needed, and means
of seeking a commutation of the death penalty in the
case of her husband. Accompanied by the child (a fine
boy of five or six years of age), she nobly devoted every
hour at her command to Gordon's comfort and to his con-
solation. They have evidently been much attached to
each other.

"Last evening the final parting scene occurred. Gordon
did not entirely lose his self-possession, but the grief of
Mrs. Gordon was of the most acute description. She was
taken away at half-past six o'clock.

"After parting with his wife, Gordon was transferred
to another cell, and his clothing thoroughly searched to
prevent the possibility of any attempt at suicide. He
then partook of some refreshments and lighted a cigar,
and, calling for pen and ink, sat down to write letters.
He thus passed the principal part of the night, up to about
four o'clock.

"About four o'clock in the morning Gordon was discovered in convulsions, and a physician was sent for, who
pronounced him suffering under the effects of a dose of
poison. The prisoner afterwards admitted that he had
taken a small powder which had been furnished him and
which he had concealed in a crack under his bench.

"He continued in convulsions until about ten o'clock
Friday morning, when the effects of the poison seemed
to subside, and he rallied materially. About eleven
o'clock he requested that a lock of his hair and a ring
should be carried to his wife.

"At eleven o'clock a despatch was received from Judge
Beebe, who had gone to Albany to see Governor Morgan,
stating that after his interview the Governor had sent a
telegraphic despatch to President Lincoln requesting a
further respite for the prisoner.

"Inside the Tombs building, and at every entrance, a
guard of marines were stationed with fixed bayonets.
They had been detailed from the Marine Barracks, were
under the command of Lieutenant Cohen, and numbered
about eighty men. The special guard was composed of

the marshal's deputies, with some police captains. A guard
of police was also stationed around the outside of the
Tombs.

"The gallows was a new one, originally made for hanging the three murderers of Captain Pyke, of the ship
'General Parkhill', but not used, as the sentence of those
men was commuted by the President to imprisonment for
fifteen years.

"The hour of twelve was fixed for the execution.
Over a hundred persons had been admitted to witness the
scene, among whom were Marshal Keyes of Boston, several State Senators, and reporters of the press.

"Gordon was taken from his cell to the gallows at a
quarter past twelve o'clock. He was supported by two
of Marshal Murray's deputies. The marshal walked on
his right. The appearance of Gordon's face was ghastly,
his fear was extreme ; but with that assumed stoicism
which had distinguished him, he walked, or was rather
carried, quickly to his place. He made no dying speech.

"As soon as the noose was adjusted the black cap was
pulled over his face. The signal was at once made, and
and in an instant he was dangling in the air. He died
easily ; but few convulsive motions were observed. He
was dead in about five minutes from the time the rope
was adjusted, but the body was allowed to remain half an
hour, when his body was taken down and placed in a
rough coffin, in which it will be delivered to his friends."

It was said that Gordon was at one time the possessor
of over $100,000, which sum he had accumulated in the
slave trade, but the expenses, etc., of his trial swallowed
up all his little fortune.

Great political influence was brought to bear on President Lincoln to commute his sentence. He had already
once respited Gordon (see Illustrated New York News,
February 22d, 1862), and the latter's friends were confident that he would not die on the gallows, but the President remained firm.

Thus did one wretched outrager of humanity pay for
centuries of misery and suffering which bare words cannot
describe.

INDEX.